HandiLand

Corporealities: Discourses of Disability

Series editors: David T. Mitchell and Sharon L. Snyder

A complete list of titles in the series can be found at www.press.umich.edu

HandiLand

The Crippest Place on Earth

Elizabeth A. Wheeler

University of Michigan Press
Ann Arbor

Published in the United States of America by
the University of Michigan Press

First published August 2019

A CIP catalog record for this book is available from the British Library.

ISBN 978-0-472-07420-4 (hardcover : alk. paper)
ISBN 978-0-472-05420-6 (paper : alk. paper)
ISBN 978-0-472-12571-5 (ebook)

The cover is a bright sky blue with white, yellow, and black type. In the center is a gaily
colored drawing that suggests a map of a theme park or summer camp and featuring
fanciful buildings. At the center is a ramped Castle of Intersectionality, and around it
lakes and woods, farm animals, a tent with a question mark on it, and a stage with two
people rehearsing. Alice in Wonderland's giant leg emerges from a little house. The
all-gender restrooms, basketball court, treehouse, school bus, and outdoor dining room
are all wheelchair accessible.

For my family, Jordan Shin, Kevin Shin-Wheeler,
and Bridget Shin-Wheeler
the founders and members of the Society for Disability Studies
and the Finnerty, Yozzo, Lee, Christou, Cooper, Elliott-Jones,
and Morrell families:
You are my HandiLand.

Acknowledgments

Thank you to the people and organizations who gave me time, room, and inspiration to write this book. The Oregon Humanities Center and its staff, Paul Peppis, Julia Heydon, Melissa Gustafson, and Peg Gearhart, provided time and blessed seclusion. Thanks also to the OHC and the University of Oregon College of Arts and Sciences for subvention funds to cover publication costs. The UO Center for the Study of Women in Society also supported writing time. For all the books and articles, thank you to the librarians and staff of the Eugene Public Library, the Knight Library at the University of Oregon, and the British Library.

Thank you to Lisa Elliott, kindred spirit, teen librarian, and godmother to our children. Lisa steered me to most of the young adult novels in this study. Talking with her about books, shows, parenting, or anything else is one of my life's chief pleasures. Thank you also for bringing Jake Jones and Avi and Briar Elliott-Jones into our lives, all of you friends who are family.

Thank you to my mother, the late Phyllis Huntley Wheeler, the first children's literature fan and disabled person I ever knew. My mother believed firmly in the good sense of children, their sovereignty over their own minds and bodies, and the importance of their upbringing for the future of democracy. Thank you, Mama, for all those nights reading *Winnie-the-Pooh*, *Little Women*, and Dr. Seuss with me, and for all the other ways we have shared an understanding.

Thank you to my wonderful editor, LeAnn Fields, and to Ally Baker and Danielle Seid for their crucial aid in manuscript preparation and research. Thank you to Robin Kaplan for the splendid picture of HandiLand that graces the book cover. Thank you to the brilliant scholars whose insights transformed this book: Kristen Anderson Wright, Priya Lalvani, Sarah Jaquette Ray, Maram Epstein, Mary E. Wood, Jay Sibara, Scott Pollard, Sharon L. Snyder, David T. Mitchell, Bethany Jacobs, Isiah Lavender III, Lisa Yaszek, Susan Burch, Stephanie LeMenager, and anonymous reviewers from *Children's Literature Quarterly* and the University of Michigan Press. Thank you to my writers' group, Anne Laskaya, Mary E. Wood, and Martha Bayless, who kept me writing during the years I had many other urgent matters claiming my attention.

Thank you to Dianna Lee for taking such good care of my children while I wrote. Dianna attended so thoughtfully to their needs and loves us all so well. Thank you also to Rachel Fellman and Charlotte Boatner-Doane for the childcare in London and your friendship.

Thank you to the Society for Disability Studies, my intellectual home. Disability studies scholars who enlighten me include Chloë Hughes, Susan Schweik, Eli Clare, Rosemarie Garland-Thomson, Mel Y. Chen, Christopher M. Bell, Jim Ferris, Ann Fox, Sami Schalk, Alison Kafer, Julie Minich, Alice Sheppard, Michelle Nario-Redmond, Peter Trojic, Russell Shuttleworth, and Cynthia Wu. Special thanks to Simi and David Linton for the warm hospitality you have shown me and so many other SDS newcomers. Thank you also to the scholars of Pacific and Western Disability Studies, especially Allison Hobgood, Joanne Woiak, and José Alaniz.

Thank you to my Eugene disability communities, many of whom graciously allowed me to tell their stories in this book. Thank you to the circle of families who have kept riding with us over many bumps in the road: Jaymason Bouwman and Cynthia Foster Finnerty; Robin, Carlo, Alex, and Duncan Yozzo; Elia, Miriam, Christos, and Nanette Makrina Christou; Carina and Hailey Cooper; Heather, Stephen, Dana, and Shanti Morrell; and Hyla Rosenberg and Barbara and Alfonso Dumesnil. Thank you to Gina Wadsworth, Karen Kline, Janice Ziegler, and Dianna Lee of the Orthopedically Impaired Preschool for showing us what real community looks like. Thank you to Mark Roberts, Mike Shugrue, Stanley Coleman, Bill Winkley, and all the actors, volunteers, and crew of the Shenanigans Theater Company and the Stray Cast, including Alana Unfried and Billy Dean Bogard, whose stories appear in this book. I look forward to many more years of making theater with you.

Thank you to the University of Oregon disability studies community, especially Heidi von Ravensberg, my partner in creating the UO Disability Studies Minor. Heidi, thank you for your expertise, hard work, and advocacy, and for keeping the faith so long with disability studies and with me. Thank you also to Deborah Olson, Doug Blandy, Karen J. Ford, Andrew Marcus, Hilary Gerdes, Veronica Vold, Judith Raiskin, Kyu-Ho Ahn, Lisa Abia-

Smith, Brian Trapp, David de Lorenzo, and Susan Sygall. Thank you to Jené Conrad, Taylor Eldridge, Rachel Alm, Jackson Darland, Nocona Pewewardy, Jennifer Syverson, Woo-Kyung Kim, Colleen Broderick, Melissa McCloskey, Elizabeth Mattar, Martina Shabram, Dean Dier, Elizabeth Peterson, Nina Moon, and the insightful students in my children's literature, comics, and theater classes.

Thank you to the friends who love and support me in all aspects of life: Wendy Simon, Laurie Ozone, Jane Boatner and Dudley Doane, Maxine Craig, Francesca Royster, Margaret Holub, Anne Williams, and Ellen Scott.

Thank you to the late Aurora Shin-Wheeler, our Havanese dog. For two of the years I spent on this book Rory was by my side: sitting on a footstool next to me, sleeping under my desk, or giving me a good reason to get up and run around the block. You have exemplified the very best in companion species. Rest in peace, pupperdog.

Thank you to Kevin Shin-Wheeler, who busts through every door, open or shut. Thank you, Kevin, for allowing me to write about our lives and for the feedback that improved this book. Thanks also to Bridget Shin-Wheeler, fellow bibliophile and Ravenclaw, who read just about every book in this study along with me and has provided such good intellectual company over the years. I knew I would love my offspring, but I never thought I'd like you both so much.

Over our twenty-four years together, my wife Jordan Shin and I have developed the philosophy of living and parenting that undergirds this book. Thank you for your smarts, humor, and devotion. Thank you for the beautiful photographs that enliven this book. Thank you for picking up vast quantities of household slack so I could disappear to write or recharge. You are the practical yet intellectual spouse scholars crave, and I am lucky and delighted to share my life with you. Your love puts a bounce in my step even on the overwhelmed days.

Chapter 4 is reproduced in altered form from *Disability Studies and the Environmental Humanities: Toward an Eco-Crip Theory*, edited by Sarah Jaquette Ray and Jay Sibara, by permission of the University of Nebraska Press, copyright 2017 by the Board of Regents of the University of Nebraska. Portions of chapter 6 first appeared in *Children's Literature Quarterly* 38, no. 3 (Fall 2013): 335–50, copyright 2013 Children's Literature Association.

Contents

Digital materials related to this title can be found on the Fulcrum platform via the following citable URL: https://doi.org/10.3998/mpub.9533468

HandiLand

Fig. 1. Jennifer Keelan at the Capitol Crawl, March 12, 1990. AP Photo/
Jeff Markowitz.

Introduction

Welcome to HandiLand

Remarkable things can happen when a child with a disability enters public space. At the age of eight, Jennifer Keelan crawled up the steps of the US Capitol and clinched the biggest legal victory to date in the American disability rights movement. In the push for passage of the Americans with Disabilities Act, protesters used the visual drama of public crawling to create social change. On March 12, 1990, activists threw themselves out of their wheelchairs and crawled up the eighty-three marble steps of the US Capitol building. The Capitol Crawl showed the literal difficulty of entering an inaccessible building and the figurative difficulty of accessing equality under the law.

Despite dozens of adult protesters, press attention focused on the lone child activist, Jennifer Keelan, a second grader with cerebral palsy. The next day the Associated Press story led with Keelan: "Using her small arms to drag her body up the Capitol steps, 8-year-old Jennifer Keelan joined some 60 disabled Americans Monday in lobbying for legislation to guarantee their civil rights. 'I'll take all night if I have to,' Jennifer said to others crawling alongside her."[1] The accompanying photo showed Keelan exhausted but determined, headed up to the Capitol dome with the Declaration of Independence rolled up in her back pocket. The sole image from the ADA fight that stayed in the public memory, this photograph helped secure passage of the Americans with Disabilities Act.[2] In a 2010 interview, Jennifer Keelan recalled her pride of accomplishment and her resolve to represent her generation in the struggle for disability rights.

> Everybody didn't want me to. It was supposed to be an all-adult thing, and they were like, "No, no, no, Jennifer, you're too young. You can't

do it." And I turned to [protest organizer] Wade Blank and I said, "I need to climb the steps. I want to climb the steps." So I got out of my wheelchair and I started climbing. Well, the next thing I know I've got fifty cameras on me and I've got mikes all over me. . . . I had international news on me, I had national news, I had local news, I had everybody. . . . Once I climbed the steps I sat down and I'm like, "Wow! I just did all that." And they say that it was the image of me climbing those steps that was the final decision to get the ADA passed. And that is one of the . . . memories that I am extremely proud of. And I knew at that moment that I was not only representing myself but I was representing my generation.[3]

HandiLand: The Crippest Place on Earth looks at the new prominence of youth with disabilities in contemporary young adult and children's literature since worldwide rights movements and laws brought them into the public sphere. As students with disabilities entered mainstream schools in the late twentieth century, they also moved to the literary forefront. For the first time, writers featured main characters with disabilities and invited young readers to identify with them and see the world through their perspectives. Finally, the disabled child no longer served only as a sidekick, sibling, or educational toy for the nondisabled main characters. The entry of young protagonists with disabilities changes public space and exposes its limitations. In the words of Susan Sygall, these characters move "from inclusion to infiltration."[4] They fan out into a multiplicity of spheres, not just the ones designated for them. They don't wait for an invitation.

This new literary canon has had a profound and widespread influence on disabled and nondisabled fans. Many of these books are bestsellers with a passionate fan base, including *The Fault in Our Stars, Turtles All the Way Down, Harry Potter, Hyperbole and a Half, Wonder, The Absolutely True Diary of a Part-Time Indian, Everything, Everything, Speak, Orleans, The Last Wild,* and *Out of My Mind.* Their genres, including graphic memoirs, picture books, fantasy, dystopian science fiction, and young adult romance, represent major growth areas in contemporary publishing. Many have become Hollywood films, while the theatrical version of *The Curious Incident of the Dog in the Night-Time* has played to sold-out audiences in London's West End and on Broadway. A real breakthrough has come with the casting of young actors who share their character's disabilities, as in the films *Wonderstruck* and *A Quiet Place* and the television shows *Breaking Bad* and *Speechless.*

Literature for young readers is the ideal viewing stand for a parade of political changes as kids with disabilities have infiltrated public space. This viewing stand allows us to see how far we've come toward defeating ableism (antidisability prejudice) and how far we still need to go. *HandiLand* focuses primarily on authors from the United States and the United Kingdom but also ventures into the young adult and children's literature of Ghana, Venezuela, and Japan. The disabilities represented range from post-traumatic stress disorder to speech impediments, chronic pain to blood-borne illness, mobility impairments to autism, and supernatural disabilities found only in the fantasy realm.

Each chapter of *HandiLand* explores the influence of particular laws on the portrayal of disability in books for young readers. In the late twentieth century, disability rights movements rose up all over the world. The global momentum began in 1981 with the United Nations International Year of Disabled Persons. Pressured by activists who took to the streets, nations rolled out disability rights laws throughout the 1990s and 2000s: the Americans with Disabilities Act (1990), Japan's Basic Law for Persons with Disabilities (1993), India's Persons with Disabilities Act and the United Kingdom's Disability Discrimination Act (both 1995), Venezuela's Law for Persons with Disabilities and Ghana's Persons with Disability Act (both 2006). While the United States has led the way in legislating access to ramps and restrooms, other nations have led with initiatives like universal health care.

Some laws had a profound impact on children with disabilities, notably their mainstreaming into public schools with the 1975 Individuals with Disabilities Education Act in the United States and the 2001 Special Educational Needs and Disability Act in the United Kingdom. However, laws unrelated to disability rights have also affected young people with disabilities. In the United States, for example, the standardized testing of No Child Left Behind (2002) has produced mass test anxiety starting with the millennial generation, while the crime bills of the War on Drugs have led to mass incarceration of young African Americans with learning disabilities.

New rights laws change the arts because they make new human experiences possible, or at least imaginable. *HandiLand* explores how national politics and laws, everyday life experience, and literature collaborate and clash with each other in the project of reimagining young people as full members of society. To make a just and decent world for kids with disabilities, we need to radically reimagine the ableist structures we have inherited. The purpose of this book, then, is threefold. First, I use children's and young adult literature and popular culture as sites for exploring contemporary understandings of disability. Second, I derive principles for understanding social justice from the everyday experiences of adults and families with disabilities, including my own. I hope that readers from many disability communities will recognize familiar events and dilemmas in these pages. Third, I offer these ideas and stories as tool kits for parents, educators, therapists, doctors, policymakers, and everyone else whose work, ideas, and hands touch young people with disabilities.

To reach these goals I have needed to write this book in a particular way. I have used the clearest language I could find to develop my theory of young people with disabilities in public culture. I have pursued complex politics and arguments in plain words and distilled my points into a handful of key terms and frameworks. Where the argument requires specialized terms, I define the terms at first use. I intend this book for scholars of disability studies and literature for young readers, but I also welcome a wider readership beyond my own small and jargon-dependent professional circle. I hand the tools of critical disability studies to everyone who builds the worlds that young people with disabilities will enter. I hope this book will help strengthen the case that humanities scholars should put their work at the service of a wide public.

How Far We've Come, How Far We Have to Go

These new books for children and young adults bring us new heroes. They take what others regard as weaknesses and redefine them as part of the hero's journey. The *Harry Potter* series, for instance, redefines chronic headache and depression as wellsprings for ethical decision-making. Harry identifies and fights evil long before others do because of his chronic pain. In Sherri L. Smith's Afrofuturist dystopia *Orleans*, Fen de La Guerre lives in a militarized quarantine zone because she and her fellow residents carry a contagious blood disease. Fen uses her vulnerability in the face of state violence to save the next generation from harm. She joins the ranks of young black heroes in African American science fiction who battle the forces that militate against their survival. Melody Brooks, the protagonist of *Out of My Mind*, may be nonverbal, but she uses a voice computer and even her physical clumsiness to challenge her school's grudging inclusion. Classmates give her a pitiful little trophy as a consolation prize for being excluded from the quiz team championships.

> I roll with laughter. My hand jerks out and hits the trophy—I'm not sure if it was an accident or not—and it falls to the floor, breaking into several pieces . . .
>
> "I don't want it!" I finally type. Then, turning the volume as loud as

it will go, I add, "You deserve it!" Still laughing, I click on the power to my chair, do a smooth turn, and roll myself out of the classroom.[5]

The new literature of disability heralds many champions who emerge out of obscurity to claim leadership, like latter-day King Arthurs. Their entry into the public sphere benefits not only themselves but their whole societies. They have heroes' roles to play, and people need them.

That said, *HandiLand* is not a story of uninterrupted progress. A body of literature does not necessarily gain enlightenment just by being recent. Older books may reach higher stages while newer books lag behind. For example, the "Fantasy" section of this book explores the mature disability consciousness of nineteenth-century British literature. Victorian fantasy fiction refutes the proposition that literature for young readers only awoke to disability politics in the late twentieth century. As I demonstrate in chapters 8 and 9, the British fantasy tradition rendered the inner experience of childhood disability and designed inclusive worlds long before realist literature or real life did.

Conversely, *HandiLand*'s explorations of contemporary literature highlight how far we still need to go to achieve full and fair representation. Contemporary literature for young readers has opened its doors to disabled protagonists. Nonetheless, this new canon also bespeaks the halfway inclusion of the neoliberal twenty-first century. Too often young characters with disabilities have to earn their inclusion through exceptional charm and intellect, sterling character and determination, heroic and athletic feats, and white privilege. College-bound, mostly white, requiring no accommodations, these new heroes fit into the narrow market-driven demographic of neoliberal education. The high-achieving main characters of the school novels I discuss chapters 6 and 7 only represent a small slice of students with disabilities. The protagonists of the picture books in chapter 4 also fit a narrow profile: they are Supercrips who win over readers with their athletic feats and heroic rescues.

Here in the twenty-first century we have brand-new forms of oppression and plenty of unfinished business when it comes to creating a just world for young people with disabilities. We have traveled a long way and still have a long way to go. For instance, disability rights have largely benefited children from richer families and cultures. Chapter 4, "Moving Together Side by Side," explores the postcolonial imbalance of power and wealth between Ghana and the United Kingdom and its consequences for children with disabilities. In the United States, African American students with disabilities are four times likelier than their white peers to be educated in a juvenile justice facility.[6] As I argue in chapter 10, lack of disability services forms the backdrop to the police killing of Freddie Gray in Baltimore in 2015. While they all face challenges, young people with disabilities live on a spectrum of privilege.

The twenty-first century has devised its own excuses to segregate students of color with disabilities out of mainstream classrooms. The market-driven model of education, in which schools compete for the highest-testing students with the most involved parents, has come to dominate education in the United Kingdom and United States since the 1990s. Sally Tomlinson's research demonstrates that this marketing model has encouraged British schools "to remove black children in disproportionate numbers from mainstream education."[7] Regarding them as "troublesome" and "difficult to teach," schools shunt black students into special education in order to "function unimpeded in the scramble to be regarded as good schools, high up in league tables of examination results."[8] The marketing model of education goes hand in hand with the testing model of disability, which also rose in the 1990s and forms the topic of chapter 5.

HandiLand

Throughout this book I use a fictional place called HandiLand as a yardstick to measure how far we've come toward justice and how far we still need to go. What would a fair world look like for children with disabilities and their families? My friend Cyndi and I used to ponder this question a lot when our boys were young. Her son Jaymason and my son Kevin were born a month apart and they both have cerebral palsy. We met when the boys were about a year and a half old. In Cyndi I found a friend who had the same frustrations and same daydreams about a world without barriers and stigmas. As she said once, "We formed a deep bond because we realized that our kids were perfect just the way they are." Our conversations led us to reflect more broadly on the social roles childhood disability plays and the kinds of support our kids would have in a perfect world. We call that ideal world "HandiLand." Cyndi tells HandiLand's origin story:

> We were talking about how wonderful it would be to live in a community where all the houses are accessible, all the houses' fronts face a parklike setting. Everybody had ramps. It was all flat, accessible. There was a community building in the middle that would be a full physical therapy gym and a resource library for families. Maybe a pool—whatever you could envision to help our children be happy and suc-

ceed. They could go there on their own or we could take them there. It's just out the front door and everybody's homes are accessible for everybody else's children. . . . I was telling [my friend Emily] about this dream about this community where nobody would judge each other, all families would know one another, everybody would be capable of having their other children just pop in for a hello, just like it should be. And she said, "You could call it HandiLand."[9]

We could add many things to HandiLand: every child gets invited to birthday parties. We all know sign language. You can have a meltdown in the middle of the community center and no one blinks an eye. The computer room gives everyone access to screen-reading and voice-to-text software. There's a free twenty-four-hour insulin bank, equipment repair center, and counseling service. The books and movies in the library reflect everyone's identities. According to Cyndi, however, it boils down to two basic principles: Families who accept their children from the start and "support systems that let families know that their child is perfect."[10] In front of Sleeping Beauty's Castle at Disneyland stands a statue of Walt Disney and Mickey Mouse holding hands. The bronze plaque underneath the statue quotes Disney: "I think most of all what I want Disneyland to be is a happy place . . . where parents and children can have fun, together." In the utopia of HandiLand, families with disabilities would have fewer hassles and more time for fun.

Given the real world's mixed landscape of new access and continued exclusion, this book traverses many moods and modes, from dystopia to play, critique to humor, anger to celebration, least crip to crippest. With this mixed legacy in mind, I have configured the book as if it were the Magic Kingdom at Disneyland: a place for children and families both ideal and real, laced with magic, rife with ironies, encircled by capitalism. Part I resembles Disneyland's Main Street, USA, inviting readers into disability community through the portal of one preternaturally wholesome American town, my city of Eugene, Oregon. The book then fans out into three parts or lands, each one representing a public space that young people with disabilities have entered in the literature of recent decades: Nature, School, and Fantasy. These three spaces mirror Disneyland's Adventureland, Frontierland, and Fantasyland.[11] *HandiLand*'s conclusion leaves characters with disabilities at the threshold of maturity: the Tomorrowland of sex and the spectrum of sexual privilege.

A Visitor's Map

Part I. Kids in Public Space: A Theory in Stories

I used to take a neurological drug for my chronic migraine that had what the warning label called "intellectual side effects." It turned out that phrase just meant "wipes out your short-term memory," but I have found that the experience of disability does have profound intellectual side effects. Children and families with disabilities develop specific *epistemologies*, ways of knowing and navigating the world. "Kids in Public Space" lays out the habits of mind and insights our children and families acquire. Each chapter focuses on a different space of early childhood: the playground, the preschool, and the public toilet. Part I conveys the flavor of life in a mixed-ability family and the challenges of entering public space. Through stories, I lay out the fundamental concepts at work when a disability goes public.

While disability studies, critical race theory, queer theory, and urban studies inform my approach, I also draw theory from my family life and interviews with other families. I root my theories in reflections on my own neurological disabilities as well as my parenting of children with cerebral palsy, asthma, and life-threatening food allergies. Through my interviews with families I trace the patterns of community, systems of mutual support, worldviews, sense of justice, and crip humor we develop as we come out in public and construct versions of HandiLand together. Out of these shared experiences I derive the concepts I apply to young adult and children's literature in the rest of the book. These concepts include cripistemology, misfitting, the prosthetic community, and intersectionality.

Cripistemology (Disability Epistemology)

When a mixed-ability family is working well, kids and parents collude together to resist the idea that disability in public is a problem. Habits of mind like body humor, access intimacy, and ferocity in the face of injustice help young people claim their right to belong. Many families use bathroom humor to help children rehearse their futures as assertive adults who understand injustice. Chapter 3, "Epistemology of the Toilet," and chapter 6, "Rehearsing the Future," show how young people with disabilities work with their parents and friends to build a repertoire of responses to ableism.

Misfitting

Every built environment makes assumptions about the bodies and behaviors of humans who will inhabit it. These assumptions become clear when an unexpected human enters the space instead. A child with a disability on your average neighborhood playground often misfits rather than fits its play structures. This child becomes what Rosemarie Garland-Thomson, who coined the term *misfitting*, calls an "agent of recognition" who reveals the limitations of the space.[12] A good solution to the problem is to change the space to fit the child, not the other way around. A better solution is to make the space ready for a wider variety of people even before they get there. A world ready for young adults and children with disabilities before they get there: that is the essence of HandiLand.

I apply this idea of misfitting to the way readers and pop culture consumers fit themselves into narratives. Is it possible for young people with disabilities to see themselves reflected in the culture around them, or do they have to force their way in with some difficulty? In the first chapter and in chapters 8 and 9, I address this question of fitting or misfitting into the culture through a look at disability fandom and the creation of fan communities. For example, the *Harry Potter* series satisfies the longing to move from misfitting into discovering a world where you fit, a world that was ready for you even before you knew it existed.

Prosthetic Community

I define a *prosthetic community* as a cluster of living beings, objects, resources, technologies, and ideas that enable full inclusion. The prosthetic community characterizes a society that works well for the disabled people in it. While we may think of prosthetics as inanimate technologies, they cannot work without people and money. Throughout this book I highlight the wide variety of wraparound supports young people with disabilities need to become full citizens of their societies. Goodwill and good intentions can't do the job alone. It takes decently paid caregivers, consistent advocacy, good health insurance, input from disability communities, and lots of creative brainstorming. Chapters 2, 4, and 7 trace the extraordinary things young people with disabilities can do if their prosthetic community supports them well. Chapter 10 details the devastating and fatal consequences of withholding prosthetic community from young people in urban sacrifice zones.

Most disabled youth do not grow up in families who share their disabilities. The solidarity of a mixed-ability family may be the closest they come. And even when disability runs in the family, young people still need peers as well as relatives. Ideally, children and young adults find or assemble their own disability communities: groups of people with the same or different disabilities who come together to celebrate, agitate, commiserate, or just hang out. A strong prosthetic community provides the kinds of support that make transition into disability community possible.

Intersectionality

If we think about disability working in tandem with other social identities like gender, sexuality, race, and class, we can have more productive and challenging conversations. Scholars call such versatile thinking *intersectionality*. Kimberlé Crenshaw, who coined the term to describe African American women's lives, explains the need to move beyond single-issue political practices: "And so, when the practices expound identity as woman or person of color as an either/or proposition, they relegate the identity of women of color to a location that resists telling."[13] When we tackle disability as a single issue, we reinforce white privilege, reduce gender to two small boxes, and deny the difference in opportunities for disabled people who have money versus disabled people who don't.

When we consider two or more aspects of identity together, problems and solutions swim into view that were previously out of sight. For instance, chapters 1 and 10 look at works of art by African American women where the disability experience could remain invisible unless we expand our definitions. Chapter 2, "Masculinity at the Orthopedic Preschool," tells a story about the need to question gender norms at the same time we question the roles of disability in society. Chapters 4 and 8 continue the exploration of disabled masculinity. Too often, literature and popular culture in the United Kingdom and the United States define disability as something that happens only to white people. Chapter 7, "One Difference at a Time," critiques the strange failures of intersectionality in young adult fiction about school.

Part II. Nature

Nature gives young people with disabilities a survival niche in human society. For instance, teenage writers with autism assert their right to be in the world through their affinity for nature. Naoki Higashida and Philip Reyes, who communicate by means of letterboards, computers, and human help, represent two of the emergent voices. At age twelve Reyes wrote, "It is common to think Autistics are in their own world. We are treated as if we don't belong here in this society. . . . I am worried someday people might want to prevent Autistics from being born."[14] Higashida and Reyes use their ecological awareness to claim a sense of belonging in a human society that extends them only a tenuous welcome.

Linking autism to affinity for nature, Higashida and Reyes refute a message common in popular culture that autism is a symptom of declining global health.[15] Both argue that their respect for nature proves their right to exist. At age thirteen Higashida explained, "When we look at nature, we receive a sort of permission to be alive in this world, and our entire bodies get recharged."[16] He theorizes that people with autism are grandfathered into the primeval history of the planet and exist to avert ecological crisis: "We are more like travelers from the distant, distant past. And if, by our being here, we could help the people of the world remember what truly matters for the Earth, that would give us a quiet pleasure."[17] Reyes argues that neurotypical people rush to get things done, while "I use my senses to enjoy God's creation. I listen closely to the sounds of nature so that I can appreciate a momentary wandering wind or the call of a robin to its babies."[18] While people with autism may seem to outside observers as if they live in another world, both writers claim they are more attuned to this world than people without autism.

HandiLand considers disability across lines of race, gender, class, and nationality, and across species lines as well. Animals and children have been natural companions in literature for centuries. This companionship takes on particular importance for children with disabilities. In the picture books of chapter 4, service and companion animals enable outdoor adventures and forays into public life. The shared movements of animals and children represent ingenuity, joy, and freedom. As I discuss in chapters 4 and 8, animals provide assistance, solace, and delight in ways that do not threaten the masculine independence of boys with physical disabilities. The kinship goes beyond companionship, however, as different species come to resemble and act like each other.

Unfortunately, human-animal comparisons can be double-edged. Comparison to an animal often comes with the intent to insult, and such insults have given license to cruel and genocidal treatment of people with disabilities. As Mel Chen writes, cross-species comparisons are fraught because of "what linguists call an *animacy hierarchy*, which conceptually arranges human life, disabled life, animal life, plant life, and forms of nonliving material in orders of value and priority."[19] Being compared to an animal means moving down the animacy ladder, so stories limit such comparisons in the interest of human dignity. In chapter 4 I critique philosophers who argue for animal rights by rearranging the hierarchy instead of questioning it, claiming that nonhuman animals possess greater worth than children with disabilities.

Many books in this study question the binary dividing human from non-human animals, including the subject of chapter 5, "Disservice Animals." In the graphic memoir *Hyperbole and a Half*, Allie Brosh upends the animacy hierarchy to claim disability solidarity with her dogs. They and she share an implacable neurodiversity that colors her whole absurdist picture of the natural world. Out of this history grows Brosh's ADHD environmental ethic, in which nature—including human and canine disability—always exceeds our ability to harness or alter it. In children's stories like *Seal Surfer*, *Sosu's Call*, and "The Little Lame Prince," comparison to animals does not disparage children with disabilities but rather makes their ways of moving seem right and natural. The more humans treat animals and children with disabilities with respect, the more they can claim their kinship to each other.

Nature has its handprints all over this book, even in the sections devoted to other public spheres. Chapter 10, "Runoff," explores the environmental justice vision of *Orleans*, Sherrie L. Smith's Afrofuturist dystopia about a Gulf region laid low by repeated floods. Smith's future vision distorts reality just enough to unearth the kinships between different urban sacrifice zones. In "Runoff" I use the science fiction metaphors of *Orleans* to illuminate the lead-poisoning crises of Baltimore and Flint, Michigan.

Like many theme parks, *HandiLand* is a water fantasy. In writing this book I found myself returning again and again to imagery of water. The buoyancy of water has a democratic tendency to even out the strengths of various human bodies. Water also spreads toxins, creating disabilities in entire communities. Floods expose the resources a community has or lacks along with the structures of inequality that underlie those lacks. In landscapes of environmental sacrifice, toxic runoff leads to running off from troops or police. Unchecked pollutions cause disabilities, and the state responds with excessive policing instead of a prosthetic community. While Afrofuturist literature, music, and visual arts feature black space travelers called Afronauts, *Orleans* introduces us to a heroine we could call an *Afroaquanaut*, who wades through alien waters here on Earth. Afroaquanauts with disabilities need the prosthetic community's life support systems to navigate hostile terrain. Real-life Afroaquanauts struggle to survive the low-oxygen atmosphere of police brutality. "I can't breathe," said Eric Garner to the police officers choking him.

Part III. School

Part III focuses on a set of twenty-first-century novels that replicate the movements of students with disabilities into mainstream classrooms for the first time. These novels include *Wonder, Out of My Mind, Face, After Ever After, Reaching for Sun,* and *The Absolutely True Diary of a Part-Time Indian.* In the United States, mainstreaming commenced with the 1975 Education for All Handicapped Children Act (later renamed the Individuals with Disabilities Education Act) and in the United Kingdom with the 2001 Special Educational Needs and Disability Act. The novels of Part III illuminate the benefits an entire community receives when disability enters a new public space. They also show the hostility a student with a disability faces when he singlehandedly desegregates a classroom or a school. Protagonists like *Wonder*'s August Pullman have to build a repertoire of responses to the challenges of bullying, staring, and exclusion. Using the tools of disability epistemology like body humor, access intimacy, and ferocity in the face of injustice, students collude with their friends and families to rehearse an assertive future for themselves. At the same time, nondisabled young allies have the privilege of choosing whether or not to face down ableism.

These novels about school show how far we've come toward equality and how far we still need to go. The new heroes with disabilities still conform to a narrow personality profile that marginalizes intellectual and behavioral disabilities. These main characters have to be book smart, charming, and quick with a comeback. Their narrow personality profile mirrors a neoliberal era that talks a big story about inclusion but only gets the job halfway done. In one book after another, young narrators claim the power to speak for themselves by asserting that they are "not retarded" and displaying their wit and intellect. I call this gesture the Not Retarded Trope (NRT). The NRT not only perpetuates the insulting R-word but also narrows the pool of potential characters who have the power to speak for themselves. It arises from the misperception that young people with intellectual disabilities have no future. This misperception, I argue, has a material base in the lack of social supports to aid their transition from school to adulthood. In both the United States and the United Kingdom, the lack of prosthetic community makes this transition much harder than it needs to be. Literature falls short of imagining full lives for young people with intellectual disabilities because society has fallen short of full inclusion.

These school stories also reveal how far we still have to go in their failures of intersectionality. As I argue in chapter 7, "One Difference at a Time," British and American writers of realist stories about school-age kids abide by a strange unspoken rule that you can't be a person of color and have a disability at the same time. If the protagonist has a disability, they make the character white or erase all racial markers. If the main character is not white, the disability vanishes by the end of the book. The exception that proves the rule is Nicola Yoon's *Everything, Everything* (2015). Created by an African American author, the novel's protagonist is a teenager of black and Asian heritage confined to her house by Severe Combined Immunodeficiency Disorder. Spoiler alert: She doesn't have SCID at all! She just has a deceitful and overprotective mom.[20] What causes this failure of intersectionality? It is a neat solution to the problem authors face: how do you get a wide general audience to identify with a character who has a very specific, stigmatized difference? Authors and publishers solve this problem by asking readers to identify with only one difference at a time.

Part IV. Fantasy

Unlike the rest of *HandiLand*, the "Fantasy" section begins not with the new disability rights laws of recent decades but in the 1860s. British fantasy fiction held a space open for disability community many decades before the community's existence in real life. The ability to imagine HandiLands does not rely on their prior existence in the physical plane. Long before rights laws and mainstreaming, British fantasy fiction captured the experience of childhood disability through ingenious metaphors. Lewis Carroll dreamed up whimsical versions of misfitting to express his own difference and amuse his disability community of brothers and sisters. Dinah Maria Mulock created a traveling cloak that solved the access problem for a young ruler with impaired mobility. J. K. Rowling's supernatural analogues for chronic pain are recent links in a long chain of resonant disability metaphors reaching back to the Victorian era. I borrow Rowling's word "portkeys" as the name for visible, tangible metaphors that transport the reader into an alternate world of human histories and feelings. Just as the significant distortions of Afrofuturism make hidden injustice visible, the portkeys of fantasy give invisible disabilities visible form and turn them into characters in the story.

How is fantasy a public space? It envisions new human orders within its pages and creates communities of readers outside them. Fantasy is a crucial realm of freedom, recognition, and solace. Chapters 8 and 9 ponder what British fantasy fiction means for readers who see their own disabilities reflected yet magically transformed. In the fantasy genre, the arts and everyday life interact to reveal the hidden complexities of both. For instance, when fans explain their identification with fictional characters, they disclose their inner experiences of disabilities. Conversely, when writers adopt and adapt the experience of disabilities into fantasy and science fiction, their artistic choices reveal the inner workings of their craft. In chapter 8 I consider the role of "The Little Lame Prince" in the reading life of the first disabled person I ever knew, my mother, Phyllis Huntley Wheeler.

Harry Potter has inspired both virtual and real-life communities involving millions of fans worldwide. In chapter 9 I assess *Harry Potter*'s importance for fans with disabilities, including myself. J. K. Rowling's fantasy metaphors refute the stigmas surrounding invisible conditions. The Potterverse functions as a wellspring of identity, community, and decision-making for the disability fandom among the millennial generation who grew up with *Harry Potter*. Fans with disabilities identify with characters who begin as targets of cruelty or ridicule and finish as heroes. *Harry Potter* provides an escape into another world, yet one resonant with the emotional truths of living with a disability. The "Fantasy" section concludes with the science fiction of *Orleans* and the ways Afrofuturism rehearses a future for young black adults even in times and places where environmental racism works overtime to foreclose their futures.

Changing Stories

Why approach the politics of childhood disability through books for young readers rather than special education or the history of social movements? When I became the parent of a child with limited mobility I realized how deeply the books I read as a child governed my perceptions and misperceptions of disability.

I was sitting on an exercise mat at the Child Development and Rehabilitation Center, my fifteen-month-old son Kevin on my lap, my husband John next to me. The doctor was explaining that Kevin had cerebral palsy. The cerebral palsy caused his brain to send unclear messages to his muscles, which impaired his motor skills. I started to cry.

"He will be able to have a full life," Dr. Fusetti said. "He will be able to play soccer and ride a bike and go to school."

"Really? He'll be able to do all those things?"

"Yes."

"Will he ever learn to walk?"

"That's hard to say at this point. We just have to work with him and see how his muscles develop."

"Could he learn to walk normally, so no one can tell he has cerebral palsy?"

"No."

I handed Kevin to my husband and went back to work, reeling. I thought about all the gyms and school playgrounds where I had been teased for being the new kid, the kid who made such awkward and ineffectual moves at kickball and volleyball. On my way into a meeting I ran into my friend Mary and told her about the diagnosis.

"I'm sure everything will be all right," she said. "After a while you'll figure out a way to add this into your picture of Kevin."

"But kids can be so cruel," I said. The thought of him in a wheelchair made me feel as if the whole family were under a curse and powerless to remove it. I feared Kevin would face a lifetime of isolation, misunderstanding, and bitterness.

Eighteen years later, Kevin uses a power wheelchair and, as the doctor predicted, he lives a full life. He has an acute sense of humor, a businesslike approach to problem-solving, and a younger sister who used to be his best friend and is now his best verbal sparring partner. He has earned the respect of his mentors, professors, friends, and employers. I have learned that being unable to walk is not a big deal. A few years ago Kevin came home from an appointment at Shriners Hospital and said, "I got so tired of all those people at physical therapy saying, 'Maybe if he does this or we do that, he will walk someday.' It was such a relief at Shriners for the doctor to say, 'You're not going to walk.'"

Why did it seem to me like the end of the world if my child couldn't walk? Because a million cultural messages taught me that a phrase like "He never walked again" can only be uttered in a tragic tone. In the time between then and now I've examined the stories I absorbed from a lifetime of loving stories. One of my favorite childhood books was *The Secret Garden*. The main character, Mary Lennox, makes friends with her cousin Colin and through her healthy influence he learns how to walk at the same time both children learn to love life. Colin's walking becomes the triumphant conclusion to the novel. It's pretty much the same story in *Heidi*, another favorite book, where Heidi's friend Clara learns, with Heidi's encouragement, to walk. It turns out all four kids just needed to get more fresh air. And that physical therapist of Kevin's who was so determined to get him up and walking? Turns out she grew up reading *The Secret Garden*, too.

Fig. 2. Kevin and Bridget Shin-Wheeler, ages twelve and ten. Photo by Jordan Shin.

Many experiences have led me to understand that living with a disability doesn't have to be tragic. Kevin's sunny disposition changed my mind, but I also learned from other happy families. As Kevin grew into a nontoddling toddler, we met other children with cerebral palsy. It was a huge relief to discover other parents going through the same experiences of joy and frustration, and it was intellectually stimulating as well. We discovered so many things together. We learned from each other's children as well as our own. While struggling against financial, bureaucratic, and physical barriers, we learned a lot more about how the world works. I have drawn from this collective knowledge base to create Part I of this book.

I also discovered the vital knowledge base of disability studies. This academic field reinforced my growing conviction that there is nothing wrong with having a disability. It helped me let go of my desire to have a "normal" family and to see that if a person doesn't fit the society, we need to change the society, not the person. Disability studies offers a framework for seeing the interactions of disability with the world and its instruments of power. It gives names to all those weird little interactions at the mall, the supermarket, and the doctor's office. Once these interactions have names, we can move on from the small moments to work on the big picture instead. One principle of disability studies I find crucial is the idea that disability communities and experiences are the wellspring of knowledge, not doctors, not physical therapists—and not parents, even though parents' knowledge is also important.

These principles have enriched not only my parenting and intellectual life but also my inward experience of disabilities. They have helped me rethink the depression and anxiety that have shared my consciousness since childhood. I developed chronic daily migraine when my kids were small, and more recently, fibromyalgia. The skills I acquired as a mother have helped me navigate my own neurodiversity: skills like persistence, seeking out community, and a heightened sense of absurdity to keep me sane when dealing with recalcitrant insurance companies. I have also used skills acquired from disability studies: learning to accept chronic pain and brain fog as parts of my identity; placing my experiences within a larger disability politics; and refusing to write myself off just because a doctor does. Through these two communities I have met people who can listen to our family's disability stories without becoming shocked or recommending some exotic miracle potion.

I went to my first Society for Disability Studies conference when Kevin was three. The whole conference was a string of life-changing moments, among them a story Simi Linton told during a panel on disability in the arts.

Simi was talking about a painter friend who had cerebral palsy. "I asked him how his CP informed his art, and he said, 'Oh, Simi, I've been passing for so long, I wouldn't know how to bring my CP into my work.'" It had never occurred to me that cerebral palsy could be a fundamental part of one's identity to accept or deny. A three-year-old comes to recognize different parts of himself by having other people mirror those parts back to him. If CP were an essential component of Kevin's identity, that meant John and I needed to find ways to mirror his CP back to him, the same way we smiled back at him when he smiled. It occurred to me that while Kevin had John's big brown eyes and my curly hair, he also had a family resemblance to other people with cerebral palsy, like the way he held his mouth open when focusing on a difficult task or splayed his fingers when reaching for something.

I had already bought Kevin picture books and dolls reflecting the Korean side of his identity. Now I started looking for portrayals of children with disabilities, and it turned out that lots had happened in children's literature since *The Secret Garden*. I found *Seal Surfer*, *We Can Do It!*, *Mama Zooms*, *Featherless/Desplumado*, and later, *Max the Champion*. In the course of Kevin's childhood more books appeared that didn't just explain disability to children but actually told good stories. I read *The Lion Who Had Asthma* to Kevin and his sister Bridget to help them understand their new diagnosis. I asked them if they liked it. Kevin said, "Yes. I liked Sean. I would like to play with him." From my point of view, the important thing about this book was its clear explanation of nebulizer treatments. From Kevin's point of view, the important thing was a main character named Sean who liked to pretend to be a wild animal and a jet pilot. I realized that children's books need not just to explain disabilities but to create characters and stories kids can imagine themselves into.

I hope this book provides companionship and food for thought to parents of children with disabilities. For parents who already belong to disability cultures, I hope you find useful parallels and contrasts to your own reflections. For parents without much prior knowledge of disability, this book offers an entry point into cripistemology, a vast and vital realm of knowledge. Children with disabilities grow up into adults with disabilities. They have much to learn that only adults with disabilities can teach them. However, nondisabled parents tend to seek support from other nondisabled parents, teachers, and service providers rather than disabled adults. This book attempts to close that gap by creating a kind of virtual community, bringing the insights of scholars, artists, and activists with disabilities to bear on family life.

Conversely, disability studies needs children. I have noticed an aversion to addressing the needs of children among our scholars. Disability studies now has a strong presence in higher education, but there are still virtually no textbooks, articles, or curricula for teaching disability studies to children and teenagers. This aversion to childhood may arise because adults with disabilities are often treated as if they were children. For instance, Tobin Siebers has written that Jennifer Keelan's participation in the 1990 Capitol Crawl ran the risk of infantilizing adult protesters and stealing the spotlight from them. "Some activists worried that the coverage pictured the image most people with disabilities want to avoid—that they are pitiable, weak, and childlike—and concluded that assuming this identity was not worth the publicity. Predictably, in fact, the cameras did pick out exhausted, eight-year-old Jennifer Keelan for special attention, twisting the emphasis from the concerns of adults to those of children."[21]

Children with disabilities are not our rivals or surrogates, nor are they weak. They are our comrades in struggle, and often they are the ones on the front lines of the battle over the social meanings of disability. They belong not only in their families but in the varied spheres of public life, including the disability community. I begin this book with Jennifer Keelan, a child activist who made the news in 1990, and conclude it with Amariyanna Copeny, a child activist who made the news in 2016. In between, *HandiLand* recounts the everyday adventures of families in my own community and accompanies fictional youth like August Pullman, Melody Brooks, Arnold Spirit, Martin Turner, Prince Dolor, Harry Potter, and Fen de la Guerre as they navigate the rough waters of taking a disability public. This book is a show of respect to all adults and children who collude in shaping a just world.

Part One

———

Kids in Public Space

A Theory in Stories

One

Play Structures

A built environment assumes a certain type of human body entering that space. This fact came home to me when I started taking my son Kevin to local playgrounds. The play structure, that assembly of slides, bars, and decks, contains another invisible play structure: the theory of the human body its designers have in mind. A play structure is a conceptual scaffold that creates a lived reality. Its assumptions often go unnoticed and unchallenged until someone with the "wrong" body type attempts to enter. Children's literature is also a play structure: a world adults create that children imaginatively inhabit. Is the play structure expecting a child with a disability before he gets there, or is that child an exception to the rules of the game?

One Saturday when Kevin was twenty-one months old, we invited our friend Cyndi and her son Jaymason to the Adams Elementary School playground two blocks from our house in Eugene, Oregon. Out of the kids with cerebral palsy we knew, Jaymason was the most similar to Kevin in abilities. The boys were the same age and didn't walk but did talk (and at less than two, Jaymason could already say things like "May I have some broccoli, please?"). The boys could take some steps if you held them up under their arms. The Adams play structure consists of wood planks on a metal frame, with a swinging bridge and flights of stairs leading up to a big yellow spiral slide. With the formidable insistence of toddlers, both boys demanded to be walked up those stairs and across that swinging bridge to slide over and over again. This long route was the only way to access the slide. Cyndi and John were breaking their backs bending down to support the boys' steps across the "fun" bouncy bridge and up those unnecessarily long and twisty and multiple

Fig. 3. The play structure at Adams Elementary School, Eugene, Oregon. Photo by Jordan Shin.

sets of "fun" stairs. Luckily I was exempt from such duty because I was well along in my pregnancy with Bridget at the time.

Both Cyndi and John had intense looks on their faces, and the main expression I saw was anger. Since that occasion I have walked Kevin up that play structure many times, and I have felt that anger and physical exhaustion. The anger rains down suddenly and drenches completely. It reveals a lot about the physicality of living with disability, but even more about the invisible play structures of children and parents in society. We were furious at the people who built this play structure and left Kevin and Jaymason out of their thinking.

Play structures often assume that children can play separately from adults. Kevin could not sit independently. When he played sitting up, John or I sat behind him with our hands around his waist, our thumbs prompting the muscles of his lower back. Modern play structures have little kid-sized spaces, like crow's nests and sandboxes, where kids can congregate for a secret tea party or club meeting. These spaces are built deliberately small to fit children but not adults. At that time I usually had a migraine, and the pain and fatigue made it difficult to haul myself around. I was also substantially overweight. If Kevin wanted to play in the sandbox tucked under the slide, I had to wedge myself in there with him. It made my head throb, and I felt pretty ridiculous, like Alice in Wonderland after she grows. Direct sun also made my head throb, and few playgrounds had adult-sized shade anywhere near the play structures. Sometimes I was happy to fold myself in there just for the shade. Rosemarie Garland-Thomson calls this contortion a *misfit*: "A misfit occurs when the environment does not sustain the shape and function of the body that enters it."[1] As I will discuss, young readers also fit and misfit themselves into the play structures of literature and media.

What bodily assumptions do different types of playgrounds make? The post-and-deck play structure at our elementary school, the one that enraged John, Cyndi, and me, came from the back-to-nature ideas of the 1970s. Bark mulch and wooden decks replaced the concrete and metal of the midcentury modernist playground. A theory of the playing child as outdoor climber and explorer prompted our play structure. Landscape architects linked the slides and sandboxes, wanting to "forge an innovative and exploratory environment." They "used a softer palette, natural stones, and abstract shapes to create entire playgrounds. Kids could scamper along walls and/or work their way up stone mounds."[2] Children became the hikers and runners the 1970s wanted us to be.

These designers envisioned a child who scampers and rock climbs, a junior version of the mountain climber who became the "wilderness bodily ideal" of the environmental movement.[3] Unfortunately, the mass-produced play structures that grew from this ideal do not only *allow* children to scamper and climb on their way to the slide; they *require* children to do so. Susan G. Solomon criticizes "the restricted options of a post-and-platform ensemble: wait, go up, go across, go down, and start all over again. The interactions among young users is limited; there is nothing to do together."[4]

Playgrounds began with the ideal of an inclusive community that plays together. In the newly industrialized and overcrowded cities of the late nineteenth century, children worked in the formal and informal labor force. Social pioneer Jane Addams wrote in 1910, "Only in the modern city have men concluded that it is no longer necessary for the municipality to provide for the insatiable desire for play."[5] Declaring that the "right to play" included immigrant and other working-class children, Progressive Era reformers invented the playground.[6] The playground movement also had its theory of the human body: the playing child represented democracy in action. The playground was a "great ethical laboratory," in the words of Luther Gulick, first president of the Playground Association of America.[7] In the sandbox, on the swings and playing fields, children had the freedom to develop fair play, mutual consent, and self-control. They taught each other the skills of citizens in a democracy.

Inclusive playgrounds extend this citizenship to children with disabilities. On another Saturday playdate Cyndi introduced us to Emerald Park. It had swings with big plastic seats and shoulder straps for older children with limited trunk control. The play structure had wheelchair and stroller accessible ramps leading to the smaller slides. These features played a part in my larger revelation: instead of fitting the kid into the space, you can change the space to fit the kid. When Kevin and Jaymason were four, RiverPlay opened at Skinner Butte Park in Eugene, and both boys got their first power wheelchairs when they were five. Not only did RiverPlay have innovative features for kids in wheelchairs and blind kids; the playground offered a theory of children with disabilities as integral members of our town and its history. RiverPlay welcomed them because adults with disabilities had a say throughout the planning process.[8]

A miniature version of Eugene circa 1865, RiverPlay nestles in the city's core between the Willamette River path and the butte where Eugene Skinner built the first homesteading cabin. To the north stands a play structure representing Skinner Butte, with metal conifers topping a rock climbing wall. As in real life, a miniature Willamette Street runs south from Skinner Butte down a row of playhouses: city hall, jail, school, Oregon Stagecoach, Bristow's Mercantile, Sloan's Blacksmith Shop, and the St. Charles Hotel. Nearby, children turn a crank to give each other rides on the ferry (est. 1847) and play in the millrace water wheel. In the giant sandbox next to the miniature river, children dig up concrete fossils from many eras of Oregon history and prehistory.

RiverPlay imagines children with disabilities as full citizens. An earth berm leads to a wheelchair ramp on the wide middle deck of the play structure, high in the air. Sitting on a bench far below and yards away, I watched Kevin zoom onto the play structure, crawl out of his wheelchair, and hit the slide on his own. Later, Kevin paddled his hands in a tiny river flowing at wheelchair height through rocky channels embossed with bronze fossils, dragonflies, and turtles for tactile play. Expensive poured-in-place rubber covers the ground instead of bark mulch, the painful and obstructive bane of crawlers and wheelchair drivers. The rubber changes color to represent the main street, bridges, and river and provide routes for children with low vision. The park has a raised map labeled in Braille. My only access quibble is the continued prejudice against playground shade; the sun beats down on

Fig. 4. The wheelchair ramp on the play structure at RiverPlay, Eugene, Oregon. Photo by Jordan Shin.

RiverPlay in the middle of summer. I can't be the only parent who fights off fatigue while sitting in the sun.

RiverPlay, however, imagines children with disabilities as white citizens only. It invites young visitors into a pioneer town where white homesteaders occupied Native American land. A replica of Eugene Skinner's 1846 homesteading cabin sits a few yards from RiverPlay, and the interpretive sign quotes his diary: "for 4 months less 3 days" his wife Mary "never saw the face of a White woman, or child except our own."[9] By 1865 the town Skinner built was full of white pioneers. The RiverPlay plan originally included a Kalapuya Indian village but it never materialized.[10] The only traces of Kalapuya history are empty tent poles and some arrowheads in the sand dig. African Americans also would have been rare in 1865 Eugene. While homesteading was technically open to free black citizens, Oregon passed several laws in the 1840s that barred African Americans from entering the territory.[11] Thus, RiverPlay pictures children with disabilities as white.

Literature for young readers is another public space that has trouble thinking about disability and nonwhite identity at the same time. In this book I have endeavored to make room for thinking intersectionally about racial and bodymind diversity at the same time.

Literature and Media as Play Structures

Youth with disabilities also infiltrate the playgrounds of literature and popular media. They fit themselves into stories. Young children in particular don't just listen to stories; they play in them, live in them, and absorb them into their DNA. Vivian Gussin Paley argues that the dramatization of concepts is young children's native language. "Play and its necessary core of storytelling are the primary realities in the preschool and kindergarten, and they may well be the prototypes for imaginative endeavors throughout our lives."[12] More than ever before, children and young adults with disabilities find themselves represented in literature and other media.

However, a portrayal does not guarantee that readers and viewers will identify with it. In the following examples from Disney movies, comics, picture books, and hip-hop, I show how children and young adults with disabilities fit themselves into stories. Sometimes readers and viewers match stories to their own with ease. Some stories appear to invite disabled readers but in fact do not. Sometimes there is a profound misfitting and young adults have to bend the bars of the stories to squeeze themselves in.

Fitting

The 2013 film *Frozen* may not seem like a disability narrative, but young people on the autism spectrum have found they fit perfectly into the character of Elsa. In Elsa's childhood and coming of age, blogger E sees "a number of parallels to my own life, especially based around my being autistic. And I wanted to recognize that, because it made me really really happy. I almost never relate to movie characters that way, but I did, and it made me smile."[13] Elsa's story parallels several young bloggers' experiences of autism, including isolation, repression, meltdowns, and self-acceptance. Fans employ the social model of disability, seeing Elsa's biggest problem in others' misunderstanding rather than the autism itself. According to Luna Lindsey, "After one mistake, her talent turns into a dark and ugly thing, not because of Elsa herself, but because of how the people around her view it."[14] Comparing *Frozen* with their own lives, bloggers expose the difficulties of living with autism in a neurotypical world. In Elsa they find a place to fit their experience of misfitting.

Frozen fans with autism identify with the repression and unleashing of Elsa's powers. Through her graceful hand motions Princess Elsa has the power to cast snow and ice wherever she aims or touches. As a child she accidentally freezes her sister Anna's face while they are playing. Their frightened parents plunge Elsa into a kind of social death, erasing Anna's memory of her sister's powers and consigning Elsa to her room, "alone, where I can be who I am without hurting anybody."[15] Elsa wears gloves at all times because they block her freezing powers. During her young adulthood, the film's villain locks up her hands in iron gloves attached with heavy chains to the stone walls of her castle.

The imprisonment of Elsa's hands serves as a metaphor for people with autism who have been told since childhood to stop stimming and act more like neurotypical people. Stimming is any repetitive bodily behavior, such as flapping hands, rocking, or tapping, considered unusual in the neurotypical world. Writer and educator Julia Bascom describes stimming as a crucial part of autistic self-expression.[16] "My hands are more me than I am." She deplores educational methods that banish stimming from the classroom. "When I was a little girl, they held my hands down in tacky glue while I cried."[17] If selfhood rests in the hands, then their confinement represents a cruel form of silencing akin to the medievalism of Elsa's iron chains.

Frozen fans on the spectrum put their own childhood stories in political context. Images of Elsa's confinement remind Jeffrey Zare and E of the ways they have been told to hide all traces of their autism. Zare feels a personal connection to Elsa because both of them live under orders to hide what makes them different. Compared to the neurotypical majority, he writes, people with autism may get emotional about different things or express their emotions differently. The majority pressures children with autism to conceal and conform. "A famous line from the movie that has meaning to me is 'Conceal, don't feel' . . . the person with autism is taught even by well meaning people that while it's healthy for others to express their emotions, when we express our emotions, it's wrong."[18] In Zare's experience, the world asks the autist to become more understandable, but it does not ask the majority to become more understanding. "I have facetiously commented before, 'Being understood is someone else's luxury.'"[19]

E calls for an educational philosophy that teaches children on the spectrum how to wield their powers constructively rather than hide them. "There isn't any help for us to learn how to work with what we are given. We don't have the opportunity to learn and grow with our powers, we are told to suppress them or there will be dire consequences."[20] Bloggers' experiences replicate long-running political struggles over the treatment of people with autism. These young people have not experienced the physical segregation of institutions, but the bad old days live on in the injunction to lock away one's differences.

Frozen fans also aim their critiques at the social construction of meltdowns. They regard the emotional meltdown, a common component of autism, as a side effect of social pressures to conceal one's true self. The repression of feelings and the need to stim build up into an explosion that can hurt other people. The emotions of a person on the spectrum are not scary by nature, but can turn that way if long repressed. To show how meltdowns happen, E reinterprets the coronation scene in *Frozen* where Elsa, frightened and upset, inadvertently freezes the whole kingdom into an eternal winter.

> When she is being crowned, and has to remove her gloves, you see her muster every tiny ounce of self-control she has, so that her hands will work the way "normal" people do. She is able to do it, but only briefly. Because that's not how her body works, and there are limits to how much anyone can do to "pass" as normal, and she is finding her limits. And when she is pushed past her limit later at the party, she has a meltdown, and her magic spills out uncontrollably. She accidentally hurts someone she loves, terrifies everyone around, and spirals into a complete shutdown, running away from everyone in the process. I'm sure I am not the only one who has had this experience.[21]

E conveys beautifully the tremendous effort required to pass for nondisabled. Nearly always, passing drives people past their limits and exacts a high price. Luna Lindsey also interprets Elsa's meltdown as the result of repression. "By stuffing her emotions, by trying to deny who she really is, by allowing social shame to consume her, she becomes explosive."[22] Like E, Lindsey sees the answer in learning to use one's powers constructively rather than suppressing them. By the end of the movie, Elsa has returned to the people she loves and freed them from eternal winter. She uses her powers for fun, conjuring up a skating rink in front of the castle. Lindsey writes, "Elsa finds her answer, and it's the answer I found. . . . It's only when she 'lets it go' and accepts who she is in spite of what others tell her, that her talent becomes a controllable force for good. The message here, for anyone with autism or Asperger's, is to be true to your autistic self."[23] Like E, Lindsey suggests that young people should be taught how to use their powers for good rather than repress them. If Lindsey and her peers had encountered this message in their early youth, it would have saved them years of struggle.

These disability interpretations of *Frozen* do not arise from raw coincidence. There is in fact a disability subtext to the characterization of Elsa in *Frozen*, revealed in documentary interviews with the film's creators. Songwriter Kristen Anderson-Lopez recounts that in earlier versions of the screenplay "Elsa was a villain. She was still probably coming down the mountain later with her army of evil snowmen to terrorize the village."[24] Then executive producer John Lasseter started thinking about his ten-year-old son, recently diagnosed with type 1 diabetes. "This little guy was being poked with needle after needle after needle . . . and he asked, 'Why me?' And I thought of Sam as I was thinking of Elsa. She was born with this. Why is she a villain?"[25] "Born this way" connotes a young person's true identity society has an obligation to respect.

Meanwhile, songwriters Robert Lopez and Kristen Anderson-Lopez were thinking along the same lines, revisiting the story from Elsa's point of view. "And we started getting into the head space of how you'd feel if you were that isolated."[26] This exercise in empathy turned Elsa's big musical number "Let It Go" from a villain's song into "this moment of exhilaration where she could finally let go of all she'd been holding inside."[27] Originally, Elsa's character corresponded to a premodern concept of disability. She was a monster. Now she fits a contemporary definition of disability as an identity worthy of social room. An "autism version" of "Let It Go" circulates on the internet. Sarah Rush's altered lyrics conclude, "I don't care what they're going to say. Let this girl stim on. The stares never bothered me anyway."[28] In a movie that has reached millions of children, young adults on the autism spectrum have seen a model of acceptance better than the repression they encountered in their own childhoods.

Melissa McCloskey, a student in my London study abroad class on graphic narratives, had no trouble at all fitting herself into Katie Green's graphic memoir *Lighter Than My Shadow*. At a British Library exhibit on comics, McCloskey looked at a page from the book and did a double take.

> It was a page that displayed a picture of a girl standing on a scale with a cloud of scribbles above her head. The picture next to it showed the same girl crouched into a ball, clearly distressed while thoughts of food, numbers, and more scribbles consumed her. I immediately knew what this comic was about because I know it all too well myself.
>
> The displayed comic was *Lighter Than My Shadow* by Katie Green and it is a graphic narrative about her own experience with having an eating disorder. As someone that has gone through several hospitalizations, residential programs, and treatment for an eating disorder of my own, this hit close to home, and hard. I stood in front of the comic for longer than I was comfortable with, longer than I have ever stood in front of something in an exhibit or museum before. I was analyzing the pain that the author drew in her face and I was putting myself into each visual aspect of the character. I could feel my own eyes squint with the girl in the text and I could feel my stomach condensing into a nauseating knot. I had never heard about this particular graphic narrative before but it allowed me to understand how people are able to connect on a deeper level to comics. The fact of the matter is that sometimes we are unable to put words to our emotions; sometimes our emotions are merely a galaxy of chaotic scribbles above our heads.[29]

What an astounding phrase: "Sometimes our emotions are merely a galaxy of chaotic scribbles above our heads." Words may not render an experience, yet body language and visual icons deliver the message. McCloskey attaches her own truths to a widely available image. Ubiquitous in the age of memes, such image-matching represents a new genre of life writing. McCloskey found that "some of my indefinable emotions were given a visual definition" through Green's images.[30] However, McCloskey also creates images of her own. "For me, there are times when I can construct a mental picture of the struggles that I have gone through easier than I can explain it in words."[31] She matches her mental pictures to those in Katie Green's book. Indeed, she matches the book's pain not only with images but with her entire body, squinting with the girl in the text, her "stomach condensing into a nauseating knot." If literature is a play structure, sometimes playing there hurts.

Lighter Than My Shadow was ready for Melissa McCloskey before she got there. Although McCloskey is American and Katie Green is English, both are white and members of the same disability community. Their experiences are so similar, McCloskey can fill in the gaps of Green's pictures with her own experience. She decodes the image of "Katie walking in long pants, a long-sleeved shirt, and a scarf even though it indicates on an earlier panel that it is summer. This was because Katie was most likely cold from a low heart rate causing decreased blood flow and from a low body weight."[32] Disability graphic memoirs play central roles in the contemporary comics publishing boom and represent an important aspect of childhood disability infiltrating public space. Firsthand accounts like Green's *Lighter Than My Shadow*, David Small's *Stitches*, Al Davison's *Spiral Cage*, Cece Bell's *El Deafo*, and Allie Brosh's *Hyperbole and a Half* are ready for young readers before they get there.

Pseudofitting

How does image-matching work for blind children? *The Black Book of Colors* translates a blind child's perceptual world into the visual form of the picture book. It speaks to experiences beyond pictures, just as *Lighter Than My Shadow* speaks to experiences beyond words. An artistic tour de force by the Venezuelan team of Rosana Faría and Menena Cottin, *The Black Book of Colors* is a monochromatic, poetic, and sensual explosion. Like many picture books, this one teaches children their colors, but here the teacher is a young blind narrator named Tomás who matches colors to nonvisual experience. The English translation begins, "Thomas says that yellow tastes like mustard, but is as soft as a baby chick's feathers. Red is sour like unripe strawberries and as sweet as watermelon. It hurts when he finds it on his scraped knee."[33] On each page, braille translation runs above the lines of text. Embossed in glossy black on black pages float feathers and strawberries, leaves and kites, freshly cut grass, and the waves of his mother's hair. Each page gratifies the fingers.

Surprisingly, however, *The Black Book of Colors* excludes the possibility of a blind child reader. The braille is too shallow to be legible, while the pictures are indecipherable unless you can see them as well.[34] Blind children might enjoy hearing the text, but the book works primarily as a disability simulation for sighted readers. In a final note the authors concede that the braille translation "due to book production demands is of a quality intended for sighted readers only."[35] As all too often, the high cost of adaptive technology excludes children with disabilities. *The Black Book of Colors* invites readers to imagine living without sight, but does not invite blind readers. Because it represents disability while excluding it, the book reminds me of the slogan "Nothing about us without us" popularized by South African disability activists Tshililo Michael Masutha and William Rowland, both visually impaired.[36]

Misfitting

Trigger warning: this section contains graphic depictions of sexual violence.

Some young people with disabilities hear themselves in hip-hop music. They experience depression and anxiety woven together with other identities, and media must reflect that multiplicity. Like many African American art forms, hip-hop tends to embed its disability narratives within stories of race. Classic songs like Grandmaster Flash and the Furious Five's "The Message," 2Pac's "16 on Death Row," and the Geto Boys' "Mind Playing Tricks on Me" lead with urban violence, but at their tender core lies a disability narrative about depression, suicide, and losing one's grip on reality. The story of psychological disabilities is there if the listener has ears for it.

In "Cleaning Out My Closet," Angel Haze tells a story of mental illness and post-traumatic stress disorder born from childhood sexual abuse. In explaining how she has recovered but will never be the same, Haze upends the ableist stereotype of black women as impermeably strong. This stereotype impedes African American women's disability claims, literally and figuratively. As Therí Pickens writes, "Materially, the perception of inherent strength and durability minimizes the availability of compassion and medical treatment. Culturally, this perception facilitates the racialized and gendered bias against the credibility of black female emotional and physical pain."[37] The icon of the strong black woman may seem like a positive image, but it can also be a roadblock.

Angel Haze enacts a misfitting in "Cleaning Out My Closet." To make room for her story she bends the bars of the hip-hop play structure as well as the bars of mental disability narrative. First she finds a way past the sexual objectification of African American women in commercial rap music, an objectification widely criticized by men and women in the hip-hop world. Hip-hop scholar Tricia Rose writes that hypersexism, homophobia, "and violent portraits of black masculinity . . . have become rap's calling cards. Relying on an ever-narrowing range of images and themes, this commercial juggernaut has played a central role in the near-depletion of what was once a vibrant, diverse, and complex popular genre."[38] Angel Haze's song "Cleaning Out My Closet" helps return vibrant complexity to hip-hop, drawing on the genre's power to reflect on her life experiences at the receiving end of black male violence. Haze also reshapes conventional ideas of disability narrative, allowing the trauma in black people's lives to be heard as stories of neurodiversity.

Angel Haze pushes her way past the misogyny of conventional rap. "Cleaning Out My Closet" uses the beats and title of a popular song by Eminem, a white rapper famous for his talent, commercial success, and graphic violence and hatred against women. Eminem is the best-selling rapper of all time and in the top ten of sales for all musicians.[39] In his version of the song he spits rage and blame toward his mother with lines like "You selfish bitch, I hope you fuckin' burn in hell for this shit."[40] Angel Haze makes Eminem testify against himself, using his beats to tell the woman's side of the story. This story is about moving beyond hatred and blame. She also reshapes the meaning of "explicit content" in popular music. Her song begins, "Now this might get a little personal / Or a lot actually / Parental discretion is advised." The warning label "Parental Advisory Explicit Content" often appeals to young music buyers because it promises the pleasures of graphic language, sex, and violence. Here, however, Angel Haze presents sexual violence as anything but desirable. Her explicit language shows that child sexual abuse is not sexy.

> My heart was pumping it was thumping with like tons of fear
> Imagine being seven and seeing cum in your underwear
> I know it's nasty but sometimes I'd even bleed from my butt
> Disgusting right? Now let that feeling ring through your guts[41]

"Cleaning Out My Closet" signals a profound interdependence of mind and body. Childhood trauma begins the lifelong struggle Angel Haze calls "the war with my mind." Years of rape permanently altered her brain development. "I never got to be a kid so that's as far as I grow / My mental state is out of date, and that's as far as I know." While she can never return to a pretraumatic state, she has owned her history and learned to love herself. Her internal struggle began with the surreal unbelievability of the first rape: "See it was weird because it felt like I was losing my mind / And then it happened like it happened millions of times." As a child she felt not only deep fear but "volcanically eruptive" hate. The surrealism of real life made it hard to tell the difference between fantasies and hallucinations. "And in my mind I'd envision that I was speaking with God / And then I'd chop his fucking fist off and beat him with mine." Once grown and out of her abusers' reach, Haze struggled with anorexia, suicide attempts, escapism, and self-loathing before she faced the past and began to heal.

> I'm not deranged anymore, I'm not the same anymore
> I mean I'm sane but I'm insane but not the same as before
> I had to deal with my shit, I had to look at my truth
> To understand that to grow you've got to look at your root
> I had to cut off the dead, I had to make myself proud
> And now I'm just standing living breathing proof look at me now[42]

The phrase "I'm sane but I'm insane but not the same as before" lies at the core of Angel Haze's disability discourse. She has recovered from trauma, but her neurodivergence is here to stay. Her scars will always tell long stories. However, she has grown beyond hatred of herself or anyone else, which constitutes a triumph. She has lived to feel, understand, and tell her tale. Like other African American writers, Haze uses melancholy as a form of resistance. Despite the denial of humanity that violence demands, melancholy asserts selfhood, subjectivity, and thus survival.[43] At the end of the song Haze reaches out to the survivor community: "Now I'm just saying this to tell you there's a way from the ground / The makings of a legend are often hidden in trials / Just be strong and just move on and just accept what you can / Because it makes your story better when you read at the end." Sharing her story for free with people who might need it, Angel Haze released "Cleaning Out My Closet" as a free MP3 download.[44]

Hip-hop is about power. That power can be misused, as in the objectification of women, or used brilliantly, as in Angel Haze's test of strength against abuse. Her rapping surges in wave after wave. Her voice rises unimpeded from viscera to throat, defying the notion that anyone ever invaded this body. "Yeah, there's a story behind every single scar that I show / This a me nobody's gotten before."

"Cleaning Out My Closet" points toward a vision of disability justice that transcends what Patty Berne calls the "cliffhangers" of the US disability rights movement: "It is single issue identity based; its leadership has historically centered white experiences; its framework leaves out other forms of oppression."[45] While the song speaks to a community that shares an understanding of neurodiversity and post-traumatic stress disorder, it also speaks to the majority of African American girls and women, over 60 percent of whom have known some form of sexual violence.[46] It is impossible to separate out the survivor community from the disability community because they are the

Fig. 5. Angel Haze in concert, Belgrave Music Hall, Leeds, Britain. Rex Features/ AP Images.

same people. Sexual violence creates disability. While Angel Haze testifies that rape altered her body and mind, the scientific evidence also testifies that sexual violence creates mental and physical disabilities. According to the most recent survey by the US Centers for Disease Control and Prevention, higher rates of chronic illness and physical and mental pain accompany a history of sexual violence.

> The prevalence of adverse mental and physical health outcomes was significantly higher among women with a history of rape or stalking by any perpetrator, or physical violence by an intimate partner, compared to women without a history of these forms of violence. This includes a higher reported prevalence of asthma, irritable bowel syndrome, diabetes, frequent headaches, chronic pain, difficulty sleeping, and activity limitations. The percentage of women who considered their physical or mental health to be poor was almost three times higher among women with a history of violence compared to women who have not experienced these forms of violence.[47]

In the past, disability studies has shied away from the circumstances that cause disability, focusing instead on the potential for living well afterward. If we contemplate the causes of disability, we run the risk of suggesting that there is something wrong with having one, and perhaps it should be prevented through selective abortion or other medical interventions. However, when it comes to the traumas of poverty, racism, and violence, disability studies must consider the causes and prevention of disability. We will never achieve real diversity without this conversation. Although there is nothing wrong with having a disability, it is wrong to give someone a disability. We need a discourse ready for all kinds of stories before they get here.

Two

Masculinity at the
Orthopedic Preschool

———

Once there was a paradise by the inelegant name of the Orthopedically Impaired Preschool. It didn't look like much from the outside, just a classroom in an unused corner of a tired brown school. What happened inside, however, was rare and enchanted. It was HandiLand. It was Camelot. Funded by the state of Oregon, the OI Preschool epitomized what I call *the prosthetic community*, a cluster of living beings, ideas, resources, and objects that enable the full inclusion of people with disabilities. The four staff members were a dream team who could troubleshoot at lightning speed. Gina, the head teacher, was also a speech therapist, Janice was a physical therapist, Karen an occupational therapist, and Dianna Lee, the instructional aide, had the best lap in the world for comforting a homesick child. Half the students had cerebral palsy and half of them were able-bodied "playmates" whose families paid a low fee.

Dianna, Karen, Janice, and Gina were more than ready for Kevin when he got there. They didn't blink an eye when I told them Kevin had life-threatening allergies and took over an hour to eat lunch. They were also at ease with other kids' gastric tube feeding, cystic fibrosis, choking, gagging, and seizures. After struggling on our own for three years, we parents breathed a sigh of relief and went out for coffee together.

Nanette Christou, mother of twins Miriam and Elia, says that the four teachers created "an environment where the girls could become their best selves." Both mother and daughters benefited from the preschool's climate of acceptance and commitment to finding what worked for each child.

I had been told and had begun to believe that Miriam's shortcomings in following directions and cooperation were because of my own bad parenting. I will forever be grateful to Karen, who somehow picked up on this, for redirecting me and liberating my understanding by simply stating something to the effect that this is from brain injury, nothing else, and especially not from bad parenting. . . . OI helped me gain perspective and reclaim my belief in my mothering, the good natured and kind hearted spirit resident in my beautiful daughter Miriam, and move forward in our journey of working through life. At OI, I felt for the first time that Miriam was not being judged, that teacher-therapists were not on fault-finding missions, and that we were safe to figure out what would work in moving forward. This has given me strength and chutzpah to stand up and advocate for both my girls and myself over the years. I do not know if I would have had the confidence to push back against the "experts" had I not been an OI mom.[1]

The OI Preschool came close to the vision of perfect inclusion that philosopher Susan Wendell describes: "I imagine a fully accessible society, [with] universal recognition that all structures have to be built and all activities have to be organized for the widest practical range of human abilities . . . everyone who is not disabled now can participate in sports or games or make art, and that sort of general ability should be the goal."[2] With their endless creativity and homemade gadgets, the four teachers devised ways for every child to cut out valentines, paint at easels, and play the hokeypokey. At recess, Gina held a tiny swing in one hand and a tiny sandbox in the other, so a child could indicate her choice of playground activity with the slightest head nod. The preschool owned a wheelchair swing, a big steel platform on heavy chains the teachers hooked on the swing set. A kid could roll onto it to swing without even leaving his wheelchair. Kevin and Jaymason raced down the play structure ramp in their walkers, yelling and shrieking. At OI Kevin unleashed his silly and gregarious self: giggling as he launched himself into his new friend Keegan's lap and knocked them both over, wide-eyed with excitement about a visit from Smokey the Bear, whom he called "Funky the Bear."

Carina Cooper, whose daughter Hailey went to the school, describes it as "magical."

OI Pre-School was magical. . . . I've never seen a team that worked together as well as those four ladies did. . . . it was just this amazing combination of women that took care of this great group of kids. Half

Fig. 6. Kevin playing with Miriam Christou. Photo by Jordan Shin.

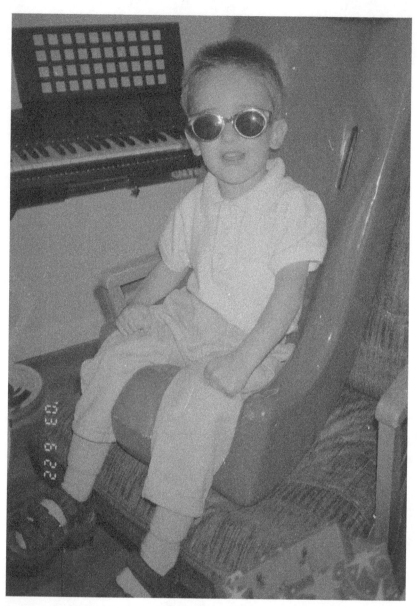

Fig. 7. Jaymason Bouwman, almost three. Photo by Jordan Shin.

typically developing pre-school kids and half with disabilities and they all played together, and in that classroom there was no difference as far as friends went. They were all friends with each other, and there was no hierarchy of the children. They were all friends equally and it was—I thought it was a magical place. There's no place like it and I haven't seen anything that came together as well as that did since then.[3]

The OI Preschool had the widest possible range of physical ability. Children with and without physical disabilities learned how to play together, equipping them for such interactions in their future lives.[4] Playmates like Keegan, Amanda, and Gina's daughter Emma would take off their shoes, get down on the carpet, and crawl around playing tag with Kevin. Hopping, bouncing, and pouncing, Kevin always left behind at least one of his socks. Nanette Christou says that the preschool taught her daughter Elia an openness to all kinds of diversity that has stayed with her through the teenage years. "I remember her saying how some of her friends could walk and some could not and how some could see and how some couldn't. It was all an equal playing field for her. She adored hanging out with Hailey Grace who could not communicate with her in any of the typical ways but in whom Elia found a great friend. . . . That openness that she experienced and that was cultivated at OI can be seen in my 19 year old Elia—in her openness to gender differences and class difference and religious diversity."[5]

The children with cerebral palsy displayed a full rainbow spectrum of differences within the same impairment. It was like a United Nations of Cerebral Palsy. Elia's very mild CP showed itself only in her left eye and slight jumpiness. Kevin was right in the middle of the spectrum, able by now to kneel, crawl, use a walker, and speak in full sentences. Joy had a gentle spirit and limited motion, and spoke with her eyes rather than words. She spent morning free time in the vertical stander, taking a break from her wheelchair. Each morning Kevin asked me to lift him into the high Tripp Trapp chair facing Joy. Her stander had a tray attached to the front, and Kevin arranged blocks and zoomed cars across the tray while Joy smiled at him with her big blue eyes.

The swift and easy inclusion of the OI Preschool stood in sharp contrast to the barriers John and I encountered as Kevin grew from birth to age three. For one thing, we had started to feel like misfits in our social circle. We knew several families with children the same age, but many of these friendships came unglued when their babies learned to walk and ours didn't. The kids we knew from the neighborhood and our birth group began to roam and climb all over the place while Kevin remained a nontoddling toddler. One Saturday morning I entered a friend's house for a playdate, holding Kevin on my right hip and looking around for a place to set him down and prop him up. Our hostess gestured toward the far corner of the living room and said, "Over there are some toys *Kevin* can play with." Day by day John and I learned the tricks and tools of inclusion, but we didn't find many social spaces beyond the family that seemed to understand.

Meanwhile John and I had begun to feel the blunt force of the delays, disappointments, and dysfunctions that often typify services for people with disabilities. As just about anyone who works with such businesses will tell you, preposterously long wait times and inexplicable incompetencies run wild in the world of disability goods and services. As John said once, "It's like living in communist Hungary circa 1953, but there's no Five Year Plan." Ann Dean, the head physical therapist at our local clinic, urged us to get on the waiting list for a revolutionary new device called a spiral brace. "The brace is coiled like a spring, so it propels the child forward with every step," Ann said admiringly. "We are extraordinarily lucky, because the inventor lives right here in Eugene. When Kevin gets that spiral brace, he will really take off." So we got on the waiting list for an appointment. And we waited. For months. Strangely enough, we kept falling off the list. Every week we checked in with Ann. Every week she said, "I don't see you on the list." So every week we put ourselves back on the list. And every week Ann said, "When he gets that spiral brace, he's really going to take off."

When our appointment finally came, the genius inventor started yelling at us in his waiting room. "You should not be here," he shouted. "Ann is supposed to come with you to see me. And this child is nowhere near ready for a spiral brace. What were you thinking?" He led us into his examining room and asked us to take off Kevin's shoes and socks. He grabbed Kevin by the right ankle and yanked his toes up as high as they would go. Kevin started crying. My gut reaction was to whisk my baby away from this botulism toxin of a man, a man capable of going into a tirade over a toddler's foot.

On the following Tuesday we had an appointment at the clinic with Ann Dean and one of the clinic doctors. They kept us waiting for an hour and forty-five minutes past our appointment time. Already aggrieved at Ann and the entire world of orthopedics, I now attempted to subdue an increasingly hungry and impatient toddler. When we finally made it into the examining room, I explained how things went wrong at the inventor's office. Ann didn't seem at all apologetic or fazed by my account. I felt bad about taking Kevin back into a clinical setting just a few days after that visit, so I was extra soothing and gentle with him. I told Ann and the doctor, "Now, Kevin's just had a rough time, so I told him I wouldn't let anyone grab him or yank his foot in here today." When we got the paperwork from this appointment in the mail, the doctor's chart notes said, "Patient is used to being indulged and will only cooperate with providers if bribed and cajoled."

At the OI Preschool nobody blamed or judged us. The preschool put into practice what disability theory calls the social model: the idea that people with disabilities don't need fixing but rather can get along just fine in a world that doesn't exclude them. As Tobin Siebers writes, the social model "makes it possible to see disability as the effect of an environment hostile to some bodies and not to others, requiring advances in social justice rather than medicine."[6] The team at OI gave us the adaptations and workarounds we needed to bridge the gap between cerebral palsy and the nondisabled world.

We were used to entering a new space and rearranging the furniture to make a place for Kevin to sit, but Janice was way ahead of us. She had five or six chairs of increasing size lined up and tried Kevin in each until she found the right one. Then she added foam pads of various sizes until he was safe, comfortable, and upright in his seat. We didn't have to do a thing.

Not having to do a thing is a rare and buoyant feeling for parents of children with disabilities. We often have a bad reputation for excess anxiety, aggression, and hovering, but we have good reasons for our vigilance.[7] Especially when our kids are small, only the wealthier and luckier among us ever get to go off duty. I think of myself as a pretty mellow, unhelicopterish mom, but my kids' disabilities have trained me otherwise. Take their potentially fatal peanut allergies, for instance. If a Fun-Size Mr. Goodbar could kill your kid at any moment, what looks to the outside world like hypervigilance looks to us like good parenting. To most people, the words "piñata" or "potluck" may conjure up images of innocuous and festive gatherings. When we hear those words, we think, "Secure the perimeter!" And we are among the lucky parents with plenty of money and respite care. So, to meet a team of caregivers willing and capable of taking over—and for free? Astounding.

The other moms were astounding, too. When I told stories about our breakthroughs and frustrations, the other moms knew exactly what I was talking about. One day, having coffee at Cyndi's house with Robin, I said, "The people I work with who are parents seem to worry about totally different things than I do." "Like what?" asked Robin. I said, "I work with this woman who has a daughter in first grade, and she's worried about her *penmanship.*" Robin and Cyndi laughed out loud.

Fig. 8. Hailey Cooper.
Photo by Jordan Shin.

"You know what bugs me?" Cyndi asked. "When you take your kid to the mall and everybody stares at you."

"Oh, I know," I said. "And the worst ones? They're the ones who think they're really subtle and wait until you've gone past them, then they turn around and stare at you from behind."

Robin said, "We should all get T-shirts that say across the back, "KEEP STARING. I MIGHT DO A TRICK."

On the mornings I brought Kevin to school, I learned along with him how to make friends, play, and communicate with people who can't speak or move much. Alex was a handsome five-year-old with curly honey-colored hair. I didn't know how much emotion he could convey until I sang "Itsy Bitsy Spider" and his face lit up. He radiated delight when his parents, Robin and Carlo, walked into the room. Alex loved to watch other kids running around, swiveling his head as far as humanly possible. Hailey Cooper, who passed away at age eleven, had a "huge personality," in her mother's words. She could only see out of the corners of her eyes, so she would look at you sideways and startle you with her deep, hearty guffaw. "Alex and Hailey kinda had their own little language without talking. They smiled at each other and they kind of had this little flirty thing going . . . we parked Hailey's wheel-chair next to Alex's and Alex's face would immediately turn red."[8] When she

Fig. 9. Alex Yozzo, age fifteen. Photo by Jordan Shin.

and Alex were lying on the carpet together, somehow they always found each other's hands.

Kevin was lucky to have two years at OI. It closed right after he graduated. During a freeze in state spending, the school district took money from programs for students with physical impairments to plug budget gaps elsewhere. Saying the OI model was too "resource rich," administrators substituted less qualified teachers. They replaced OI with a "highly structured environment" open only to preschoolers with little speech or independent movement, essentially segregating them.[9] Ironically, they called the new school Circle of Friends while cutting many friends out of the circle. When I asked Carina what she would change first to make life easier for kids with disabilities, she replied, "The people making decisions for these children, the administrators or whoever is in charge—I would like to see that they worry more about the well-being of the children, and what these children can do in society, rather than what it's going to cost."[10] I am grateful for Kevin's two years at OI, and wish many more children and families could experience a community like that.

Although we fit in beautifully at OI in most ways, there was one way in which our family misfit, and that way had to do with gender. The story I'm about to tell illustrates why it matters to think about identities like disability, gender, race, and class together at the same time. Scholars often call such versatile thinking "intersectionality." Although sometimes criticized as too rigid or schematic, intersectionality yields indispensable truths.[11] Kimberlé Crenshaw, who coined the term to describe African American women's lives, explains the need to move beyond single-issue political practices: "And so, when the practices expound identity as woman or person of color as an either/or proposition, they relegate the identity of women of color to a location that resists telling."[12] When one looks at two or more aspects of identity together, problems and solutions swim into view that were previously out of sight. "Intersectionality" refers specifically to combined types of oppression, while Michael Hames-Garcia uses the term "multiplicity" to indicate any blend of identities.[13] My story about masculinity at the orthopedic preschool shows how families, not just individuals, form multiple, complex identities.

Our gender misfitting at the orthopedic preschool began with Kevin's clothes. Resisting masculine norms, my husband John dressed Kevin in pink and purple and wanted his hair kept long. Not that I'm a big gender square myself; my favorite school outfit for Kevin was a leopard print turtleneck with black velveteen bellbottoms. The other moms teased me about our fashion choices. Although OI made room for a wide spectrum of abilities and disabilities, it didn't have a wide gender spectrum. The preschool parents and teachers, while open-minded, were straight and cisgender. Many of the moms who became my dear friends were conservative Christians, either Orthodox, Catholic, or fundamentalist.

If the OI Preschool was a deeply gendered place, it was not alone in this. Preschool is a key construction site for gender. Sociologist Emily W. Kane writes that the preschool age range "is the period when most children begin to develop a clear understanding of the gender expectations around them."[14] In Kane's interviews, preschool parents expressed fear that their sons would face harsh judgments if they failed to uphold the ideal of traditional masculinity. They saw preschool as "an important, foundational moment, often projecting into the future as they expressed concern about the risk of gender assessment."[15] This fear shows up in the exaggerated gender differences between boys' and girls' clothing. When shopping for Kevin I found it very difficult to find gender-neutral clothing in preschool sizes. The T-shirts all had pictures of football players or fairies. In her study of 112 children at five preschools, Karin A. Martin found clothing was a key way "the preschool as an institution genders children's bodies."[16]

> The clothes that parents send kids to preschool in shape children's experiences of their bodies in gendered ways. Clothes, particularly their color, signify a child's gender; gender in preschool is in fact color-coded. On average, about 61 percent of the girls wore pink clothing each day. Boys were more likely to wear primary colors, black, fluorescent green, and orange. Boys never wore pink.[17]

And there was Kevin, dressed in pink and purple among his male playmates in navy blue and camouflage. At the preschool Halloween party there were lots of boys in Oregon Ducks football uniforms and girls in ballerina tutus. Karin A. Martin concedes that "parents are not solely responsible for what their children wear to preschool, as they are constrained by what is available and affordable in children's clothing. More important, children, especially at ages three to five, want some say in what they wear to preschool and may insist on some outfits and object to others."[18] Fashion conformity may have been even more exaggerated at the OI Preschool, where many of the children could not declare their clothing preferences or dress themselves. Here was a way in which disability intersected with gender.

Toys also come with gender expectations, and preschoolers get the message loud and clear. Karen, the occupational therapist, had received a grant to start a toy library at the OI Preschool. Each child could choose a toy and take it home for a week. She asked me to be the toy librarian on Thursdays, helping children select their toys. A boy named Hunter, one of the playmates, was the rowdiest kid in the bunch. He stood in front of the toy cabinet wearing a T-shirt that read, "My Grandpa Rides Motorcycles and Someday I Will, Too." Hunter loved to play dress-up. The toy he was returning that week also lent itself to dress-up play: a boy bear with a shirt you could lace up. Hunter looked longingly at the girl bear with a dress you could lace up, but finally chose a toy golf set instead.

This anxiety about gender moved into my heart as well. One day John said to me, "I'm leaving my identity, Betsy." He wanted to transition to female. It didn't come as a complete shock. I always knew he liked to cross-dress while puttering around his home office or working at the computer. He had been pushing down his desire to become a woman since his early teens in Korea, and now it came knocking more and more insistently at his door. He asked if it would be all right with me if he started taking testosterone-blocking hormones. He made it clear he was content with our life together, still wanted me and our family above all things, and would not transition if it harmed us in any way. The decision would be his and mine together. I started doing some long, slow thinking.

I worried about social ostracism, gossip, and pity. As an interracial couple with one of our kids in an orthopedic walker, we already attracted plenty of stares in lily-white Eugene, Oregon. I could only assume that an interracial lesbian couple with one of our kids in an orthopedic walker would attract even more stares. However, I concluded that worrying about what other people think is the fastest way to ruin family happiness. I was also still smarting from the loss of our friends with nondisabled children. Would this new kind of difference cause us to lose our new friends from the OI Preschool? Just because people accept some kinds of bodily difference doesn't mean they accept all kinds.

I worried about my own sexuality, but found a deep well of queerness and bisexuality inside myself, along with my abiding love, passion, and respect for Jordan, the new name John chose. I worried about my ability to handle another change amid the stresses of two young children, cerebral palsy, anaphylactic food allergies, an aging mother, my career, and an almost constant migraine. (One morning at the preschool Robin Yozzo took me aside and whispered, "Do you know your pants are on inside out?") On the other hand, it was clear to me that something monumental was happening to Jordan that might trump the immediate stressors.

My last worry concerned both our kids but especially Kevin. He already had a bundle of identities commonly branded unmasculine. He had a physical disability, asthma, and life-threatening food allergies. He was Korean American, and as David L. Eng writes, "The Asian American male is both materially and psychically feminized within the context of a larger U.S. cultural imaginary."[19] Was I going to take his Asian American male role model away from him, too? In the midst of these deliberations I found my fears expressed in a psychology book called *Beyond a Physical Disability: The Person Within*.

There is a difference in a male helping another male compared to a female taking care of a male. One danger is that the development of the male ego can easily be impaired. This is not as likely to happen when there is a male role model in the home. Such a role model can easily point out to the disabled teenager necessary masculine traits.

Just because the teenager has a disability is no reason for him to be stripped of his masculinity.[20]

I wanted no part in stripping Kevin of his masculinity. The risk to his romantic life seemed to bother me the worst. I pictured him thirteen years in the future, home alone on prom night. (As you can tell, I am a world-class worrier.) Then one day at work I came across a disability studies article by Russell P. Shuttleworth, who interviewed men with cerebral palsy about their dating lives. Shuttleworth found three things that helped men with CP move into the world of romantic and sexual relationships. The first was a "supportive context" of people who see you as whole person. I thought, yes, Jordan and I can facilitate that, especially now we have the affirming community of the preschool. The second was the ability to see negative views of the disabled body as society's problem, not yours. Critical thinkers by temperament and education, Jordan and I could definitely facilitate that. The third was a category called "expanding the masculine repertoire." Shuttleworth wrote,

> Those men who attempted to conduct themselves in rigid accordance with hegemonic masculine ideals and who measured themselves against these ideals were more apt to remain immobilized or socially to withdraw when they fell short; and, indeed, much of the blame for their failure in love was shouldered by their inability to measure up. Those men, however, who perceived hegemonic masculinity as less a total index of their desirability and who could sometimes draw on alternative ideals such as interdependence, prioritizing emotional intimacy, becoming friends first, allowing the other to make the first move sometimes . . . , could better weather rejection and remain open to the possibility of interpersonal connection and sexual intimacy. In this expanded masculinity, ideals often associated with femininity take their place in the masculine repertoire alongside more hegemonic ideals in subjects' psyches and interpersonal practices.[21]

Looking up from the book and out my office window, I had a revelation. Jordan's gender transition could actually be good, not bad, for our son. Clinging to the ideals of traditional masculinity could make Kevin's life harder, not easier, robbing him of resilience and versatility. I started thinking about the problem intersectionally. Kevin benefited if his family saw negative views of disability as society's problem, not ours. Perhaps, then, Kevin would also benefit if his family saw negative views of gender nonconformity as society's problem, not ours. My mistake lay in thinking of identity as a scoreboard, as if he needed the home run of masculinity to wipe out the two strikes of disability and race.

I needed to envision a spectrum of masculinity as wide and inclusive as the spectrum of ability at the orthopedic preschool. Rather than turning Kevin into a social outcast, the relaxing of gender conventions around our house could help him expand his masculine repertoire, just as the inclusive world of the preschool had helped us expand our horizons of what someone with cerebral palsy could do. He was already a patient, loving, acutely aware, and hilarious little boy. Like Jordan, he could become anyone he wanted to be.

I knew Cyndi had similar worries about Jaymason's future as a man with cerebral palsy, so I told her about Russell Shuttleworth's article during a party at the Yozzos' house. She got tears in her eyes. "Our boys may not be good at walking up to the door and ringing the bell, but they'll be great with the candy and flowers."

Three

Epistemology of the Toilet

One of the many ways my family is unfit for polite society is that we talk about poop at the dinner table. Among the four of us, we have three family members with irritable bowel syndrome and serious food allergies, one who needs assistance in the bathroom, and one (me) with anatomically induced constipation. Perhaps not coincidentally, we also have a rich family tradition of potty humor and open talk. The same is true of our circle of friends who also have kids in wheelchairs. My mom friends and I joke that whenever we get together, within thirty seconds we're talking about poop.

This chapter explores the political philosophy of toilet talk. We build an important epistemology, a distinct way of knowing and understanding the world, as we joke and hang out in the bathroom together. Our comfort reflects the understanding that caregiving is not an act of martyrdom and disability is not a tragedy. As Stella Young once said, "Having to rely on someone else to wipe your bum may not be something anyone aspires to, but I'm quite sure it's never killed anyone."[1] In forming this epistemology of the toilet, I draw on my own family's experience as well as interviews with our circle of friends. Obviously the interests and subject positions of young people and their parents are far from identical; and we know there are abusive and clueless caregivers. However, I focus here on the moments when the buttwiper and the buttwipee join in dialogue.

This epistemology marks what I call a *family with disabilities*, a kinship group in which members share a critical consciousness even if they don't all share the same disability. Sometimes only one family member experiences disability firsthand while the others are allies. Sometimes most or all family members have stutters or asthma or ADHD. Some families are gardens of neurodiversity, where one member may have autism while others have fibromyalgia or schizophrenia instead. What marks a family with disabilities is that they share some degree of fluency with disability culture and an awareness of misunderstanding and ableism in the society at large. Families collude together against the arrogance, absurdity, and exclusion of the normate world. For those whose disabilities permit some degree of independence, families rehearse the children's futures as assertive adults who understand oppression.

Toilet talk plays a crucial part in this alliance because in families with disabilities toileting is often a shared rather than solitary activity long after a child's first years. Through toilet talk we assert our belonging in public space as we negotiate barriers and intrusive or hostile strangers. With shared laughter and open talk, we resist the idea that disability in public is a problem. The body is not shameful, and neither is the stuff that comes out of it, but it is shameful to hinder or interrogate a child's free, comfortable, and unremarkable use of public space.

The three stories I tell here illustrate how toilet talk is an important branch of political philosophy. Bathroom humor allows families with disabilities to declare their solidarity. It equips kids who can communicate with the sass and self-confidence necessary to become full citizens. It proves that public space fails to fit us; we do not fail to fit public space. It demonstrates that families with disabilities can live together in good humor. However, toilet talk also shows the limits of mixed-ability solidarity, because some people in the family have more freedom of movement than others. Through toilet talk we map out our comparative privilege, our respective areas of choice and restriction.

Unless we want to stay home or court kidney stones, we all use public toilets. They are necessary spaces for the full range of the population. Indeed, "Access to toilets is a prerequisite for full public participation and citizenship."[2] However, even though we all need to go sometimes, some people get in more easily. Through signs and stall size, restrooms specify who fits and who doesn't belong. Therefore, toilet talk is a good way to make privilege obvious. It also shows how identity categories like disability and gender identity overlap and intersect. For example, disability and transgender activists can work together "to undo the gendered conventions of the toilet as part of our larger struggles for access to public space."[3] The restroom is a good place to think about intersectional politics.

My first story, which comes from the Morrell family, shows how toilet talk can help a child rehearse her future as an assertive adult. Heather and

Stephen Morrell are the parents of Dana and of Shanti, who uses a wheelchair because of a genetic condition. Shanti's frequent surgeries have resulted in increasingly long stretches of postoperative constipation. Shanti and her mother are used to hanging out in her room at the Ronald McDonald House, watching TV and making fun of laxative commercials while she spends some quality time on the commode.[4] This particular story, though, takes place in a parking lot. Heather tells how Shanti uses her own comfort with toilet talk to assert a sense of belonging in public.

> So one time Shanti and I went to pick up her brother from basketball, and we used a disabled parking permit spot. And she and I got back to the car long before he actually came out, so we were just sitting in the car. Her wheelchair was already loaded up in the car. And a woman walked by—our window was open, it was summertime—and looked at me with a very disgruntled look and said accusatorily, "Are you disabled?" . . . [M]y first response—'cause I'm a good girl and I don't like confrontation—I was like, "Oh, no, no, but my daughter is." And then she walked away, and I was like, "Wow." I said to Shanti, I was like, "That was rude." She's like, "Yeah." I was like, "I wish I had thought of something better to say when she said that," 'cause it felt really invasive and intrusive. And we've talked together about how the feeling somebody puts into a question really has an effect on how you feel in answering it because she often has people ask questions and we're often very cheerful and happy to answer them, but the way that this woman was speaking to us really felt really negative. So I was like, "Yeah, we should think of something equally invasive and intrusive to ask her that's really none of our business." Shanti's like, "Yeah. It's like what if we ask her, 'When did you last poop?'". . . It was after the fact, so we didn't do it, but . . . we got a good laugh out of that.[5]

This is a great moment of flipping the script, where a mother and daughter imagine how to be intrusive back at an intrusive questioner. As the story makes clear, Heather is not disabled, but she and her daughter collude together against an ableist challenge. Heather's initial response was conciliatory. However, in her follow-up conversation with Shanti she doesn't justify the woman or convey any shame. Rather, she names the rudeness and invites Shanti to help her think of a snappy comeback. Shanti comes up with a great one. They don't make the joke to the woman's face, but they rehearse together for Shanti's future as an assertive adult. They talk, not just this once but

Fig. 10. Shanti Morrell, age eleven.

over time, about people's questions and attitudes. They develop a repertoire of possible responses that become strings for Shanti's bow. Heather relishes Shanti's sassiness and wit. And while Shanti is a kind, conscientious, and fair-minded person, she does not suffer fools gladly.

Heather says, "We got a good laugh out of that." Healthy families with disabilities figure out ways to have fun with the moments in life no one would choose. Their resilience is specific to families with disabilities, but it also shows how they are just like families in general—they laugh together. It's what healthy families do. Why is Shanti's snappy comeback a poop joke? Because poop is funny and kids like poop jokes, but also because poop is supposed to be private. The joke reminds the questioner that she is poking her nose into other people's business, and that she has a body, too. Poop is also associated with shame, so poop jokes are a good way to shame ableism.

Bathroom humor can expose the moments when public space fails to fit our needs. Sometimes the restroom is a "place where disabled people are made absent, and where this absence is regarded as irrelevant."[6] My second story, from the Yozzo family, makes disability present and inaccessibility relevant. There is a very literal misfit between the child and public space. Robin and Carlo Yozzo are the parents of Duncan and of Alex, who has cerebral palsy and wears a diaper. Robin tells how she was waiting outside a restroom at the Denver airport when it was relatively new and full of much-advertised state-of-the art technologies. It was taking forever for Carlo to change Alex's diaper, so she finally went into the restroom to find both Carlo and Alex drenched in water. The changing table was designed to fit a baby or toddler, not an older child like Alex. The sink was too close to the changing table, and his legs stretched out way beyond the table and kept setting off the automatic faucet.

CARLO: And we had Alex laid out and when he was getting to be so long and every time his feet would go down the water would go on. Hysterical. And Alex would crack up. And we would crack up but it didn't make it any easier to do.

ROBIN: Right, and he's just struggling. And then the toilet would flush, someone would move and the toilet would flush. We were just cracking up because all of this new electronic stuff. You couldn't move, you get the sink going off, the toilet's flushing.

CARLO: You couldn't adjust it—turn it off.

ROBIN: Exactly. But again, we just cracked up.[7]

This story raises an important question about disability comedy: Who is the target of the joke? In one interpretation of this story, the wrong one, I believe, Alex's body is the target. It is excessively and absurdly big and doesn't belong on a baby's changing table. This incongruity is the source of the humor. I don't think that's the right reading, however. To my mind, it's the Denver Airport that's preposterous, with its brand-new baggage carousels that kept breaking down, automatic faucets that kept going on and off, and its architects who thought changing tables were only for babies. When my disabilities show up in public I often feel excessively and absurdly big, sweaty, awkward, and conspicuous. However, I've concluded I usually feel this way when the space has failed to get ready for me before I get there. So this story laughs not at disability, but the absurdities of a world built wrong.

This story, like Heather and Shanti's, also shows that a healthy family with disabilities listens to the children in it. While Alex is nonverbal, he is in on the joke: he was cracking up, too. He and his parents were all laughing together. The Yozzos go together: they go to the restroom together, and they work beautifully together as a team. Their shared laughter asserts a sense of belonging in public, even soaking wet and struggling with the changing table. Then they have shared the story with other families with disabilities like mine, who get it and laugh, too, and have formed a community through the sharing of stories like this. Such conversations represent a worldview Rosemarie Garland-Thomson calls "the solidarity born of misfitting."[8]

My third and final story comes from my own family. Our public toileting became more complicated when Kevin was a little boy and his dad began transitioning to female. We no longer had a same-sex caregiver to take Kevin to the men's room. Through her own coming out, my wife Jordan served as a model for Kevin to rehearse his own future as an assertive adult who understands oppression. Jordan has demonstrated how to ask your family to accept the new emerging parts of you, even if it requires some discomfort on the family's part and some rearranging of the world rather than rearranging or hiding yourself. This transition has brought home to me the ways that disability and gender identity intersect in "pee privilege," and the mixtures of privilege and discrimination we experience in our mixed-ability family.[9]

During Jordan's transition Kevin would ask, "Why can't we use the men's room any more?" Jordan explained that a transwoman can't use the men's room because of the threat of violence, and that the kids should stop saying "Dad" in public for the same reason. Kevin quickly grasped this concept. Usually we went to ladies' room with Kevin, but when he and I used the men's room I entered and exited as swiftly as possible, aware of my misfitting.

However, I still retained a great deal of privilege. No one questioned me in the men's room because I was a "typical mom": white, middle-class, cisgender, escorted by a son in a wheelchair. My presence was uncontroversial. To wash my hands I quickly retreated into the ladies' room, where I fit in just fine.

As a thought experiment inspired by Samuel Lurie, I once tried using the men's room when I was by myself.[10] However, I turned around and left just as soon as I entered because I was scared and embarrassed. I told Kevin about this and he asked me, "When you left, were you thinking that you didn't have to do it?" and I thought to myself, yes, I was. Then I thought, he knows a lot about choice as a form of privilege. Through toilet talk we map out our respective areas of choice and restriction.

When Kevin was fifteen I asked him about embarrassment, and his answers reflected the view that there is nothing wrong with having a disability but there is something wrong with public space. He said he didn't find it embarrassing to have his caregivers help him in the restroom. However, he did find it embarrassing to have to use the ladies' room, or have a female caregiver with him in the men's room if other people were there, too. When the ladies' room and the men's room were the only two choices, he couldn't avoid that embarrassment.

We appreciate all the activists in the past and present who advocate for family, gender-neutral, and wheelchair-accessible restrooms, and we use them whenever we can. However, there still are not enough of them. And for my son to be embarrassed to use the restroom: that's no joke and it is a shame.

Part Two

———

Nature

When we look at nature,
we receive a sort of permission to be alive in this world,
and our entire bodies get recharged.
  —Naoki Higashida

Four

Moving Together Side by Side

Human-Animal Comparisons in Picture Books

Involvement with animals is a central way kids with disabilities connect with the world and play an inextricable part in it. This involvement forms the centerpiece in an international canon of picture books I have found. In these picture books, animals form part of a prosthetic community, defined in chapter 2 as a cluster of living beings, ideas, resources, and objects that enable disabled children's full inclusion. The human-nonhuman relationships transcend service and companionship, however. These books compare children with disabilities to animals, and different species come to resemble each other. Adults as well as children can use these books as models toward an important goal: recognizing the personhood of animals and children with disabilities, and their common membership in the living world. The greater this recognition, the more humans can claim their kinship to nonhuman animals.

One image repeats frequently across this canon of picture books: a child with a disability and an animal moving together side by side. The pictures compare human and nonhuman bodies as they surf, crawl, fly, dance, climb, and play. Their movement represents ingenuity, joy, and most of all, freedom. At these moments the characters claim their place in the world, expressing their relationship to nature through their bodies. These images usually serve as the climax of the book and the solution to the problem.

In this chapter I will focus on two picture books from this canon: *Seal Surfer* by Michael Foreman of Britain and *Sosu's Call* by Meshack Asare of Ghana. Disability activism and public debate provide the social context for both picture books. Both appeared in 1997 during the era when their respective countries engaged in vocal controversy over disability rights. Disability issues became public matters and nationally shared concerns as never before. Founded in 1987, the Ghana Federation of Disability Organizations gained a boost for its advocacy under democratic reforms in 1992–3 which brought a new constitution, freer civic association, and the return of free and fair elections.[1] In the United Kingdom of the early 1990s, hundreds of disability rights activists took to the streets. Their protests aided the passage of the 1995 Disability Discrimination Act (DDA).

> Disabled people chaining themselves to public transport, wheelchair users blocking streets, chanting loudly and being lifted from their chairs by police and laid down in the roads to stop them, protesters shouting out for civil rights—these were powerful images on the TV news in the early 90s, and a far cry from how disabled people were often represented (when they were represented at all), as passive and grateful recipients of charity.[2]

In both countries disability rights stayed in the public conversation well past 1997. The protests and civic involvement of the Ghana Federation of Disability Organizations led to the passage of the Ghana Persons with Disability Act of 2006 after a twelve-year struggle.[3] The British Parliament continued to strengthen disability rights and finally rolled the DDA into the Equality Act of 2010.[4] Ghana and the United Kingdom were both early signatories of the United Nations Convention on the Rights of Persons with Disabilities (2006).[5] Both *Sosu's Call* and *Seal Surfer* portray disability inclusion as a matter of shared concern all children should understand. *Sosu's Call* stars a mobility-impaired main character, hidden at home in response to social stigma, who becomes the celebrated hero of his Ghanian fishing village. *Seal Surfer* shows readers what inclusion ought to look like through the experiences of a mobility-impaired boy who enjoys nearly ideal levels of access in his Cornwall fishing village.

While the main characters share similar impairments and landscapes, the two picture books sit on opposite ends of the postcolonial legacy. Given the two nations' unequal resources, the prosthetic community looks very different in Britain than it does in Ghana. This economic disparity is no coincidence. A former British colony, Ghana can trace the longest roots of its poverty back to colonial policies of underdevelopment. For a hefty part of the nineteenth and twentieth centuries, the British colonial state in Ghana prohibited manufacturing, created reliance on expensive foreign imports, and transferred sources of wealth from African to European ownership.[6] Nonetheless, both nations have adopted disability rights laws in the late twentieth and early twenty-first centuries that enable children with disabilities to infiltrate wider worlds. *Seal Surfer* and *Sosu's Call* reflect the new presence of children with disabilities in outdoor public space.

Moving together side by side, animals and kids with disabilities express a freedom that is not only physical but also political. Human-animal comparisons solve problems. They establish kinship across species. They challenge human domination. They express the interdependence valued in kids' culture, disability culture, and environmentalism. They unsettle social norms. Human-animal comparisons help us rethink our ideas about capability, agency, and belonging.[7] As Sunaura Taylor points out, "The big questions in disability studies seem equally relevant to the animal rights debate: How can we create new meanings for words like 'dependent' and 'independent'? How can those who are seemingly most vulnerable within a society be perceived as also being useful, strong, and necessary?"[8] Human-animal comparisons address another question as well: How can the vulnerability of disabled people be perceived as part of our shared vulnerability on the planet, and the vulnerability of the planet itself, rather than a unique and separate kind of weakness?

Human-animal comparisons also create problems, however. There is the devastating, even genocidal history of comparing people with disabilities to animals. Given this history, stories often contain kinship across species as soon as they express it. *Sosu's Call* must contain the human-animal resemblance more quickly than *Seal Surfer*, given the racist legacy of comparing Africans as well as people with disabilities to animals. There is also the long history of using animals as beasts of burden. Animals often bear the unfair burden of proving the humanity of children with disabilities, just as children themselves bear that unfair burden. In this canon of picture books, including *Seal Surfer* and *Sosu's Call*, animals bear the specific burden of proving the masculinity of boys with disabilities. Some of these assertions of masculinity are more traditional; others widen the masculine repertoire to include more vulnerability, flexibility, and cooperation.

In this exploration I have drawn on ideas from animal studies and disability studies, since one field affirms the equality of nonhuman animals and the other affirms the equality of people with disabilities. However, I have discovered a problem in bringing these fields together: the ableism, or antidisability bias, in animal studies. The personhood of children with disabilities is still a fragile construct, even among those committed to animal rights.

Ableism in Animal Studies

Disrespect for children with disabilities runs through the philosophical wing of animal studies. This disrespect shows itself in the frequent use of disability as a hypothetical test case for the limits of personhood. The obvious example is Peter Singer, whose *Animal Liberation* (1975) and *Practical Ethics* (1979) sparked the field of animal studies. In *Practical Ethics*, his hypothetical examples support the argument for redefining nonhuman animals as persons. Defining personhood as the capacity to make choices and imagine a future, Singer argues that a chimpanzee qualifies as a person, while some newborn humans do not. "So it seems that killing, say, a chimpanzee is worse than the killing of a human being who, because of a congenital intellectual disability, is not and never can be a person."[9] Singer pits children with disabilities against animals in a kind of personhood contest.

Peter Singer is the most notorious example of ableism in animal studies, but he is far from alone. Philosophers often question the limits of the human by invoking hypothetical examples of people with disabilities, especially children. While these philosophers think consciously about race and gender, their comparisons between disability and animality seem unconscious. Human disability haunts the margins of the animal studies imagination, ready to hand as a rhetorical counterexample but not as a subject of ethical inquiry.

The same antiquated, ableist phrasing circulates from one generation to another, often as jokes. Although Cary Wolfe criticizes Singer's ethics as a "utilitarian calculus," he neutrally summarizes Singer's view that "the hydrocephalic child" fails the test of personhood, and uncritically adopts the term "human vegetables" from Luc Ferry.[10] Wolfe compares the struggles for animal, racial, and women's rights but ignores disability justice, even though hypothetical children with disabilities help make his case. Donna Haraway argues for the importance of human-canine coevolution by making a cognitive impairment joke: "How might stories about dog-human worlds finally convince brain-damaged US Americans, and maybe other less historically challenged people, that history matters in naturecultures?"[11] In *The Animal That Therefore I Am*, a founding animal studies text, Jacques Derrida also invokes cognitive disability when he concurs with René Descartes that the idea of the animal soul is "the prejudice of children or of 'feeble minds.'"[12] Vicki Hearne argues for the advanced level of communication between dogs and their trainers by disparaging people with schizophrenia: "I can go a lot farther with my dog than I can with a schizophrenic, or a Nazi, if only because my dog doesn't bore me."[13] Over and over, rhetorical figures of disability appear as animal studies philosophers compare human and nonhuman animals.

Why this disparagement in the defense of animal rights? The impulse arises from the relative ranking of human adults, children, people with disabilities, and nonhuman animals. Mel Y. Chen writes, "In spite of their regular co-occurrence with humans, nonhuman animals are typologically situated elsewhere from humans, as in the linguistic concept of an animacy hierarchy, a scale of relative sentience that places humans at the very top."[14] While they may not be conscious of their preoccupation, animal studies scholars have disability on their minds because animals and people with disabilities are often seen as competing for the bottom rung on the evolutionary ladder.

Children take part in this fictive competition as well. The field of child development has its origins in child study, a movement that emerged around 1900 and bore the influence of Darwinism. Children assumed increasing importance for Progressive Era psychologists like James Sully: "Nearly all the early psychologists articulated the idea that child study mattered because by observing children and 'the lowest races of mankind,' 'we are watching the beginnings of things. . . . Our modern science is before all things historical and genetic, going back to beginnings so as to understand the later and more complex phases of things as the outcomes of these beginnings.'"[15] If you add the category of "disability" to the category of "child," you get an especially fierce contest for the bottom rung of the evolutionary ladder.

I want to contrast this image, the battle royal at the foot of the evolutionary ladder, to the picture-book images of children with disabilities and animals moving side by side. These images show that animal rights do not have to come at the expense of disability rights; rather, the opposite is true. The greater the social acceptance of disability, the more freedom there can be to claim animal kinship.

The key task is not to establish the correct threshold of personhood. Rather, the key tasks are adaptation and cooperation, two organizing principles of many disability cultures. We work together to make it work. The prosthetic community evident in children's literature includes service and companion animals; wheelchairs and adaptive sports equipment; technologies like text-to-speech synthesizers and news media; friends, family, and paid caregivers; decent income and health care; disability rights; and resources of the creative mind, like brainstorming, fantasy, and activism. These solutions rely on local knowledge in specific ecosystems. The beauty of the prosthetic community is that a disabled person does not have to rely exclusively on one overburdened source of support. The richer the prosthetic community, the more humans with disabilities can compare themselves to animals without risking their status as persons.

The Problem with Human-Animal Comparisons

As things stand, human-animal comparisons create problems. Over centuries they have justified the murder, subjugation, and locking-up of people with disabilities, ethnic minorities, and colonized populations. This history is so destructive, Isabel Brittain lists "forging links between the character and animals" among "The Six Pitfalls of Disability Fiction."[16] Sunaura Taylor describes how this history of harm trespassed on her own childhood. "I remember knowing that my kindergarten classmates meant to hurt my feelings when they told me I walked like a monkey, and of course they did. . . . I understood that they were commenting on my inability to stand completely upright when out of my wheelchair—my failure to stand like a normal human being."[17] As Taylor explores, people with disabilities often hear animal insults.

> When I ask members of the disabled community whether they have ever been compared to animals because of their disabilities, I receive a torrent of replies. I am transported to a veritable bestiary of frog legs and penguin waddles, seal limbs and monkey arms. It is clear, however, from the wincing and negative interjections, that these comparisons are for the most part not pleasant to remember.[18]

Being compared to an animal, however, is only an insult in a context where animals endure widespread mistreatment. We can help remove this stigma by advocating for animal and disability rights in tandem. Taylor concludes, "I am also convinced we cannot have disability liberation without animal liberation—they are intimately tied together."[19] For instance, both factory farm chickens and some disabled children live in cages. Ninety-five percent of laying hens in the United States spend their lives in battery cages, squeezed in too tightly to move. Designed to increase profits, their immobility causes mental and physical disabilities.[20] In Paraguay and Greece, state-run institutions keep children with disabilities locked in cages.[21] At the KE-PEP Center in Lechaina, Greece, the cages seemed preferable to strapping the children to their beds, the prior practice, since low staffing levels made it impossible to provide adequate supervision. The center cannot increase staff levels because the European Union and the International Monetary Fund imposed a hiring moratorium after Greece's economic bailout.[22] The center locks up children not because they are cruel or ableist, but because the prosthetic community lacks resources.

The obvious way to criticize the Greek and Paraguayan governments is to say that it is wrong to keep children caged like animals, but this criticism misses half the point. It is also wrong to keep chickens caged like animals. Questioning the overall flow of capital—the profit motive in one case and the lack of resources in the other—might increase freedom for both animals and children with disabilities. Certainly the global flow of capital underlies the differing resources of the two boys in *Seal Surfer* and *Sosu's Call*.

Human and nonhuman lives leak into each other if nothing stops them. For Mel Y. Chen, "kinship formations between animals and humans" represent "the unsteadiness of categorical hierarchies and the legitimacy afforded to some of their leakages." Yet "biopolitical governance . . . steps in over and over again to contain these leaky bounds."[23] These picture books reveal both the leakage and the containment, a containment spurred not only by animacy hierarchies but also by the terrible history of comparing people with disabilities to animals. The containing wall comes down harder for some children than others, depending on the degree of stigma and the age of the child. Small children are free and encouraged to imitate various animals. However, while an older child can swim like a seal or fly like a bird, she cannot eat like a pig or crawl like a dog without courting insult. I found no picture books that compared a child with a cognitive disability to an animal. The deep stigma attached to cognitive disability prohibits that human-animal comparison.

However, I did find many picture books comparing children with physical disabilities to animals, including the two I feature here: *Seal Surfer* by Michael Foreman and *Sosu's Call* by Meshack Asare. Asare and Foreman are both distinguished and prolific writer-illustrators. The human-animal leakages in *Seal Surfer* and *Sosu's Call* happen in literal cascades of water. Both books take place in Atlantic fishing villages, one in Cornwall, West Britain, one in Ghana, West Africa. Both stories present animals and boys with disabilities as heroes in order to assert their belonging in changing nations.

The Supercrip and the Beast of Burden

Sunaura Taylor is right about the key question: "How can those who are seemingly most vulnerable within a society be perceived as also being useful, strong, and necessary?" The next question, however, is "Useful to whom?"

Animals and kids with disabilities become heroes by proving their usefulness to human society and thus their right to exist. The burden of proving one's own personhood gives rise to two mythological figures: the Supercrip and the Beast of Burden. The Supercrip signifies a hero with a disability who performs astonishing and admirable feats. The Supercrip never acts for himself alone; he exists to inspire or admonish others. Usually the story contains elements of magic realism, falling silent on the adaptations required to achieve seeming miracles. The Supercrip is a close cousin to the idea of passing, which in the case of disability refers to doing more than you really can in an effort to meet social expectations.

I am using the term Beast of Burden to signify a nonhuman animal who bears the burden of triangulating relationships between humans.[24] Families often triangulate their relationships through animals, "deflecting to pets or routing through pets emotion and communication intended for other family members."[25] Animals also perform this type of emotional labor in public, and the triangulation can work to the advantage of kids with disabilities. For instance, a pet or service dog can deflect attention away from the disability and give the child a different story to tell. In *My Buddy*, a picture book about a service dog for a boy with muscular dystrophy, the narrator testifies: "Before Buddy, I didn't like to go places. People stared at me. Now people look at *us*—and ask about my dog."[26] These picture books frequently transfer the focal point from the disability to the nonhuman animal. In other senses, too, kids with disabilities use animals to leverage greater status for themselves.

This canon of picture books showcases a particular variety of triangulation: animals establish the masculinity of boys with physical disabilities. They enable traditionally masculine actions like physical courage and outdoor adventures. In *Sosu's Call* and *Seal Surfer*, the protagonists are the sons and grandsons of fishermen who establish their belonging in the male line of the family through their outdoor sojourns. Of the thirteen picture books I found featuring animals and kids with disabilities that had the same protagonist for the entire story, all the main characters were boys.

Human-animal partnerships allow these boys to act like the independent, adventurous heroes of so many classic picture books, from *Harold and the Purple Crayon* to *Where the Wild Things Are*.[27] Apparently animal help does not foreclose independence in the same way human help does. The narrator of *My Buddy* says, "Before Buddy, Mom and Dad helped me. Mike and other friends helped, too. But friends sometimes get tired of helping. And I wanted to do things on my own."[28] A dog's help doesn't count as a form of dependence. Animals allow boys with disabilities to prove themselves in nature without dependence on other humans.[29] Chloë Hughes writes, "Picture-books that are successful in challenging ableism seem to extend social capital toward characters with disabilities."[30] These picture books grant boys many varieties of social capital, including autonomy, friendship, courage, quick wits, athleticism, and masculinity.

My assertion that human-animal bonds reinforce traditional masculinity may seem to contradict recent work in animal studies that asserts the queerness of those bonds. For Jack Halberstam and Donna Haraway, human-animal bonding is queer because it represents a form of family building not based on biological reproduction, kinship, or lineage.[31] For Mel Y. Chen, such bonding is queer because, like same-sex human partnerships, it represents "improper affiliation, so that queerness might well describe an array of subjectivities, intimacies, beings, and spaces located outside of the heteronormative."[32]

For children, however, close bonds with animals are not queer but normative. Take for example the commonplace "There's nothing like the bond between a boy and his dog." If you want a kid with a disability to look conventional, make him a boy and give him a dog. The narrator of *My Buddy* describes his dog as "just one of the guys."[33] Pet ownership is a conventional feature of life in American and Western European families; kids may feel left out if allergies or finances prevent them from having a pet. "Companion animals and children literally go together": 70 percent of all households with children younger than age six and 78 percent of all households with children older than age six have pets.[34] While animal companionship may be normative for children, however, another relationship to animals skates close to queerness, especially as children get older: resembling an animal. In a study of Australian college students, psychologists found that comparing animals to humans "expands moral concern, not only to animals but also to human outgroups," while "comparing humans to animals maintains the status quo."[35] Both these picture books reveal the interplay of leakage and containment, queerness and convention, when it comes to animal resemblances.

Seal Surfer: The Prosthetic Community

Michael Foreman's *Seal Surfer* concerns Ben, his grandfather, and their shared love of the ocean. The book takes place among the surfers and fishermen of St. Ives, Cornwall. One of Britain's best-known picture-book authors, Michael Foreman grew up in the fishing village of Pakefield, Suffolk, and now divides his time between London and St. Ives.[36] *Seal Surfer* glows with intimate knowledge of the British coastline, its steep cliffs, waves, and seasons. Ben's rich prosthetic community includes a wheelchair, crutches, and adaptive surfboard. While Ben's surfing prowess represents to some degree a Supercrip need to impress the viewer, the story leaves plenty of room for physical vulnerability and interdependence.

Leigha McReynolds writes that the introduction of an animal body in a prosthetic relationship allows disabled human characters "to thrive in an embodiment that exists beyond the ableist myth of an impermeable, bounded self."[37] Permeability and boundlessness saturate *Seal Surfer*, from the leakage between animal and human identities to the immersive watercolors. The interdependence of the prosthetic community extends to a larger sense of interdependence with the natural world. The ocean seems boundless, and so does the boy's ability to connect with nature. The watercolor paintings render a translucent sea, the human and seal characters visible within it and sharing its colors. In traditional portrayals, men's bodies are impermeable while women's bodies leak. *Seal Surfer*'s paintings of the sea permeating Ben's body may indicate a new masculinity in the making.

Ben's disability is only one small part of this big picture. Michael Foreman expresses this relative importance literally in the book's first two pages, set in the spring. While the text talks about the grandson and grandfather collecting mussels and spotting a seal who seems to be injured, the opening picture focuses on something else: the larger natural world all three mammals share. The big picture is a spectacular landscape in bright, layered watercolors reminiscent of Claude Monet. The massive rocks are not gray, but built out of purple, turquoise, ochre, and chartreuse, resolving into a deeply observed recreation of Britain's west coast.

The two human figures and the seal are tiny in this landscape, which could diminish them. Instead, these proportions establish their belonging and naturalize the boy's disability. We see the three figures from far above; as picture-book scholar Perry Nodelman observes, "Figures seen from above become part of an environment, either secure in it or constrained by it."[38] *Seal Surfer* emphasizes the security rather than the constraint. Ben's comfort outdoors and his ability to collect mussels with his grandfather show his belonging in this family of fishermen. Indeed, the book never shows physical constraint. The text says, "Ben and his grandfather carefully climbed down to a rocky beach."[39] The picture, however, doesn't show that careful climb. The boy is already lying down on a tall rock near the shoreline, his crutches lying next to him. At the very top right of the picture, on the tall, jagged cliffs, sits a wheelchair.

How did the boy get from his wheelchair down the rocky cliffs on his crutches? The picture refuses to answer that question. Instead, it takes the boy's presence in nature for granted. Ben wears shades of blue and green, like the sea and the grass. The light from the sea turns the wheelchair shades of purple, blue, and pink along with the rocks next to it. The text never refers to the mobility equipment shown in the pictures. In another form of naturalization, the colors of the wheelchair and crutches always match the landscape: gray like the sea wall of the harbor in the evening, pink like the sunset, transparent blue like the spring ocean. The adaptive equipment is so tiny in the vast landscape it might seem inconsequential, but young children love to scan pictures for the tiny details irrelevant to adults.

These opening pages suggest the kinship between humans and seals, through physical likeness and a transfer of focal point. The second two-page spread moves down to a closer view of the seaside rocks, where Ben looks at the seal again and sees "a flash of white. A newly born seal pup nuzzled her mother."[40] Ben lies propped up on his elbows on one flat rock, just as the baby seal lies propped on her flippers on the next. From the left corner of the picture, Ben and his grandfather stare in awe at the newborn seal. Ben's body juts out diagonally, his feet facing the viewer. Perry Nodelman observes, "A character on the lower left with his back turned to us will receive the most sympathy, for his position is most like our own in relation to the picture."[41] The glance curve moves up Ben's body to his intent, smiling face, then across his sight line to the seals in the right-hand picture. The viewer identifies first with the boy, then with the seals.

Ben's connections run many ways, from his grandfather, the seals, his human friends, and his multiple assistive devices, to his love for the ocean. His prosthetic community includes peers. The second beach summer starts with Ben on a typical Saturday at Surf School. As usual, the book emphasizes Ben's abilities rather than his disability: "He was a strong swimmer, and after much practice he and the other new surfers were ready to catch some waves."[42] Ben walks across the sand to the water in a row of four students. The author draws Ben's crutches in subtle, thin lines. The boy next to Ben is chatting to him while carrying Ben's board along with his own. Because the boys are talking and because there are four kids and four boards in a row, Ben's disability is inconspicuous. The other boy's help seems completely casual and natural. This casual familiarity also appears in a picture of the third spring. The grandfather is dead and gone, but a group of three friends cluster around Ben's wheelchair, looking at the sea from the high cliffs. Ben moves comfortably from the companionship of family to friendships with peers.

The prosthetic community also includes a variety of adaptive equipment available to a First World child, especially one covered by Britain's National Health Service before the last rounds of austerity cutbacks. It is helpful that *Seal Surfer* shows a child with a physical disability moving back and forth between different types of equipment, since such ambidexterity confuses many people. It can even lead to accusations of fraud. The book clarifies that different technologies work for different uses and seasons. Even the other kids' nonadaptive surfboards could be seen as prosthetics, since humans cannot surf without them. Tim Jordan has argued that the surfboard could also be seen as a companion species. He concedes that the surfboard does not have changes of expression or body language, "Yet a board does react back and can be part of joy."[43]

Ben and the young seal share physical likeness and the same sport. The book reaches its climax as the boy and the seal pup, now grown, surf a huge wave together. The wave absorbs nearly the whole picture from top to bottom, the crest curling along the top edge. Foreman captures the moment just before the wave breaks and the white water falls on the two surfers. From the steep angle it looks as if the water is going to break hard, on them and on the viewer. The boy and the seal share kinship as amphibious mammals. Both of them move adequately on land but more elegantly in the sea. Both of them fish. Their bodies and wakes are parallel as they surf down the same wave. On his board Ben is horizontal and tripedal like the seal. His webbed gloves resemble flippers and his surfboard echoes the shape of the seal's snout. This animal comparison does not disparage the boy, nor does his resemblance to a female animal. On the contrary, the comparison establishes his fluency in the ocean environment.

Their shared vulnerability before the power of the ocean also creates parallels between the seal and the boy. So does their elders' assumption that they can be independent despite danger. Like the young seal who braved his first winter storms, Ben hits a big wave that pushes him into a rock. The wave smacks him off his surfboard. Just as Ben was concerned for the seal's safety, the seal is concerned for his. Ben is sinking into the depths when the young seal rescues him. "Sunlight shone through the water onto Ben's face as the seal pushed his body up. With a final heave she flipped Ben onto his board. He held on, and the next wave carried him to shore. His friends crowded around to make sure he was all right."[44]

In the rescue the seal becomes a kind of feral service animal, but not an overburdened one. This pairing of traits shifts the meanings of both "feral" and "service." "Feral" loses its connotation of savagery, while "service" loses its

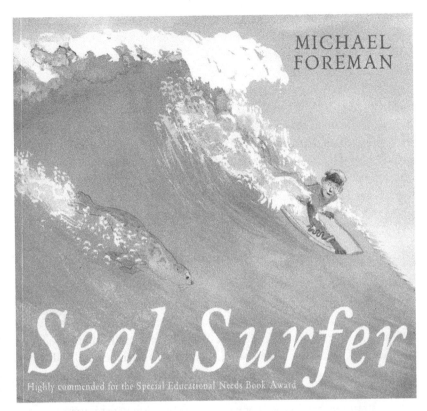

MICHAEL
FOREMAN

Seal Surfer

Highly commended for the Special Educational Needs Book Award

Fig. 11. Ben and the seal ride a wave side by side. *Seal Surfer* by Michael Foreman, Andersen Press, 1996.

connotation of obedience. In the picture, the seal hoists Ben onto his board while a cluster of three human friends paddle close to the pair, concern evident on their faces. This prosthetic community means that the seal does not have to act alone to make the boy independent or valuable to his peers. Nor does the animal have to integrate the boy into human society. That integration has already happened. The seal is just doing a favor for another surfer. It is a friendship of equals.

Ben's surfing and other ocean adventures reinforce his masculinity. Surfing is cool, surfing with able-bodied human friends is cool, and surfing with a seal friend is pretty cool, too. In his seal surfing, fishing, and hunting mussels, Ben's proficiency with marine animals brings him closer to a respected elder, his grandfather. We also see him move into his grandfather's role. At the end of the book Ben assumes his late grandfather's old fishing spot below the sea wall in the harbor. More elders, the fisherman of his village, look on as Ben greets the young seal, now mature. She doesn't look like Ben anymore; now she looks like his grandfather. "Ben cheered as he saw the once young seal—now as whiskery as Granddad—with *her* young pup."[45] On the last page of the book, Ben imagines himself as a male elder: "And maybe one day he would lie on the cliff tops with his own grandchildren and together they would watch the seals."[46] Ben's three grandkids lie on a rock like seal pups, propped up on their elbows. Ben sits next to them, his crutches leaning behind him. He will continue the male line of the family, and subsequent generations will continue their relationships with the seals. Ben's prosthetic community allows a connection to nature sustainable over the seasons and years. In a translucent Atlantic, he thrives and takes risks.

Sosu's Call: Social Change and the Prosthetic Community

Sosu's Call depicts a new prosthetic community in the making, symbolizing the social changes in Ghana over the past twenty-five years. The picture book reflects how children with disabilities have claimed public space. *Sosu's Call* is a Supercrip story where a mobility-impaired boy's relationship to an animal helps him move into a wider world. With the encouragement of his dog Fusa, the protagonist Sosu performs a heroic rescue, gains status in his coastal village, and leaves his previous isolation behind. Meshack Asare, the writer and illustrator of *Sosu's Call*, is one of Africa's best-known children's authors. The book has won many awards, including the 1999 UNESCO first prize for Children's Literature in the Service of Tolerance. In 2002 a jury from thirteen African countries chose *Sosu's Call* as one of the twelve best African books of the twentieth century.[47] These prizes acknowledge not only Asare's talent but also the increasing prominence of disability rights in Africa.

The Ghanaian disability activism of the 1990s forms the context for *Sosu's Call*. Asare's picture book appeared in 1997, in the midst of a twelve-year struggle culminating in the passage of the Ghana Persons with Disability Act (2006).[48] The Persons with Disability Act has enabled new access to quality education, health care, employment skills, small business capital, barrier-free buildings, social life, voting, and public office.[49] In this political context, Sosu's bravery consists not only in his physical feats but also in his request for inclusion. Like the real-life Ghanaian disability activists of his day, Sosu makes the news. When the TV and radio journalists come to his house and ask him what he would like the most, he says he wants to go to school.

At the end of the story Sosu heads to the local school in his new wheelchair, an emblem of the changes at work in Ghana. "Prior to the 1990s, very few students with disabilities in Ghana were included in regular education classrooms." Ghana's Education for All policy has now opened the school doors.[50] According to Ghanaian Deaf and disability community leader Christie Yaghr, "The new educational measures in Ghana have indeed improved the lives of children with disabilities. This is because these measures have opened the chance for children with disabilities to go to school. It is unlike the past where nobody paid attention or gave recognition to the importance of their education."[51] Unlike Ben in *Seal Surfer*, however, no one can take Sosu's education and equipment for granted.

It is still unusual for children with physical disabilities in rural Ghana, like Sosu, to attend their local schools. In a postcolonial nation like Ghana, rural schools lack accessible buildings and special education teachers. The cost of wheelchairs is prohibitively high. Parents "cannot purchase wheelchairs for them to commute to and from school," and "government funding for wheel-chairs for persons with disabilities is either not enough, absent, or to a selected few who are rather well to do."[52] The happy ending of *Sosu's Call* represents a best-case scenario rare in the real world.

The desire to be useful motivates Sosu's heroism. This goal respects Ghanaian tradition and overturns Ghanaian prejudices. *Sosu's Call* refutes two of the attitudes that frustrated and delayed passage of the Ghana Persons with Disability Act. The Ghanaian disability studies scholar Ato Quayson details these ableist attitudes. The first is the idea that people with disabilities have received a divine curse and can alter others' luck. The second is the idea that people with disabilities have no useful labor to offer and can survive only as disparaged beggars. On the streets of Accra live people with motor impairments much like Sosu's:

> The vast bulk of beggars on intersections and street corners are persons with various kinds of disability, thus making the link between the two almost natural in the minds of the nondisabled. Indeed, a local Akan saying, "*e ti se bafa ne fom*" (it is like the cripple [*sic*] and the ground), which is used to convey the inseparability between the two entities, derives from the observation that persons with severe motor impairments are often seen dragging themselves on the ground, begging for alms at street corners and elsewhere.[53]

Sosu's Call evokes these stereotypes in the process of overturning them. Although Sosu's family supports him, several pictures show him in the role of the beggar, sitting alone and idle on the ground outside the family house.[54] Sitting in his yard, Sosu asks himself, "What good is a boy without a pair of good, strong legs?"[55] The repetition of this image conveys the dullness of his existence. Sosu appears in the left-hand observer position with which the viewer identifies, wearing a bright orange shirt that makes him stand out as the protagonist. Thus, the viewer identifies with Sosu's idleness and exclusion and sees them as problems rather than the inevitable results of his disability.

By contrast, a flashback shows Sosu in an active and capable role with his father in their fishing canoe. Father and son stroke their oars in parallel lines, embodying the smooth passage of the fishing livelihood from father to son. They are out in the peaceful lagoon, the space of men's work and the "kind mother" to the village that supplies many delicacies.[56] However, two older men in another canoe pull up beside the father and son, saying, "We don't think it is wise to bring that boy of yours out here. It is unlucky enough to have the likes of him in the village. We doubt if the Lagoon Spirit is pleased to have him sitting here as well! We think you must keep him in your compound."[57] Thus the reader learns that Sosu wasn't always idle and excluded. One stigma has led to another in a vicious circle. The community excludes a disabled person from useful labor because it regards him as bad luck. Then it stigmatizes him for being idle.

Usefulness is a central virtue for Ghanaian children. "No child is useless" is a slogan of Education for All.[58] An eldest son, Sosu would normally take a central role in caring for his family as he grows into manhood. As a Ghanaian special educator explains, it is a huge loss if a child cannot grow up to take care of his parents.

> I think the role of the child right from the beginning is to grow up and to look after the adult. . . . We have a saying in Ashanti, literally it means "I have cared for you for all your teeth to grow so now you care for me for all my teeth to drop out." . . . So if you have a child who is not going to be successful or they are not going to be able to do that then that is a really big loss, that is a massive loss.[59]

Sosu finds a way to fulfill his social role, taking care of the old and very young and thus proving his usefulness.

Like the other books in this canon, *Sosu's Call* depicts an animal and a child with a disability whose bodily movements resemble each other. Side by side they solve a problem, and that solution leads to a new vision of inclusive community. However, *Sosu's Call* contains the human-animal comparison more firmly than *Seal Surfer* does. The stronger containment arises from the greater stigma attached to resembling a dog versus a seal and also from the different social context. In a poor nation where wheelchairs are rare and most people with physical disabilities beg and drag themselves across the ground, dignity is more fragile. Therefore, it is more important to contain the animal resemblance. The postcolonial racist legacy of comparing Africans to animals also casts its shadow on the comparison of a Ghanaian boy to his dog. For example, Vivian Yenika-Agbaw critiques the charity Heifer International for trumpeting in its publicity how "a goat saved an African child," and describes the outrage across Africa when an African village was exhibited at a German zoo in 2005.[60]

Nonetheless, *Sosu's Call* depicts an African boy who saves his village and establishes his human worth by moving like a dog and following a dog's lead. Breaking the barriers between human and nonhuman animals also breaks down barriers for human beings. Initially, however, movement creates contrast between Sosu and the family dog Fusa: the dog can leave the family home while Sosu cannot. Like many Africans, Sosu's family lives in a house surrounded by a wall, and the yard within the wall hosts domestic activities. Sosu sits on the ground right outside his house, looking up at the narrow patch of world he can see above the wall, when Fusa comes bounding into the yard. Fusa has accompanied Sosu's brother and sister to school: "The dog was always back puffing and its eyes shining with the satisfaction of having been outside! It was this more than anything else, that made him envious."[61] The dog has the free range of the village denied to Sosu.

On the day when "all of that changed," however, Sosu's body language starts to resemble the dog's, and this resemblance continues throughout their rescue of villagers. Their shared movements indicate when they become a team. Sosu has nearly always appeared in the lower left corner, where viewers identify with him. Now Fusa joins him in the corner, and viewers can identify with the pair. Both dog and boy have their necks stretched up and out, looking at the coconut palms "as their tops bent and swayed desperately in the wind" of a sudden, violent storm.[62] In the next double-page spread, both dog and boy pull back in alarm as "the old wooden gate shot across the yard like a massive kite!"[63] Sosu and Fusa figure out together how to respond to the storm.

Fusa's help is not physical, as one might expect; rather, theirs is a thinking partnership. "Something had to be done. And fast. But what could he do? The only other people in the village at this time were those who were too old and frail to do anything. There were many like that in the village. Often, they were left with very young children. They could all be trapped and drowned if the sea continued to rise."[64] Fusa's listening seems to pull a good idea out of Sosu's mind, as often happens in creative partnerships. While Fusa looks at him with "a knowing and reassuring look in its eyes," Sosu hits on the idea of crawling to the drum shed and drumming. His drumming will notify the working adults to return to the village and rescue those trapped by rising floodwaters.[65]

Fusa becomes a human's working partner like dogs throughout the centuries, including service dogs. Stephen Kuusisto says of his guide dog Corky, "Although we move as one, we are more than that. Guide dogs and their human partners must each trust the other's bravery and judgment."[66] Fusa supports and shares Sosu's bravery and judgment: "The look in Fusa's eyes did not only say that it knew where to find the drums. It also said, 'Don't be afraid! We will be all right!'"[67] Sosu becomes a hero by moving on all fours like a dog. In the book's climactic picture, Sosu and Fusa head for the drum shed on all fours, "leaning into the howling wind and sloshing through churning water."[68] The boy and the dog resemble each other in their poses and earthy colors. The viewer is down at the ground level, too. Sosu has one hand in the air while Fusa raises the corresponding paw. The dog looks back at the boy reassuringly and wags his tail, their communication in sync despite the stress of the storm and the need for swift action.

Sosu acquires the dog's freedom to roam, and his entrance into wild nature signals his new freedom in human society as well. When Sosu crawls out of the family compound to the drum shed, he infiltrates the forbidden world of work. Alerting the adults about the flood, Sosu saves the lives of the village's children and grandparents. By rescuing those "too old and frail to do anything," he demonstrates that he himself is neither frail nor incapable.

In this village, joining the human community means going outdoors. To be fishing in the sea or lagoon is to be a man. When the men in the canoe say that Sosu displeases the Lagoon Spirit and must stay at home, they exclude him from the nature at the center of their work and spiritual worldview. However, when the churning tide of water spills into his yard, the sea comes to him. Crawling through that tide, Sosu joins the useful world of men in water. However, he doesn't do the same job as the men who come running home to carry the grandparents and babies out of the flood. In the crisis he invents a new job that a young man with a physical disability can do, and thus widens the definition of useful labor.

Floods often enter this village on its narrow strip of land between the sea and the lagoon. The villagers accept the inevitability of flooding in their

Fig. 12. Sosu and Fusa, side by side through the rain. *Sosu's Call* by Meshack Asare, Sub-Saharan Publishers, 1997.

ecosystem. Their vulnerability is part of the social contract. Sosu comes into this shared vulnerability instead of being seen as helpless in a way separate and different from the rest of his society. His rescue forms part of the natural cycle of humans responding to their wetland home. Sosu embodies nature in his drumming. At first he is uncertain because he has never played a drum before. Then he becomes the voice of nature, bringing the villagers running to him because he enacts the story of the storm through his hands:

> But suddenly, the storm, the pounding waves of water, the young children, the sick, the old, the animals, the crashing fences and snapping trees, all came rushing to him like moving pictures!
> So he struck the drum harder and faster until he heard it above the shrieks and howls of the wind:
> Belem-belen-belem! Bembem-bembem-bembem![69]

At his moment of human acceptance, Sosu's body language stops resembling the dog's and he comes up off the ground. The men realize that Sosu has drummed the call that brought them home in time to save the village. "He was soon riding on strong shoulders, with Fusa leaping into the air to reach him!"[70] In the last two spreads, Sosu talks to the press and receives his wheelchair while family and neighbors cluster behind him. He sits up high with the dog on his lap or next to his chair. Fusa has become his pet rather than his partner. Thus, the animal-human comparison is paradoxical in *Sosu's Call*. Moving like an animal has enabled Sosu to become a useful and respected member of his village, yet he must leave the resemblance behind for other humans to accord him full dignity. The book has to break the association between him and the ground in order to cut the ties between disability, begging, and uselessness.

Sosu's Call is not just a Supercrip story about individual accomplishment. It also tells the story of a village that can change its mind. The book refutes the stereotype of African villages as immune to change. Vivian Yenika-Agbaw writes, "The representations of West Africa in children's books seem to make Africans' efforts to modernize invisible to all who are not there."[71] She asks, "Should African children accept every single tradition that has been handed down to them by their elders?"[72] Sosu's village is not the stereotypical one where children follow every tradition, even the most destructive ones. Instead, tradition and modernity come together, represented by the village chief who presents the gleaming new wheelchair. The last pages of *Sosu's Call* shows the chief in his traditional robe, bracelets, and headwear, shaking Sosu's hand as the boy sits in his new chair. The chief joins Sosu on the left page, where he has so often been alone, and a half-circle of villagers stand behind them.

A collective exclusion becomes a collective inclusion. Celebrating their survival at a village festival, everyone finally wears the same bright colors as Sosu, and the same bright umbrellas cover them all. Sosu has joined the human community—or rather, they have joined him. It is fitting that the chief presents the wheelchair, since chiefs had been "unwitting guardians of prejudice toward disabled persons" and their support has been crucial in the struggle for disability rights.[73] The last page shows elements of Sosu's new prosthetic community: his family, neighbors, and leaders; his wheelchair; and his dog. The village has also changed the infrastructure, smoothing a new wheelchair-accessible path from Sosu's house to the school. We might also consider the journalists' microphone and camera as part of Sosu's prosthetic community, since the news coverage has enabled all the other changes.[74] In Sosu's struggle as in others, media coverage can contribute to human rights.

Through his bodily movements, Sosu forms a creative partnership with an animal, embodies the power of nature, and infiltrates the human community—even though his bodily movements were the original basis of his exclusion. The animal and human worlds resemble each other. Nonetheless, the story must disavow this resemblance for Sosu to take his place in the human community. The disability-positive message at the happy ending of *Sosu's Call* contains the leakage. Yet the animal-human comparison floods into the middle of the text and creates the fertile ground for that happy ending.

Freedom of Movement

Sosu and Ben find their freedom with nonhuman animals in wild nature. It's just too bad they have to work so hard for it, and the animals do, too. Their adventures demonstrate their skill and bravery. The problem is the *need* to prove their worth, to readers and other characters. Sosu and Ben, the dog Fusa and the young seal, have to perform Supercrip athletic feats and heroic rescues to demonstrate their personhood. Appreciation for animals, both wild and domestic, often comes through stories of gratitude for their service to humans. It isn't enough for animals to exist for themselves. Similarly, kids with disabilities face the task of meeting the benchmarks adult humans set. In Ben's village in Britain, the benchmark is self-fulfillment; in Sosu's village in Africa, the benchmark is service to the community.

As boys with disabilities, Sosu and Ben also bear the burden of demonstrating their masculinity. Both boys come from fishing villages where physical courage and outdoor adventures are prerequisites for joining in male elders' pursuits. However, the animals enable two different kinds of masculinity, one quite old and the other quite new. In the older kind, traditional masculinity steps in to erase and replace disability as the standard of personhood. If you can prove you are traditionally masculine, your disability no longer threatens your status as a person. The newer kind of masculinity, however, is a masculinity-with-disability that widens the gender roles to make more room for vulnerability, partnership, and adaptability at work and play.

In their moments of freedom, however, child and animal have nothing to prove to each other. They have learned to trust each other's judgments through partnerships in play and problem solving. That trust is more important than the world's judgments. Children with disabilities and animals belong together in the natural world. Through surfing and responding to floods, both boys dive deeply into their watery ecosystems. The vulnerability of disability is no different from our shared vulnerability before the power of water. Animals and humans work together to save lives, and this cooperation could extend to saving the ocean itself.

For Ben and Sosu, getting out into nature requires a robust human world.

Wheelchairs, individual feats, and service animals can't do the trick on their own. It takes a prosthetic village to raise a child with a disability. *Seal Surfer* sports a prosthetic community so rich, it can afford to take nature access for granted. *Sosu's Call* displays the kind of social change necessary for kids with disabilities to come outside into the world. In a diverse prosthetic community, people with disabilities don't have to lean so hard on service animals that they become beasts of burden.

A British picture book takes wheelchair ownership as a matter of course, while a Ghanaian picture book takes wheelchair ownership as a cause for mass celebration. This difference in access has its roots in Ghana's history as a British colony. The legacy of underdevelopment plays a role in the daily lives of people with disabilities in contemporary Ghana, where a wheelchair is a luxury item.

The greater the climate of social acceptance and the availability of resources, the more children with disabilities can claim their resemblances to animals. In *Sosu's Call* and *Seal Surfer*, bodily movement forms the basis of the human-animal comparison. The dog and seal have tremendous freedom of movement, and this range of motion transfers metaphorically to the boys. Their resemblance to animals does not signify lower status, but rather, the freedom to roam. Many animals and children with disabilities lack this freedom. If we opened the cages, we would see the capacities for joy, problem-solving, partnership, and adventure we find in these picture books.

Five

Disservice Animals

Hyperbole and a Half's *Test Anxiety for Dogs and Humans*

———

This chapter on canine-human failure offers a refreshing break from the previous chapter's animal-human pairs excelling in perfect tandem. Allie Brosh's beloved graphic memoir *Hyperbole and a Half: Unfortunate Situations, Flawed Coping Mechanisms, Mayhem, and Other Things That Happened* (2013) grew out of her web comic of the same name. The book stars two dogs and a dog owner who all have disabilities. The mayhem of her household serves as a corrective to the romanticism of animal studies writers like Donna Haraway and Vicki Hearne, who base their understanding of cross-species partnership on training high-performing animals for work like scent tracking and agility trials.[1] By contrast, Brosh and her dogs fail spectacularly to be Supercrips. Nonetheless, they serve as a shining example of a cross-species family with disabilities.

Hyperbole and a Half has never been marketed to young readers, so why talk about it in this study of children's and young adult literature? I have two reasons. First, this chapter contributes to childhood studies by redefining the social construction of disability for the millennial generation in the United States. The turn of the twenty-first century has seen the rise of a *testing model of disability*. The millennials were the first American students to experience the consequences of national standardized testing. I place *Hyperbole and a Half* in the context of two American pandemics: the sudden celebrity of attention deficit hyperactivity disorder (ADHD) in the 1990s and the test anxiety epidemic of the early 2000s. Brosh's vision of epic failure grows from her feelings of missing the mark as a child with ADHD in the 1990s and resonates with the text anxiety generation of young adults in the 2010s.

My second reason is that young adults do not confine their reading to books labeled and marketed as "young adult," especially when it comes to web comics and other graphic narratives. Profane, hilarious, and brutally honest, *Hyperbole and a Half* has been a favorite among young adult readers.[2] Students in my college classes, especially those who struggle with anxiety and depression, connect with Brosh's mock-heroic saga of her repeated failures. The book lends itself well to readers' imagining themselves into its stories because of Allie Brosh's deliberately simple artwork and uncanny knack for conveying mental states that are commonly experienced but seldom rendered well. In this way *Hyperbole and a Half* has formed an imagined community for young adults with disabilities.

Hyperbole and a Half represents another cultural moment in which new laws sway the portrayal of young people with disabilities. Brosh's understanding of her own attention deficit hyperactivity disorder derives in part from new social and legal constructions of ADHD at the turn of the twenty-first century combined with new legal mandates for standardized testing. Interestingly, though, Brosh wields and parodies this new millennial vision of the tested child not to reconceive school or human society, as one might expect, but to reconceive nature. Brosh's epistemology of nature, her way of knowing and understanding it, includes human and animal disabilities. She upends the animacy hierarchy through crip solidarity with her dogs. They share an implacable neurodiversity that colors her whole absurdist picture of the natural world. In Allie Brosh's ADHD epistemology, nature always exceeds human efforts to control it.

Humans often admire animals through praise songs to the services they provide. But do animals still have intrinsic value when they fail to serve our practical and emotional needs or follow our commands? *Hyperbole and a Half* dwells on the scary, funny parts of nature that defy human expectations. This nature includes woods, wild animals, and dogs, but also human disability. For instance, Brosh describes the harsh self-scrutiny of depression as "traipsing around in your deep brain-wilderness like a reckless idiot."[3] Dog training makes a mockery of techniques for testing and managing disability. Brosh administers a (failed) doggie IQ test to her first dog after finding that "not only is training my dog outlandishly difficult, it is also heartbreaking."[4] Brosh and her partner adopt a second dog as a service animal for the first, only to find that the second dog's moods pose even greater challenges than the first dog's cognitive limitations.[5] In Brosh's universe, human and nonhuman disabilities closely resemble each other and represent the power of nature that cannot be altered or harnessed.

Allie Brosh's cripistemology of nature dwells on the moment of failure. *Hyperbole and a Half* has an eccentric sense of time, insisting on the extreme moments of missing the mark rather than the long stretches when things go well. Comics, a time-based art form, help Brosh inhabit the intensity of the moment. She slows time down in panel sequences that proceed minute by minute, elucidating the paradoxes of a troubled train of thought. She draws vignettes of disorder rather than a long story arc ending in order restored. She divorces cause from effect, before from after, problem from solution. By cutting the cord between cause and effect, Brosh questions the assumption that humans actually understand the laws of cause and effect. Disability leads the questioning, underscoring that hard work does not always yield results.

Allie Brosh will never be head cheerleader on the disability pride squad. She brands herself and her dogs as abnormal and lacking. She calls her first dog by the hurtful word "retarded."[6] Yet Brosh has produced some of the most vivid and accurate depictions of depression, anxiety, and ADHD. In her harsh self-mockery, Brosh may seem to do herself a disservice. However, her disparagement mirrors the feelings of shame and inadequacy that can accompany disabilities like ADHD, anxiety, and depression. She puts into words moments that many people feel but few have been able to articulate. Readers have found recognition and relief in her honesty about her own mental contortions. *Hyperbole and a Half* topped best-seller and critics' choice lists and had an initial printing of 350,000 copies, while her blog of the same name has drawn millions of readers.[7] Because she is white, Allie Brosh has been able to expose her vulnerabilities and still receive only praise online instead of the vicious trolling that often meets women of color when they blog about their lives.

The ADHD Generation and the Testing Model of Disability

How do Brosh's ADHD and test anxiety influence her view of the living world? Brosh's ADHD epistemology of nature proceeds from what I call *the testing model of disability*. Most stories in *Hyperbole and a Half* repeat the same pattern: a human or canine protagonist faces a test with impossibly high standards and their failure to pass the test opens the door to nature's chaos. For instance, in "Lost in the Woods" Brosh's mother tries to avoid scaring her two little girls by pretending they are still in the woods by choice. She sets them the task of finding pine cones. "We had spent hours combing the forest for the biggest, brownest, heaviest, cleanest pine cones it could offer, hoping that maybe, just maybe, if we found exactly the right ones, our mother would let us go home. . . . Several hours later, we had come no closer to meeting our mother's ludicrous standards. We were beginning to lose hope."[8] Not only do the girls fail the test, but the test itself fails to shield them from a northern Idaho forest that looks ever darker and more frightening.

In her preoccupation with test anxiety, Allie Brosh shares a concern widespread among American young adults in the early twenty-first century. Studies conducted in the 2010s have shown a dramatic upswing in anxiety of all kinds among college students. Between 2009 and 2016, anxiety outstripped depression as the main reason prompting US college students to seek counseling, with 54 percent of college students surveyed reporting they had "felt overwhelming anxiety" in the past year.[9] Another study concluded, "Anxiety continues to be the most predominant and increasing concern among college students (50.6%)."[10] The legacy of high-stakes testing has played its part in this anxiety epidemic and in twenty-first-century young adult literature. Jonathan Alexander and Rebecca Black note the frequent depictions of testing in young adult fiction from 2004 to 2014. In young adult dystopias, "The competition for survival is often framed as a series of tests that individuals must face for inclusion into a community or even for educational advancement. The stakes for failure are often extraordinarily high."[11]

I posit that Allie Brosh's preoccupation with failure grows from her experiences of navigating childhood with ADHD and resonates with the test anxiety generation. Although she doesn't name the disability in *Hyperbole and a Half*, she declares on her blog, "I have hardcore, legit, currently-unmedicated ADHD."[12] Like many children and teenagers with ADHD, Brosh struggled with the demands of a regular school schedule and feelings of missing the mark. As a teenager she didn't know how to "do the things that show people you can be one of them, like they see you and they're like, 'There's something wrong here.'"[13] Although she did well academically, Brosh almost failed to graduate from high school due to low attendance during a rough patch of family life. Her comics career has been a godsend because "I've always had a problem with schedules." Although she works hard to approximate social norms, understanding them does not come naturally. "I have to reverse-engineer it: 'This is how I would feel if I were a normal person.'"[14] Although the disability itself presents challenges, the deepest anxiety comes from misfitting social expectations.

Brosh is a member of the ADHD generation. Born in 1986, she spent kindergarten and high school in the years when ADHD became such a prominent feature on the American public landscape we might call it a pandemic.[15] In the 1990s, the disability acquired a sudden celebrity and a rate of diagnosis in the United States much higher than other industrialized nations. By the year 2000 researchers estimated that at least 5 percent of the school-age population had a form of attention deficit disorder.[16] In September 1991, the month Allie Brosh started kindergarten, ADHD became eligible for special education under the Individuals with Disabilities Education Act of 1990 (IDEA), with further legal guarantees in 1997. These decisions came in response to lawsuits and pressure by parents and other ADHD advocates. The new eligibility for services made the ADHD diagnosis skyrocket.[17] Neurobiological and chemical explanations came to the fore at the same time, and prescriptions for the ADHD drug Ritalin (methylphenidate) also skyrocketed. From 1990 through May 1995, the annual US production of Ritalin increased 500 percent.[18] Boys received the ADHD diagnosis much more often than girls, which makes Brosh's account even more valuable.

Disability studies scholars have trained their critiques on the overuse of medical explanations and prescription drugs for ADHD.[19] However, the traditional disability studies dichotomy of medical versus social model may not sufficiently describe the experiences of the millennial generation. Americans born after 1980 focus their critiques on standardized tests. With disabilities or without, young Americans from the 1990s onward have faced an educational system dominated by high-stakes testing. "In the 1990s, elected officials of both parties came to accept as secular gospel the idea that testing and accountability would necessarily lead to better schools."[20] By 1994 forty-three states had implemented statewide tests in elementary schools and by the year 2000, every one but Iowa had mandated testing.[21] This political movement culminated in No Child Left Behind, signed into federal law in January 2002, which mandated standardized testing and tied federal school funding to students' success or failure.[22]

In addition to the wider testing culture of the United States, students with disabilities take more rounds of tests. To make a diagnosis or claim for accommodation, a team of professionals first identifies a child's gaps and lacks. For instance, the Individualized Education Plan at the heart of IDEA gives students indispensable rights, but requires setting annual goals for the student ("Will be able to walk in walker for 15 feet"; "Will be able to read at the rate of 100 words per minute") before pledging services to meet the goals. Students with ADHD undergo their own kinds of scrutiny. Throughout the 1990s, a proliferation of testing instruments for ADHD accompanied the rise in Ritalin production. Students wore pedometers to track their activity levels.

The Matching Familiar Figures Test measured the ability to resist tempting impulses. Parents and teachers filled out behavioral checklists.[23] Indeed, the medical model of ADHD depends on the testing model. As Pamela Beth Whitt and Scot Danforth write, an ADHD diagnosis turns teachers into "medical reporters."[24]

Hyperbole and a Half lampoons the standardized tests of US education in general and ADHD special education in particular. The phrase "flawed coping mechanisms" in Allie Brosh's subtitle echoes formal evaluations of students' ability to cope with ADHD symptoms. *Hyperbole and a Half* is chock-full of behavioral checklists and timed tests that precisely identify the dogs' and the author's gaps and lacks. The failure of the timed tests mocks orderly progress and foregrounds Brosh's eccentric sense of time.

The Art of Disorder

Allie Brosh takes the test anxiety of her generation and turns it into an art form. Nearly every chapter of the book contains a failed test. Brosh's sense of failure reveals an internal anxiety about norms, but also a critique of testing itself. The test itself fails to register the world's complexities. As Brosh declares, "Reality doesn't give a *shit* about my rules, and this upsets me."[25] The same pattern governs almost every story. First, the narrator labels a human or canine protagonist as abnormal, irrational, or doomed to fail. With dogged persistence, she keeps applying testing standards that do not apply. From there the story unleashes itself into the full chaos of the "deep brain wilderness."

Brosh refuses to become a medical reporter assembling a coherent case history with a clear-cut diagnosis. Disability and nature do not become recognizably disordered in *Hyperbole and a Half*. Elke Emerald and Lorelei Carpenter use the term "recognizably disordered" to describe how schools sometimes see children with ADHD. After overlooking a student's needs, a school may finally grant her accommodations once she has an ADHD diagnosis and becomes "recognizably disordered."[26] By contrast, Allie Brosh rejects the category "recognizably disordered" by omitting explanations of odd behavior. The stories mention her childhood hyperactivity and struggles with impulse control, but never name her ADHD.[27] Similarly, she omits the histories of abuse that could account for her dogs' disabilities. On her blog she explains that "both of our dogs were rescued from abusive situations and we've had to do substantial rehabilitation work with them."[28] However, in *Hyperbole and a Half* both Brosh and her dogs appear unrecognizably disordered. In blog conversations Brosh is happy to use diagnostic terms, but to do so in her comics would soften the impact of her humor, which relies on errant moments and deep weirdness.

Refusing to explain herself or her dogs, Brosh releases the tremendous emotional and comic energy that makes her work compelling. Stephen Greenblatt has observed such a "strategic opacity" in Shakespeare, who found "that he could provoke in the audience and in himself a peculiarly passionate intensity of response, if he took out a key explanatory element." This "strategic opacity . . . released an enormous energy that had been at least partially blocked or constrained by familiar, reassuring explanations."[29] Through strategic opacity, Brosh unleashes a larger sense of mayhem that forms the basis for an ADHD epistemology of nature. The disorder of life is not an individual problem to be treated with Ritalin. It is, rather, a fundamental part of animals and landscapes. Comedy lies in the gap between human expectations and the world's deep weirdness.

Brosh's art form, the web comic, suits her anatomy of disorder. Starting life as blog posts, her stories are vignettes of mental contortions rather than overcoming narratives. Brosh plops readers in the middle of uncomfortable feelings happening now, with no philosophical clarity grown over time. Just as people often do not outgrow ADHD, Brosh's stories never graduate from youth to adulthood. *Hyperbole and a Half* zigzags back and forth between child and adult memoir, and Brosh draws herself the same way at different ages: hot-pink sack dress, stick arms, and a yellow triangle on her head that could be a shark's fin or a dunce cap but is probably a blond ponytail. Her Paintbrush digital pictures are deliberately childlike, their wavering lines and simple faces alive with expression.

The art of failure expresses itself in this artistic and narrative zigzagging between childhood and adulthood. Brosh's aesthetic undergirds her critique of impossible norms and standardized tests. As Jack Halberstam writes, "Failure allows us to escape the punishing norms that discipline behavior and manage human development with the goal of delivering us from unruly childhoods to orderly and predictable adulthoods. Failure preserves some of the wondrous anarchy of childhood and disturbs the supposedly clean boundaries between adults and children, winners and losers."[30] The comics form of the panel sequence blurs boundaries between childhood and adulthood. Hilary Chute argues that comics lend themselves to childhood memoirs because the art of assembling words and images with gaps between them "mimics the procedure of memory." In women's graphic memoirs, "The comics form not only presents a child protagonist and an adult narrator but also gives voice simultaneously to both perspectives, even within the space of a single panel, layering temporalities and narrative positions."[31] Many facets of Brosh's aesthetic, from panels to time frames to drawing style, reinforce the connection between the child's kinetic energy and the adult's mental contortions.

Allie Brosh uses the time signatures of the panel sequence to transmit her ADHD epistemology and her anatomy of disorder. The panel sequence serves as artistic corollary to the behavioral checklist as well as parody of it. Brosh records her own swing from superego to id with painful honesty. In "This Is Why I'll Never Be an Adult," Brosh breaks down what happens during the "few times a year" when "I spontaneously decide that I'm ready to be a *real* adult." She presents herself with a sudden benchmark "which always ends terribly for me."[32] As usual, the narrator imposes ridiculously high standards doomed to failure. A comedian of hyperbole, Brosh charts not the majority of the time when things stay under control but the times they go haywire.

Although she doesn't mention her ADHD, the visual sequence in "This Is Why I'll Never Be an Adult" parodies the Individualized Education Plan and ADHD adaptation tests. She begins with a hand-drawn graph, mapping her capacity for responsibility on the x-axis and exceeding her capacity on the y-axis. A sequence of panels shows her meeting new goals like email, grocery shopping, and "go to the motherf*cking *bank* like an *adult*."[33] In the panel "clean *all* the things!" the manic energy starts to rise. A yellow splash of resolve explodes behind her. She has one fist pumped up, a broom in the other fist, and a toothy mouth ready to attack those chores like a hungry shark.[34] After a few panels showing her self-satisfaction, she crashes. Brosh cowers in the corner of a long gray panel, peering over her shoulder and clutching her trophy for being a responsible adult.[35]

Brosh's honesty prompts empathy and discomfort in readers. Her cartoon alter ego feels guilty that she cannot meet her own impossible standards: the kind of external and possibly irrelevant standards pervasive in the culture of standardized testing. "Then the guilt from my ignored responsibilities grows so large that . . . [i]t takes up a sizable portion of my capacity, leaving me almost completely useless for anything other than consuming nachos and surfing the Internet like an attention-deficient squirrel on PCP."[36] She taps on her laptop with a manic smile, head and arms flailing.[37] Accepting one's own limitations is one of the principal struggles of having a disability. Internalized standards fan the fire of self-blame. Comparing herself to "an attention-deficient squirrel" is the closest Brosh comes to disclosing her ADHD. This pseudodiagnosis turns her into an absurd, small, and cartoonish animal.

While the image of a squirrel surfing the internet suggests random nervous energy, PCP (phencyclidine) adds a whiff of "danger to self and others."

"This Is Why I'll Never Be an Adult" showcases Brosh's eccentric sense of time, with its repeating cycles and severed connections between cause and effect. She flees from the crushing weight of a failed test into rebellion, without the recognizable disorder of ADHD. However, the lack of a disability claim also unleashes the emotional intensity that prompts the story's broad appeal. The "clean *all* the things!" image has become a widely shared and reworked meme, testimony that many of us are subject to fits of high resolve.[38] A strong crip humor underlies this comic sequence that is also a repeating life cycle of resolve and collapse. Self-care is always a work in progress.

Like a Dog

In "This Is Why I'll Never Be an Adult" Brosh compares herself to "an attention-deficient squirrel on PCP." She likens herself to an animal at the moments her disabilities come to the fore. The awareness of internal or external norms prompts such comparisons. Either reality defies her arbitrary rules, or she realizes that an outside observer might judge her abnormal. In the previous chapter I discussed the long, terrible history of comparing people with disabilities to animals. Brosh courts this terrible history when she diagnoses her deep identification with animals as a symptom of abnormality. However, this kinship also reveals the cross-species solidarity at the heart of her epistemology of nature. "Warning Signs," the first chapter of the book, replies to a letter she wrote her future self when she was ten years old. Most of her questions to her adult self express canine concerns. The first question is, "Do you still like dogs?"[39] The chapter illustrates Hilary Chute's observation that "the comics form not only presents a child protagonist and an adult narrator but also gives voice simultaneously to both perspectives." The drawings capture Allie at various stages of childhood, like snapshots from an odd family album. In blocks of text she reinterprets the images from an adult's perspective.

The adult diagnoses the childhood self, and her harsh judgments riff on the testing model of disability. For instance, a strong identification with animals is a warning sign of emotional disturbance. The entry "Dear Ten-Year-old" starts with a drawing of a happy, unself-conscious Allie and her dog Murphy sitting on the floor smiling up at the camera. Looking down at them from high above, the angle reinforces the sense of happy childhood play and also echoes the text's adult scrutiny. Allie's pink dress says, "I heart dogs," she is playing with two toy dogs, and a book titled *Dogs* with tiny pictures of dogs on the cover sits between Murphy and Allie.[40] The narrator says to Allie, "Wow, you really like dogs. In fact, you like dogs so much that I'm not even sure it's emotionally healthy."[41]

The testing model of disability proliferates further and further. The narrator concludes that it is normal to like dogs, but acting like a dog indicates developmental delay. "Normal children don't walk around pretending to be a dog nearly as much as you do, for example. You're ten. It makes people wonder about your developmental progress when you growl and bark at them."[42] Here is a double outside judgment: other people's imagined standards pile on top of the narrator's disapproval. The child isn't acting like a snuggly puppy, but an aggressive dog who growls and barks. The wilder side of pets doesn't belong on the human behavioral checklist.

Timed tests, common in the era of high-stakes evaluation, appear frequently in Brosh's work to signify the failure of orderly progress. If a strong identification with animals is a warning sign of developmental delay, so is a human child's desire to take an ability test designed for an animal. "Fine, you want to train your dog to run through an obstacle course. That's pretty normal. What isn't normal is making your mother time *you* as you crawl through the course on all fours, over and over and over again. You're making Mom think that she did something wrong to make you this way."[43] The training that turns a dog into a Superdog turns a girl into a subhuman. Wanting to succeed as an animal means the child fails. The accompanying drawing has a hapless quality. With her stick limbs and misshapen oval body, Allie looks more like Kafka's beetle than a mammal. She crawls out of a tunnel and prepares to jump over a gate, but is too close to the gate to clear it. In the background stands the helpless, small figure of her mother, looking woeful.[44]

Do we take the narrator at her word that identifying with animals is a sign of disability, and that disability and animality are both abnormal? That conclusion would set back the disability and animal rights movements a few decades each. The piling of test upon test, harsh judgment upon harsh judgment, is so extreme it may lead us to question the standards themselves. The hyperbole produces reader resistance and empathy: What's wrong with wanting to be a dog? Furthermore, Brosh depicts herself and her dogs in such similar ways, it appears she hasn't surrendered her beliefs in cross-species kinship and crip solidarity. As Laurel Braitman writes, "Humans and other animals are more similar than many of us might think when it comes to mental states and behaviors gone awry—experiencing churning fear, for example, in situations that don't call for it, feeling unable to shake a paralyzing sadness, or being haunted by a ceaseless compulsion to wash our hands or paws."[45] As

Brosh and her dogs go on about the business of behaving wrong, *Hyperbole and a Half*'s anatomy of failure blurs the lines not only between childhood and adulthood but between species as well.

Dogs: Cause and No Effect

Brosh's stories about her two dogs begin in the confines of the behavioral checklist then jump the fence into the vast, messy realities of the world. These dog stories best illustrate Brosh's ADHD epistemology of nature, with its simultaneous adoption and critique of the testing model. Disability, nature, and pet ownership run on parallel courses: disability eludes cure, nature outstrips human control, and pet ownership defies romantic visions.

Canine disability mirrors human disability in *Hyperbole and a Half*. "The Simple Dog" comes right after "Warning Signs" and serves as its mirror image. In "Warning Signs" Brosh takes a canine agility test, while in "The Simple Dog" she gives a dog a human IQ test. Brosh played the child with a disability in the previous chapter, and here she plays mother to a canine child. The dismay on her face when she tests her dog matches the dismay on her mother's face when she tests Allie. This chapter rehearses many different models of disability, starting with deficit and pity. The first line of the story is "A lingering fear of mine was confirmed last night: my dog might be slightly retarded."[46] Brosh's process, from fear and hunch to confirmed diagnosis, mimics and parodies the journey of many parents. Brosh's use of the R-word follows a common pattern in disability narratives. Intellectual disability presents itself as an anxiety that must be confronted or dismissed. A Victorian discourse of pity and charitable uplift accompanies her use of the R-word, which signals self-parody but also allows Brosh to distance herself from intellectual disability. "Accepting the noble responsibility of educating this poor, underprivileged creature, I spent hours tenderly guiding her up and down the staircase."[47]

The simple dog's schooling reflects Brosh's own test anxiety. In the IQ test pictures, Brosh plays the tester while the simple dog plays the striving student who always misses the mark. The dog has a vitality, sweetness, and work ethic that make her so much more than a score. She sits at attention, tail wagging and ready for a command. In the big first-grade printing and unorthodox syntax of Brosh's canine grammar, the dog says, "Can be good dog. Yes. What Want?"[48] Brosh tries to teach her to sit in a sequence of ten moment-to-moment panels that slow the action to a crawl. The slowness confirms that the dog is a slow learner but also confirms her lovability. Brosh spends five panels issuing a "Sit" command, the dog owner's eyes and mouth narrowing and arms dropping in growing exasperation. A separate panel of the dog follows each command, in a cause-and-no-effect sequence. The dog stands in the same spot, tail happily up, motionless except for her turning neck: "But when turning her head at an extreme angle fails to produce a life-altering epiphany, she usually just short-circuits and rolls onto her back."[49] In the last panel the dog offers the reader an upside-down smile and a wave of the paw.

These cause-and-no-effect sequences mock the discourse of charitable uplift and the assumption that effort yields results. The next testing sequences come from a dog IQ test Brosh finds on the internet. She puts a blanket over the dog and times how long it takes her to escape (she doesn't). Across three panels, Brosh looks at her wristwatch while her mouth moves from a smile to a black hole of alarm.[50] In the final test the dog is supposed to find a biscuit hidden under a cup. "If she knocked over the cup to get the biscuit within a certain amount of time, she'd pass the test . . . She didn't understand but she knew she was supposed to do *something*, so she just started frantically doing things because maybe—just maybe—one of those things would be the right thing and the magical wizard cup would let her know where the treat went."[51] Like Brosh herself, the dog has an errant policy of doing all the things. She does a different random, adorable thing in each panel: jumping over the magic cup, crouching as if to play chase, holding a tennis ball in her mouth, and ending up on the floor upside down.[52] Her supine position at the end of each test seems to confirm Brosh's hunch that this dog is always threatening to devolve into "a species with a different number of legs—like maybe a starfish or a snake."[53]

Brosh never opts out of standardized tests, but she does lower the stakes at the end of this story. And the stakes could be the life or death of the dog. Being put down or returned to the shelter is a real possibility for a rescue dog who had "spent most of her life confined to a small kennel because her previous owners couldn't control her."[54] IQ tests have their roots in the eugenics movement, which underscores the high stakes of testing. In the end, however, the stakes are not very high. Brosh spares her dog the bad feelings she associates with standardized tests. "I finally accepted that she was not going to pass any part of the test, and yes, she was most likely mentally challenged. But damn it, I was not going to let my poor, retarded dog feel like she had failed."[55] In the penultimate panel she lifts the cup so the dog can see the treat, and in the last panel the dog looks delighted. Cheating on a test is a declaration of love. It also mocks the concern that testing accommodations for students with disabilities constitute a form of cheating.

"The Helper Dog Is an Asshole," the story of adopting a second dog, realizes the worth of animals even when they offer no practical or emotional benefits. Brosh and her boyfriend Duncan begin with ludicrously high expectations, fancying that they can train the shelter's "most hopeless, psychologically destroyed dog-monster" to be a service dog for their other dog.[56] "The helper dog—who earned that title on the car ride home while we were gleefully entertaining the notion that this new dog could act as a service animal for the simple dog—did not appear overly interested in interacting with us."[57] Brosh's ridiculous optimism shows up in her cartoon dialogue: "It's a great idea! There's nothing love and hope can't fix!"[58] Again, the characters misunderstand cause and effect; love and hope cannot fix a disability because a disability cannot be fixed. Here as elsewhere, the humor comes from piling disability upon disability, problem upon problem. Not only does the new dog fail to help the other dog; she hates the very thought of other dogs. "From what we can tell, the helper dog holds a firm belief that other dogs should not exist. The fact that they do fills her with uncontrollable, psychotic rage. Even the slightest hint of another dog's existence will throw her into a hysterical fit of scream-barking."[59]

As with the first dog, Brosh applies a harsh diagnostic label. In this case, the label "psychotic" taps into a common trope in *Hyperbole and a Half*: nature as scary movie. In "Lost in the Woods" the young Allie tries to talk her mother out of the woods by describing the plot of *The Texas Chainsaw Massacre*: "We should go home because . . . what if there's a man out here, and he has a chainsaw, and his face looks like meat?"[60] In "Dinosaur (The Goose Story)," a goose that gets into their house looks quite innocent and affable, but Brosh describes it as a serial killer: "Most geese are dangerous psychopaths that become extremely violent for absolutely no reason."[61] Brosh and Duncan trap the goose and take it outside of town: "I know it's there, lurking just below the surface of the murky pond, watching the children throw bread crumbs, waiting for them to get just a little too close to the edge of the water."[62]

"The Helper Dog Is an Asshole" falls into the revenge genre of scary movies. The helper dog shows every sign of having a violent plan. When Brosh tries to engage with her in the car, "It was sort of like being the taxi driver character in a Bruce Willis movie. You try to make small talk with Bruce Willis on his ride home from prison, where he spent the last nine years becoming hardened and vengeful, but he is finally free to pursue his plan and he doesn't give a *shit* about small talk."[63] The pictures make the helper dog look really scary. A walk in the park turns into a miniature horror movie. In a sequence of four camera shots, the helper dog freezes when she hears another dog, then turns her head. The third shot renders the dog's profile in close-up. Her pupils become enormous as the evil plan activates. The last shot switches to the dog's viewpoint. The landscape turns from peaceful green to angry orange as the dog bares her teeth, leaps up, and strains against her leash. Over the scene the dog's thought is scrawled in big letters: "MUST :(STOP :(OTHER DOG."[64]

There is no way to tame wild nature, just as there is no way to cure a disability. Brosh runs through the behavioral checklists and time-tested interventions "and one-on-one training classes and socialization and positive reinforcement and timely corrections and special leashes and self-esteem boosters and mind tricks" to show how they don't work.[65] "Everyone told us, *'Oh, it's easy to train dogs! You just give them a treat when they do something you like!'*"[66] This sort of well-meaning advice from inexperienced people reminds me of the days when my migraine was continuous and intractable and people would ask, "Have you tried acupuncture?" The treat technique only spreads the bad behavior to both dogs. They move the helper dog's bed to the upstairs hallway, where she can't see the neighbor's dog through the window. However, their efforts to block the stairs fail dramatically: "We were awakened at the stroke of five by both the baby gate AND the vacuum cleaner AND the helper dog crashing down the stairs."[67] The stroke of five is one of those extreme moments.

Brosh recapitulates the behavioral checklists and scientific approaches, but this time to declare them null and void. The pictures mock neurobiological and testing models of disability. A cartoon scan shows the dog's brain largely swallowed by the STOP OTHER DOGS lobe. A behavioral checklist includes categories such as "pulling on leash hard enough to win the motherfucking Iditarod, which would be cool if we were competing in the Iditarod, but we aren't. We're walking to Safeway" and "makes creaking and groaning sounds when understimulated. Possibly made out of boards."[68] However, the magic words "even though" precede all this scientific data. After the scientific data come the other magic words, "She is our dog." They keep looking for "tiny, almost imperceptible good qualities" because she belongs to them and they want to love her.[69] Whether child or adult, Brosh answers yes to the question, "Do you still like dogs?" even if this liking can't fix a thing.[70]

One picture captures the power of nature to transcend the diagnostic checklist. The picture illustrates the claim that "if you could stack the helper dog's problems one on top of the other, they would reach all the way to the moon."[71] The helper dog rockets up into the starry night sky, shooting past a moon wearing a frowny face. The motion lines look like the tail of a comet and the dog looks like a superhero. The cosmic quality of the dog in the night sky exceeds the factual recounting of multiple disabilities. She has a natural magic also suggested by the moons and stars on her dog bed, one of the few images in *Hyperbole and a Half* drawn in fine detail. The story ends with the dog lying on her cosmic bed in the bathtub, which they accidentally discover has calming powers. Contained space also calms many humans with disabilities such as autism, depression, and post-traumatic stress disorder. The words on the bathtub picture ask, "Is the bathroom magical? Do you *like* the bathroom? Are there more secrets to helping you that we don't know about?"[72] The bathtub wraps around the dog like a prosthetic community. This community includes Allie Brosh and her boyfriend Duncan, the dog's service animals.

Like a Wild Animal

Allie Brosh imagines herself as a wild animal to explore the power dynamics of tester and test subject. Brosh writes up her own "Thoughts and Feelings" as if she were a wild animal trapped in a lab cage, her movements observed and recorded in a notebook entitled "What Is It Doing and Why Is It Doing It?"[73] In this chapter Brosh oscillates between subject positions, showing how fear motivates both tester and test subject. The tester aims to free herself from the anxiety of a world beyond her comprehension and control, while the test subject aims to free herself from the anxiety of being trapped and scrutinized. Both subject positions have ethical implications for human relationships with the natural world.

As a test designer, Brosh specializes in the ludicrous and inadequate standards we have seen before in *Hyperbole and a Half.* "I have a subconscious list of rules for how reality should work. I did not develop these rules on purpose, and most of them don't make sense—which is disturbing when you consider that they are an attempt to govern the behavior of reality—but they exist, and they play a large role in determining how I react to the things that happen to me."[74] She makes up random rules and expects reality to follow them, which of course dooms her expectations to failure: "Reality doesn't give a *shit* about my rules, and this upsets me."[75] Brosh layers test upon test, picturing an imaginary researcher scrutinizing her scrutiny of reality.

Like her dogs, reality refuses to comply with her behavioral training.

The comics panels proceed in a sequence akin to the failed training of the simple dog. For instance, the imaginary researcher writes, "Caught subject trying to punish birds today. Was mad at the birds because needed to concentrate and birds were making too many sounds."[76] The two pictures, drawn, dated, and captioned like Polaroids taken in the field, form a cause-and-no-effect sequence. In the first panel Brosh peers out the window, "Thinking bad things directly at the birds." In the next panel, three birds sing on the telephone wire in a clear blue sky: "The birds continued to make as much sound as they wanted."[77] Nature refuses to honor her desire to concentrate.

Brosh fails to be rational in a manner akin to the helper dog. Neither is content to just hate something. They both have to stare very hard out the window at the thing they hate as if staring could control it. These cause-and-no-effect sequences lambaste the notion that scrutiny is the same thing as intervention. The researcher's notebook reports, "A garbage truck awakened the subject several hours before subject planned to be awake. Subject hates the garbage truck for what it has done. Hates it so much that had to get up and look at it."[78] Brosh stands at the window in three-quarter profile, fearsome frown lines on eyes and mouth, looking out the window determinedly. "The subject dislikes the sound the garbage truck is making and is trying to hurt the garbage truck with its mind."[79] The helper dog stares out the sliding glass door in a similarly intent three-quarters profile: "The helper dog is a psychotic, creepy dog-bear-beast and she *wants* to see the neighbor dog and feel all the feelings that it makes her feel." The caption on the dog's picture reads, "Come out . . . *yes* . . . yes, dog . . . come out, come where I can see . . . I *want* to see."[80] No matter how hard and hatefully they look out the window, they can't control the world outside. The neighbor dog and the garbage truck remain indifferent. By focusing on her own quirks and those of her dogs, Brosh refutes the scientific fallacy that all lab animals are identical and produce identical, reliable test results.

Why establish rules that are destined to fail? Brosh's experiments in reality testing show why someone would want to be a tester in the first place: fear. "The illusion of control makes the helplessness seem more palatable. And when that illusion is taken away, I panic." The accompanying picture shows Brosh looking fearful in a swirl of mist. The caption reads, "It is dark. Subject cannot see what reality is doing. Fears reality may attempt to do something bad while unsupervised." The gray shadows look like the scary forest in "Lost in the Woods."[81] Nature is frightening sometimes, and even arbitrary rules can ward off the feeling of helplessness. "Because deep down, I know how pointless and helpless I am, and it scares me. I am an animal trapped in a horrifying, lawless environment, and I have no idea what it's going to do to me."[82] If wild animals can be scary, they can also be scared.

Brosh plays the part of the test subject as well as the tester, comparing herself to a trapped animal whenever she entertains the thought of someone observing her irrational thinking. She draws a picture of herself in a box with an air hole, flailing her arms around and looking up at a bewildering, giant, invisible threat.

> And to me, it feels perfectly logical to be feeling these things. But if someone were to observe me in my natural environment—having all the thoughts and feelings my natural environment causes me to have—I would seem much less logical. In fact, I might seem sort of like a wild animal trying to adapt to an alternate reality that it some-how became trapped in.[83]

Randomly trapped in an alternate reality: this sounds like Brosh's description of life with ADHD, having to reverse-engineer her thoughts and feelings because the rules of this world don't make intuitive sense to her. Her panic at the thought of being studied reveals a drawback of the testing model that came of age during her childhood and early adolescence. It doesn't feel good to be a test subject. "I would be horrified to discover that someone was observing me with the intention of learning about my silly rules."[84] These "silly rules" resemble the "thinking errors" of ADHD, anxiety, and depression. The test subject doesn't just dislike being scrutinized; rather, she feels ashamed of herself.[85] The researcher notes, "Subject has become suspicious. Senses that it is being observed. Humiliated by self."[86] She runs away, "making terrified noises."[87] Scientific observation does not necessarily enact good change in the world. The conceit of the imaginary research notebook draws a parallel between the testing of people with disabilities and the harm done to lab animals.

What are the consequences here for an epistemology of nature? First, humans try to control nature, including human disability, because it is frightening and bigger than we are. Second, it can be frightening and humiliating to be a test subject, whether human or nonhuman animal. However, nature will always exceed human attempts to train its behavior. In the case of *Hyperbole and a Half*, nature includes canine and human neurodiversity.

Disservice Animals

Allie Brosh's art embodies an ADHD epistemology of nature, especially in its sense of time. *Hyperbole and a Half* ignores the majority of the time when things go smoothly. Instead, in keeping with its title, the book pinpoints the extreme moments when coping mechanisms fail and mayhem ensues. What are the consequences of eliminating the routine moments when living with human and canine disability works just fine? First, the comic exaggeration feeds the prejudice that disability is abnormal. Brosh slaps many harsh judgments on herself and her dogs, which could invite readers to do the same. Nonetheless, by refusing to explain herself Brosh unleashes a tremendous artistic force. Rather than sitting in judgment, her large audience connects with her graphic honesty. Readers see themselves in her failures to match a Supercrip image of suave accomplishment. We all know what it feels like to look stupid.

Brosh's graphic honesty expresses itself through her comic timing: comic in both senses of humor and art form. Her panels play with time in several ways: cause-and-no-effect sequences, moment-by-moment sequences, behavioral checklists, and timed tests. She has a rare ability to capture a convoluted thought process, breaking it down paradox by paradox. She explodes the scientific accuracy of the standardized test by pushing it meticulously to ridiculous extremes. By divorcing cause from effect, she questions the limits of human control over the animal world, our own selves, and the larger natural order.

Disability varies from moment to moment. We have good days and bad days. Cycles of self-care and self-harm repeat themselves. The moment-to-moment panels in *Hyperbole and a Half* capture the moment-to-moment nature of crip time. By lighting on the extraordinary moments, Brosh eliminates the possibility of an overcoming narrative. No problem gets solved once and for all. There is no one-way street from childhood to adulthood, rowdy puppy to mature service dog.

Each chapter of *Hyperbole and a Half* repeats the same cycle of ridiculously high standards followed by failure. Dogs and people fail many tests, but the tests fail, too. Brosh turns her harsh light not only on herself but also on the testing culture that has dominated the US educational system since the 1990s. Her critique of the testing model makes a unique contribution to disability studies. A checklist can never capture a lived reality that is always so much more than a score. As Brosh shows, not only are tests inadequate, they make people feel wrong, ashamed, and small.

Like mania and impulsivity, failure has its moments of wild magic. Although *Hyperbole and a Half* portrays disability as abnormal, it also justifies disability as an integral part of nature. The dogs have disabilities, too, and their failure to become trained suggests that nature does not exist to serve or obey humans. Nature exceeds our ability to harness it. Just as there are moments in human life when you can't get your blood sugar right or I can't get my head on straight, there are moments when the water overflows the levees or Shamu takes a big bite out of the trainer. Nature doesn't give a shit about our behavioral checklists.

Part Three

———

School

My teachers were nice, most of the time,
but they would've needed X-ray vision like Superman
to see what was in my head.
    —Melody Brooks, *Out of My Mind*[1]

Six

Rehearsing the Future

The twenty-first century brought a seismic shift to literature for young readers. In the United Kingdom and the United States, a steady flow of novels featuring main characters with disabilities infiltrated best-seller lists for the first time. Writers, publishers, teachers, parents, and librarians finally invited young readers to identify with disabled characters who told their own stories in the first person. These storytellers sparked great intimacy with readers. A glowing *New York Times* review said that reading *The Absolutely True Diary of a Part-Time Indian* "becomes more like listening to your smart, funny best friend recount his day while waiting after school for a ride home."[2] Most of these novels were school stories, and their protagonists retraced the movement of actual young people with disabilities into the public space of mainstream schools.

The next two chapters spotlight a cluster of novels where twenty-first-century protagonists follow in the paths of their real-life peers in the 1980s and 1990s, serving as the first students with disabilities to desegregate a mainstream school or classroom. In *Wonder*, the novel discussed in depth later in this chapter, the awareness and adaptive skills of a family with disabilities spread to the school to create a community with disabilities. These young adult novels and middle-grade chapter books demonstrate how far we've come and how far we still need to go in integrating disabled students into schools—and into books for young readers as well.

These school stories replicate the movement of actual students from separate schools into the mainstream. In the United States, mainstream education commenced with the Individuals with Disabilities Education Act (IDEA), enacted in 1975 as the Education for All Handicapped Children Act and revamped in 1990, and with the Americans with Disabilities Act (ADA) of 1990.[3] While the ADA opened up buildings and public spaces, IDEA mandated that "to the maximum extent appropriate, children with disabilities . . . are educated with children who are *non*disabled."[4] In the United Kingdom, changes toward more inclusive education began in the 1980s and gained traction with the Disability Discrimination Act (1995), addressing access for all people with disabilities, and the 2001 Special Educational Needs and Disability Act. However, a high proportion of students with disabilities in the United Kingdom still attend separate schools.[5] Indeed, in the breakthrough best seller *The Curious Incident of the Dog in the Night-Time* (2003), the brilliant protagonist Christopher Boone attends a school for students with disabilities.

Mainstreaming isn't always easy. Becky Taylor was one of the first students to be mainstreamed after passage of the Education for All Handicapped Children Act in 1975. Taylor had little trouble with teachers but recalls loneliness and taunting. Other students followed her around and yelled at her.

> I am surprised now to think that I put up with face-to-face teasing for so many years. Did I accept it as part of mainstreaming? In my mind, did I somehow think I deserved it? I could plainly see that no one else was being teased quite as much. The only explanation I can think of for having accepted such behavior is that it was the only thing I knew about.[6]

Just as their real-life peers tried to win over a hostile or clueless school, fictional characters win over their readers as they enter the public space of best-selling novels. Their adventures show how far we've come and how far we still need to go in welcoming young people with disabilities into public life. Like schools themselves, novels for young readers accommodate some students and some disabilities better than others. This canon's protagonists are nearly always brilliant, immensely likeable, and white. Even when protagonists cannot speak, as in *Stuck in Neutral*, *Speak*, and *Out of My Mind*, readers are privy to their wit and intelligence.

Between the lines of these novels hovers an implied mainstream reader who may be reluctant to accept the word of a disabled narrator. Ato Quayson suggests that "there is always an anticipation of doubt within the perceptual and imagined horizon of the disabled character in literature" and "this doubt is incorporated into their representation."[7] Anticipating reader resistance, young narrators claim the power to speak for themselves by asserting, while showcasing their wit and intellect, that they are "not retarded." This moment happens with startling frequency. I call it the Not Retarded Trope (NRT). This tactic not only perpetuates the insulting R-word but also narrows the pool of potential disabled characters who have the power to speak for themselves and potential disabled readers who get to hear and see themselves. Despite this narrow personality profile, however, these novels still illuminate the benefits the entire community receives when disability enters a new public space. They show how a family and community can help young people with disabilities rehearse an assertive future for themselves—that is, the subset of young people with disabilities who have that degree of language and independence. Such are the benefits and pitfalls of entering the mainstream.

Smart, Charming, and Quick with a Comeback

Although they all face challenges, young people with disabilities live on a spectrum of privilege varying with factors like income, race, nationality, and type of disability. These twenty-first-century best sellers do not represent the full range of that spectrum, even though they represent a giant advance for disability in young people's imagined communities. To be a main character in this genre, you have to be witty, articulate, quick with a comeback, and utterly charming. Above all, you have to be really smart: a genius, an intellectual Supercrip, or at least an academic achiever.

Nicola Yoon's *Everything, Everything* begins, "I've read many more books than you. It doesn't matter how many you've read. I've read more. I've had the time."[8] In *The Curious Incident of the Dog in the Night-Time*, Christopher Boone declares, "I am going to prove that I'm not stupid. Next month I'm going to take my A level in maths and I'm going to get an A grade."[9] By the end of the book Christopher has aced his A level, the first in his school to even take the exam. In *Wonder* the school principal says to Auggie Pullman, "I know academically it's been a great year for you. You're one of our top students. Congrats on the High Honor Roll."[10] *Out of My Mind*'s Melody Brooks, the star of her school's champion quiz team, tells us early on, "Here's the thing: I'm ridiculously smart, and I'm pretty sure I have a photographic memory. It's like I have a camera in my head, and if I see or hear something, I click it, and it stays."[11] These protagonists don't just have brains; they have superpowers.

This genre sidelines the intelligence, humor, and appeal of young people who may take a little longer to make or get the joke, sink the basket, charm the principal, or gain high marks. Abbye E. Meyer notes how contemporary adolescent literature portrays disability as an identity worthy of pride and social inclusion, but does so by showcasing "disabled characters who normalize themselves and find acceptance from their peers by asserting that they are smart and 'not retarded.'"[12] Thus, fiction for young readers marginalizes intellectual disability, echoing the marginalization of people with intellectual disabilities in other forms of community life.

Dropping the R-Bomb

It is remarkable how often the R-word appears in American twenty-first-century movies and novels. If the plot features a character with a nonintellectual disability, you can place a safe bet it will include the Not Retarded Trope. The NRT works like this. You have a main character with a disability. Let's call him Bob. Bob has something that could be confused with an intellectual impairment. He might have autism, cerebral palsy, or hearing loss. Now let's invent two more characters we'll call Lane the Loser and River the Role Model. The dialogue goes something like this:

> LANE THE LOSER (TO BOB): What's the matter with you? Are you [insert R-word here]?
> RIVER THE ROLE MODEL: No, you idiot, Bob has [insert actual disability here]. He is really smart.

The NRT has two assets. It settles any doubts about the main character's intelligence, and it allows the reader or viewer to feel superior to a loser like Lane who would use the R-word. However, the NRT has two drawbacks. It defends Bob's honor by belittling people with intellectual disabilities and it perpetuates the R-word yet again.

Ironically, the NRT gained prominence in fiction while the rest of the nation was consigning the R-word to the trash heap. In her history of intellectual disability in the United States, Allison Carey writes that at the end of the twentieth century "the new image of the self-determined citizen with intellectual disabilities was very positive, stressing group pride and demanding self-determination. In this context, the label 'mental retardation' . . . seemed inappropriate and even offensive. Self-advocates resented this label, referring to it as the 'R' word, and demanded that organizations serving them stop using it."[13] In 2005 the national organization SABE (Self Advocates Becoming Empowered) issued a statement to other advocacy groups:

> We have told you what is important to us
> Get rid of the infamous and hurtful "R" word, do not label us
> We will not put up with the "R" word continuing as part of an
>   organization's name even as initials
> If you are working with me and for me then do not disrespect me[14]

US federal regulations followed suit. In 2010, Rosa's Law changed "references in federal law to mental retardation to references to an intellectual disability."[15]

In the same era, fictional narrators use the NRT frequently to refute the charge of intellectual disability leveled against them. In first-person stories like those under discussion here, the narrator takes on the role of the person who says the R-word as well as the person who refutes it. The R-word is always the "opening gambit" for bullying in the United States. As Stephen Kuusisto elucidates, once the R-word comes into play, anything goes.

> Blind, wandering the playgrounds of childhood I was routinely called retarded and beaten by bullies who loved the "R" word—moreover the "R" word was always their opening gambit as even a six year old knows that once you've called a person "retarded" you're free to do anything you want to him. You can dismiss him. You can punch him. You can push him down flights of stairs. You can put gum in his hair. You can poke him with sticks. You can push him to the ground and rub snow in his ears. You can follow him down the street chanting the foul poetry of scorn.[16]

Therefore, the disabled narrator refutes the R-word in order to gain the trust of readers assumed to be nondisabled. However, this opening gambit also forces the narrator to scorn intellectual disability. Shawn McDaniel in *Stuck in Neutral*, who cannot speak, reports that "one bad news deal is that in the eyes of the world, I'm a total retardate. A 'retard.' . . . I do sometimes wonder what life would be like if people, even *one* person, knew that I was smart and that there's an actual person hidden inside my useless body."[17] The reader takes on the role of River the Role Model, becoming the one extraordinary person who knows Shawn is smart. That knowledge draws the reader into a circle of intimacy with him. By marginalizing intellectual disability, the novel flatters readers into considering themselves tolerant and understanding.

When the main characters face ableism at school, sometimes a classmate plays the part of River the Role Model. In *Reaching for Sun*, Josie Wyatt's new friend Jordan is the only one who understands the R-word does not apply to her. When Jordan asks her what is the hardest part about having cerebral palsy, Josie replies, "Everyone thinking I'm retarded." He protests, "But Josie, you know tons of stuff! Anybody who talks to you knows that."[18] Jordan stands in for the reader as the one attentive person who can tell the difference between physical and intellectual disability. He also assumes that people with intellectual disabilities do not know tons of stuff.

While the R-word is not a common insult in the UK, *The Curious Incident of the Dog in the Night-Time* summons other disability insults in order to refute them. The narrator Christopher Boone says, "All the other children at my school are stupid. Except I'm not meant to call them stupid, even though this is what they are."[19] Christopher wants to take his A levels to "prove I'm not stupid" and thus defy the children from another school who shout "Special Needs! Special Needs!" when he and his classmates get off the bus.[20] His academic goals reflect the need to separate himself from the other kids at school: "I'm not a spazzer, which means spastic, not like Francis, who is a spazzer, and even though I probably won't become an astronaut, I am going to go to university and study mathematics or physics, or physics and mathematics (which is a Joint Honor School), because I like mathematics and physics and I'm very good at them."[21] A string of jokes in the novel plays on Christopher's desire to distance himself from his classmates. Like the animal studies philosophers discussed in chapter 2, Christopher defends the worth of an animal's life at the expense of a disabled child's. To find this joke funny, the reader must identify with Christopher or his aide Siobhan, not with Steve or his mother:

> I also said that I cared about dogs because they were faithful and honest, and some dogs were cleverer and more interesting than some people. Steve, for example, who comes to the school on Thursdays, needs help to eat his food and could not even fetch a stick. Siobhan asked me not to say this to Steve's mother.[22]

Auggie Pullman in *Wonder* uses the words "idiot" and "freak" as well as the R-word to assert he belongs at a mainstream school event. His sister Olivia doesn't want him to come see her act in a play because she hasn't told anyone at her new high school about her brother's unusual face. When he realizes that his mother and Olivia are steering him discreetly away from attending the play, he calls them out: "You're both liars! You're lying to my face like I'm an idiot!"

> "You think I don't know what's going on?" I yelled. "You just don't want your brand-new fancy high school friends to know your brother's a freak!"
> "Auggie!" Mom yelled. "That's not true!"
> "Stop lying to me, Mom!" I shrieked. "Stop treating me like a baby! I'm not retarded! I know what's going on!"[23]

This argument hits viscerally. Nearly any reader can identify with being left out of the party. It is one of many turning points that fix readers on Auggie's side. At the start, Auggie's mother does baby him, and he enjoys being treated like a baby. When he enters school for the first time he begins a slow and steady assertiveness training. His confrontation with his mother and sister marks one of his shining moments in learning to speak up for himself. The novel invites the reader to share Auggie's justifiable anger at his usually accepting family, and beyond this, comes to identify with the politics of disability inclusion. This solidarity comes at a price, however, for this inclusion politics excludes intellectual disability. In order to identify with Auggie, the reader has to overlook the use of slurs.

Why the R-Word?

Why continue to use the R-word and others like it in the twenty-first century? The reasons reach backward to the past and forward to the future. Michael Bérubé argues that "the specter of intellectual disability" haunted twentieth-century narrators just as it haunted the twentieth century, the era of eugenics, involuntary sterilization, institutions, and the transformation of the IQ test into a weapon.[24] The specter of intellectual disability continues to haunt twenty-first-century narrative, but in its own peculiar ways that match the contours of a new era. Twentieth-century fiction evokes then disavows intellectual disability to segregate it from nondisabled people. By contrast, twenty-first-century fiction evokes then disavows intellectual disability to segregate it from people with other disabilities. This tactic mirrors an era that talks a big story about inclusion but only gets the job halfway done.

How does this partial inclusion feel to the young people who experience

Fig. 13. Billy Dean
Bogard. Photo by
Jordan Shin.

it? In the twenty-first century, bullying makes the point that students with disabilities don't belong to the school. In my life story theater classes, many students with intellectual disabilities have told of facing mockery and violence in their K-12 years. For Billy Dean Bogard, the beatings and ridicule started during elementary school. Even though he is a creative and thoughtful young man who bonded with his teachers, he started skipping school to avoid the abuse.

> I was always picked on for the way I talked and because I was overweight. People would beat me up and stuff, call me names, and then I'd get in more trouble, 'cause I'd go and talk to the principal because I was always the good kid who was like, "I'm not gonna punch those people in the face, 'cause that's gonna get me in trouble." . . . I was skipping school a lot because I didn't want to go to school. I didn't want to get ridiculed or bullied.[25]

Fig. 14. Alana Unfried onstage performing in *Heroes from Another Earth*, 2018. Photo by Nicolas Walcott.

Alana Unfried has a terrible trove of stories about high school bullying. Football players and cheerleaders, the kings and queens of the school, routinely trapped her inside lockers and poured milk all over her lunch tray. In Alana's story about riding the school bus, the feeling of exclusion came not only from one boy tripping her but from the rest of the kids laughing. After this upsetting event she says she watched *Born This Way*, an A&E reality TV show about young people with Down syndrome. She turned to virtual community to comfort herself for the lack of face-to-face community at school.

In high school, I got picked on. I was making up my bed in my room and my mom says, "Alana, it's time for breakfast!" and I said, "Okay, I'm coming down." I got up on the school bus and suddenly I tipped over. . . . [A] young boy stuck his feet out in the [aisle]. He tripped me on the ground. And I got up, sat in the seat crying, and all the people in the school bus made fun of me. Sad to say, all the others, they laughed. Sometimes I'm really sad about my life, that I tripped over in the school bus once. I went to . . . my high school, and I was really sad. I started crying. And when I got home I watched *Born This Way* on TV. So that's my life.[26]

Entering a mainstream school, young people with disabilities in real life and fiction often face ableism. In fiction they fit a narrow personality profile of charm, wit, and high achievement to prove their human worth to the school within the novel and the readership outside it. While some forms of ableism reach back to old prejudices, others arise from the misperception that people with intellectual disabilities have no future. The word "retarded" literally means a failure to move forward. Parent Rachel E. Adams critiques "the way many people perceive Down syndrome: Not only do they believe that my son's disability allows us to know what his future holds, but that it is a future in which he will be limited and burdensome."[27] This misperception about the future goes much deeper than attitudes. Its structural and economic roots lie in the dearth of opportunities available to young people when they transition out of special education. Literature falls short of imagining full lives for young people with intellectual disabilities because society has fallen short of full inclusion.

When they age out of mandated benefits, young people with intellectual disabilities often fight hard and wait a long time for the supports they need to become as independent as they can be in adulthood. For example, one young man faced an eight-year wait to move from his mother's house into a group home.[28] In the United States the funding for job training, housing, care services, and supported employment varies from region to region and depends on the vagaries of state budgets. In her interviews of American young adults with intellectual and developmental disabilities and their families, Valerie Leiter found that "funding was *the* key issue" in transitions. "Adults with intellectual disabilities who were eligible for adult services through DDS [Developmental Disability Services] might receive all the services they and their families wanted, some of those services, or none."[29] Higher-education programs for students with intellectual disabilities exist in the United States but are few and far between.[30] Valerie Leiter heard widespread concern about the future from young people and their families.

Youth had envisioned much larger lives than staying home and watching TV all day, but transportation and other supports might not be available to facilitate employment and other meaningful adult activities outside the home. This situation—in which youths maximized their abilities throughout childhood and adolescence but could face limited adult opportunities after leaving high school—is like being all dressed up with no place to go.[31]

Both Britain and the United States lack work opportunities between the segregation and subminimum wages of the sheltered workshop and the challenges of mainstream employment. The United Kingdom assures more lifelong supports for people with disabilities, but nonetheless the adult future remains a source of anxiety. "Nearly a third (27 percent) of disabled young people are not in education, employment or training. . . . Beyond school, those disabled people who were unable to find work continued to be offered very limited day service choices, with most day centres serving as warehouses or repetitive low paid workshop-type environments."[32]

Like our societies, our novels define success narrowly as a university degree leading to professional employment. High school freshman Melinda Sordino, protagonist of *Speak*, coins a great name for this ideology: "wearehere-togetagoodfoundationsowecangotocollegeliveuptoourpotentialgetagood-joblivehappilyeverafterandgotoDisney World."[33] David Brooks writes, "The whole thrust of the information age has been to reward education and widen the income gap between the educated and the uneducated." Success in the neoliberal economy requires not only higher education but a nimble, innovative mind and a casual likability. "But in America today it's genius and geniality that enable you to join the elect."[34] Therefore, twenty-first-century best-selling novels about young people with disabilities feature protagonists who have the requisite genius and geniality. This narrow personality profile reflects the new yet limited mainstream acceptance of disability. The canon of twenty-first-century best sellers with disabled protagonists reflects the halfway inclusion characteristic of the neoliberal century.

Wonder: How Far We've Come and How Far We Need to Go

Wonder (2012) exemplifies the crop of twenty-first-century best sellers that reenact the history of mainstreaming, sending a character with a disability to desegregate a school for the first time. August Pullman, the hero of *Wonder*, is a ten-year-old boy with a conspicuous craniofacial disability caused by a rare genetic condition. "I know ordinary kids don't make other ordinary kids run away screaming in playgrounds. I know ordinary kids don't get stared at wherever they go."[35] Homeschooled because of frequent surgeries, August goes to school for the first time in fifth grade. The reader follows Auggie as he gains the skills necessary to manage staring and bullying and thrive at school despite them. Smart and endearing, August fits the personality profile of the genre. In the course of the novel he becomes quick with a comeback, but more than this, he learns to speak up for himself and others when it really counts. *Wonder* packs a forceful inclusion message and sugarcoats it at the same time.

Released in February 2012, *Wonder* has been immensely popular. The novel has sold over two million copies and spent many years on the *New York Times* best-seller list.[36] It frequently appears on school reading lists. August Pullman's mixed-race background sets him apart from the predominant whiteness of the genre, although his family's affluence masks his race to some degree. August's father is Jewish and mother is Brazilian American, and the novelist, Raquel Jaramillo Palacio, is Colombian American.[37] However, in the Hollywood film version the white actors Jacob Tremblay, who does not have a craniofacial disability, and Julia Roberts play the roles of Auggie and his mother.[38]

Wonder shows how far we've come and how far we still need to go in integrating young people with disabilities into school and society. By adhering to the genre's narrow personality profile, the novel shows the need for continued social change. Its happy ending offers easy solutions to the structural problems of disability politics. Nonetheless, the novel also shows how far we've come in its rich portrayals of community. As Auggie moves from home to school we watch the movement outward of a welcoming society. Families with disabilities can sometimes be models of inclusion the larger society would do well to follow.[39] In *Wonder* R. J. Palacio uses a family as a template for an inclusion that spreads to the school. Each family member's particular skills, from humor to opposing injustice to adapting the physical world, transfers to a member of the school community. *Wonder* offers a window into the political changes of the past forty years, revealing the benefits and bruises of mainstreaming. A middle school serves as a microcosm of a changing world.

Wonder presents a fairy tale, more realistic at some times and less at others, of school life before and after the Individuals with Disabilities Education Act. The scenario is deliberately oversimplified and exaggerated. On one hand we have a child entering school for the first time in fifth grade, one of the most norming moments of social existence. On the other hand we have a private school completely void of any connection to disability.

This scenario is like a carefully controlled lab experiment. From this experiment we learn what happens when a child with a disability singlehandedly desegregates a school. In this case, able-bodied people gather a community around the child and come into disability consciousness. They become a *community with disabilities.*

A Fairy Tale

Part of *Wonder*'s appeal comes from old-fashioned inspiration. At the novel's climax, a middle school graduation ceremony, the principal gives August Pullman an award as the student "whose strength carries up the most hearts by the attraction of his own."[40] The entire audience rises to applaud the underdog hero who finally receives his due. "Not just the front rows, but the whole audience suddenly got up on their feet, whooping, hollering, clapping like crazy. It was a standing ovation. For me."[41]

There are three problems with this inspirational discourse. The first is that it is clichéd. We have seen these standing ovations in far too many movies and TV shows. Patricia A. Dunn calls this a "Rudolph the Red-Nosed Reindeer" story "because, in the end, the individual who was formerly mocked or ignored becomes a hero who saves the day."[42] Second, if August had entered a friendlier setting he would not have had to perform the Herculean task of lifting up so many hearts. Instead he could be a regular guy: "I feel ordinary. Inside."[43] Third, this scene reflects the novel's preoccupation with winning hearts rather than civil rights.

To become more accepting, the school only needs a change of heart. It doesn't need to change the way it goes about its business. The novel details August's surgeries and challenges in eating and hearing; however, the family does not ask for a single accommodation. The school doesn't have to spring for expensive equipment. The students don't have to learn a new way of communicating. The teachers don't have to modify their instruction. They don't even have to rearrange the furniture. As Sharon Snyder and David Mitchell write, neoliberal explanatory systems "enshrine those bodies different yet enabled enough to ask nothing of their crumbling, obstruction-ridden infrastructure."[44] Inclusion usually requires adaptations of curriculum, pace, communication styles, or physical space, and additional help from staff. In response to the protesting parent of another child, the school principal declares that August "does not have special needs. He is neither disabled, handicapped, nor developmentally delayed in any way." Furthermore, "Auggie is an extremely good student."[45]

Beecher Prep is a private school with no inclusion mandate, so the rules of IDEA don't apply. They don't have to guarantee August services in an Individualized Education Plan, so it's a good thing he doesn't seem to need them. Palacio represents August as having no access challenges even though sometimes he wakes up choking on his own saliva and gets hearing aids in the course of the novel.[46] Even though he is hard of hearing, August immediately understands every word teachers and peers say, and the novel's moments of pain and triumph depend upon this ability. Nor does August experience any pain or complications from his long surgical history. When August starts Beecher Prep his mother only needs to get over her own nervousness. She doesn't have to remind teachers to use the microphone looped to his hearing aids. She doesn't have to fill out endless permission forms for a regime of medications. She doesn't have to teach the school nurse how to suction his lungs.

Wonder's message of "choose kindness" is important but insufficient to creating inclusion.[47] As Stella Young put it, "You know, no amount of smiling at a flight of stairs has ever made it turn into a ramp."[48]

Creating a Community with Disabilities

Despite these shortcomings, however, *Wonder* offers a compelling vision of a community transforming itself. The novel shows how the public presence of people with disabilities benefits a whole society, caught in the moment when disability first goes public. We also see how families and communities help young people rehearse their futures as assertive adults. A family with disabilities practices certain habits of mind, including specific forms of humor, ferocity, and intimacy. In the course of *Wonder* these habits of mind infiltrate the entire community. Disability awareness expands from private to public space.

As I defined it in chapter 3, a *family with disabilities* is a kinship group of people that develops a disability consciousness even if it includes nondisabled members. When children are fortunate, family members become their allies. If I can walk but my sister rides a wheelchair, I may notice curb cuts and steep driveways even when my sister is not with me. Some nondisabled parents view adult disability culture as irrelevant to or remote from their family life. Others build bridges to it and learn from it even when the learning curve is steep. Family members sometimes become fierce advocates, like Mothers from Hell, "a national group of parents, relatives, friends, and anyone who just plain 'gets it' fighting chipped tooth and broken press-on nail for the appropriate education, community acceptance, desperately needed services, rights of and entitlements for people with disabilities."[49] Novelist Brian Trapp's late brother had an intellectual disability and cerebral palsy. He remembers getting angry as early as third grade at people's ignorance. "I used to flip my retainer upside down, turn it into fangs, and hiss at people who stared at my brother."[50]

Solidarity and acceptance also characterize a *community with disabilities*, a circle of people with and without disabilities allied through their experiences with bodymind difference and injustice. Neither a family nor a community with disabilities is the same thing as a *disability community*, a group of people with similar or dissimilar disabilities, often peers, who come together to celebrate, commiserate, agitate, and self-advocate. Most children with disabilities have little acquaintance with adult disability cultures. Families and communities with disabilities are the closest they come. However, these group formations can help prepare young people for future involvement in public politics and culture.

In *Wonder*, habits of mind like access intimacy, body humor, and ferocity in the face of injustice move out from a family with disabilities to create a community with disabilities. *Wonder*'s multivoiced narration aids this transfer of mind-set. The story begins with the intimacy of the first-person problem novel, then keeps switching young narrators in an ever-expanding community like ripples in a pond. We begin with the voice and thoughts of August Pullman as he enters school and encounters hostility, then move to his older sister Via and his new school friends Summer and Jack. As the community grows, *Wonder* pulls more and more distant characters not only into the task of narration but also into the role of August's defenders against hate. The ripple effect of this community with disabilities even laps the shore of disability community. Via's boyfriend Justin becomes one of the defenders, and he refers a couple of times to his tics: "when i get nervous my tics come out. i mean, my tics are always there, but they're not like they used to be when i was little: nothing but a few hard blinks now, the occasional head pull. but when i'm stressed they get worse."[51] After bringing in a disabled peer, the narration comes full circle back to August.

Body humor is a disability habit of mind that translates from the private sphere of the family to the public sphere of the school. In chapter 3 I demonstrated how families with disabilities use toilet humor to help rehearse their children's futures as assertive adults who understand oppression—if the children have that degree of language and independence. *Wonder* portrays August Pullman as rich in these capabilities and also reveals the political importance of body humor. Auggie's dad uses body humor to help his son brave public space. Once Auggie is in that space, the same role falls to his new friend Jack. Both of them help Auggie rehearse an assertive future in public.

At first Auggie entreats his parents not to send him to Beecher Prep: "'Everyone will stare at me at school,' I said, suddenly crying."[52] His father changes Auggie's mind, however, with his jokes about the principal, Mr. Tushman.

> "Auggie, you know, you should go to that school just so you can hear his name said over the loudspeaker!" Dad said excitedly. "Can you imagine how funny that would be? Hello, hello? Paging Mr. Tushman!" He was using a fake high, old-lady voice. "Hi, Mr. Tushman! I see you're running a little *behind* today! Did your car get *rear-ended* again? What a *bum* rap!"
>
> I started laughing, not even because I thought he was being that funny but because I wasn't in the mood to stay mad anymore.
>
> "Who's Mr. Tushman?" Via said groggily. She had just woken up.
>
> "He's the principal of my new school," I answered.[53]

The novel groups Auggie's allies into pairs to show the transition from a family with disabilities to a community with disabilities. In each pair, a friend from school takes on the role previously occupied by a family member. For instance, body humor transfers from August's dad to his new school friend Jack Will. August is right that everyone at school will stare. Jack uses bathroom humor to help Auggie build his tool kit of responses to public scrutiny. Early in the novel, August reacts to the public gaze by staring at the floor and keeping his mouth shut. Jack encourages him to speak up: "But, dude, you're gonna have to talk."[54] August hones his public speaking skills through jokes with the distinctly fifth-grade flavors of slug juice and dog pee.

Body humor is one form of what Rosemarie Garland-Thomson calls "staring management." "Starees must insist on recognition as fellow humans by wielding an array of interpersonal techniques that the commonly embodied need not acquire."[55] Walking next to August down the hall, Jack learns why people with visible disabilities need to manage the stare. Jack acquires a "next to" identity through shared experiences. You can learn a great deal walking through a public place next to someone whose minority identity you don't share. Headed to classes with Auggie, Jack experiences the staring for himself. His new anger at society's treatment of people with disabilities signals his entrance into the community of allies. Back in the classroom, sitting next to each other, Jack and Auggie conspire to manage the stares through humor.

Jack whispered, "Do you ever want to beat those kids up?"

I shrugged. "I guess. I don't know."

"I'd want to. I think you should get a secret squirt gun or something and attach it to your eyes somehow. And every time someone stares at you, you would squirt them in the face."

"With some green slime or something," I answered.

"No, no: with slug juice mixed with dog pee."

"Yeah!" I said, completely agreeing.[56]

Jack converts his anger into a bonding moment with Auggie. Most kids enjoy gross-out humor, but it has a special place in the lives of kids with disabilities. It is a reminder that everyone has a body, not just the kids whose bodies draw extra attention. Garland-Thomson writes, "Another psychological dread that staring ignites in the starer is an unsettling awareness of our own embodiment."[57] If this is true, then gross-out humor turns that awareness from dread to laughter. So many people become jumpy and hyperserious at the sight of a white cane, a short stature, or a different face, the temptation to mess with them is almost irresistible. Mikhail Bakhtin argues that body humor reverses social hierarchies. Bathroom humor upends humanity's deepest fears: "In the sphere of imagery cosmic fear (as any other fear) is defeated by laughter. Therefore dung and urine, as comic matter that can be interpreted bodily, play an important part in these images."[58] Body humor provides a way to make room for disabilities in ableist society.

In the example above, Jack takes the lead in making fun of starers. A minute or two later, though, August will take the lead and keep it for the rest of the novel. He comes to excel at managing the stare through humor. Skill with a punch line is a family trait that August has inherited along with his rare gene mutation. By joking around with Jack at school the way he jokes around with his dad at home, August moves from a family with disabilities to a community with disabilities.

We nodded and looked down at our books. Then Jack whispered: "Are you always going to look this way, Auggie? I mean, can't you get plastic surgery or something?"

I smiled and pointed to my face. "Hello? This *is* after plastic surgery!"

Jack clapped his hand over his forehead and started laughing hysterically.[59]

Jack asks a question steeped in the medical model fantasy of curing a disability through surgery. Auggie replies with a bodily realism so blunt it's funny. Jack has gotten close enough to Auggie to ask a personal question like this, but the conversation could easily become maudlin. Instead, Auggie steers the conversation away from pity and self-pity. In doing so, he reveals his growing maturity. All these conversations serve as rehearsals for August's greatest moment of self-assertion. He speaks up not only to defend himself but to defend Jack, too. On a school camping trip, older kids from another school threaten August and Jack in the dark woods. "The look of total horror on the girl's face when she first saw me. The way the kid with the flashlight, Eddie, looked at me as he talked to me, like he hated me."[60] Jack steps forward to defend August, and Eddie knocks Jack down. August responds with quick thinking and courage. It's hard to believe this is the same boy who started the year with his eyes to the ground and his tongue still.

> "Look," I said, stepping in front of Jack and holding my hands up in the air like a traffic cop. "We're a lot smaller than you guys . . ."
>
> "Are you talking to me, Freddie Krueger? I don't think you want to mess with me, you ugly freak," said Eddie. And this was the point where I knew I should run away as fast as I could, but Jack was still on the ground and I wasn't about to leave him.[61]

August and Jack are rescued by three of their former tormentors from Beecher Prep who have undergone a sudden conversion into the community with disabilities. However, becoming a youthful ally isn't always a sudden or easy process. As we see in the cases of Jack and Auggie's sister Via, that identity shift can be a rocky and zigzag climb. Just as the use of humor moved out from the private space of the family to the public space of the school, so does the process of becoming a peer ally. Jack replicates the stages of Via's disability consciousness. They are the two people who feel the most intense anger when people stare at Auggie. Via spent her childhood getting "mad when they stared. Mad when they looked away. 'What the heck are you looking at?' I'd say to people—even grown-ups."[62] Jack takes over the role of Auggie's ally.

Via and Jack both fall prey to the fear of ostracism. Via tries to avoid having August come to her school play, while Jack denies his friendship with Auggie to the popular kid / chief bully: "I mean, he always follows me around. What am I supposed to do?"[63] Because August has learned to assert himself, calling Via out and breaking off the friendship with Jack, both Via and Jack have the opportunity to reflect, ask forgiveness, and build better relationships with Auggie. As Stacy Clifford Simplican argues, practicing alliance means making mistakes, mistakes that often expose the power dynamics between disabled and nondisabled people. "Making mistakes in public and then disrupting activities to correct these mistakes is a vital component of practicing alliance."[64] August renegotiates his contracts with Via and Jack by disrupting social activities, prompting them to examine their own ableism.

Both Jack and Via turn their backs on August in the midst of learning to be allies. One of the contradictions of having a "next to" identity is that you are both inside and outside the experience of oppression. You may receive a stigma along with the person you love, yet you also have the option of walking away. Other boys at the school direct a hate campaign at Jack because of his friendship with August. As Auggie points out to Jack in one of his quick comebacks, when it comes to ostracism Auggie got there first. He's an old veteran. Nonetheless, Jack has entered the world of disability discrimination through his "next to" status. Although Auggie sarcastically welcomes Jack to his world, it's also the truth.

> "It just feels so weird," I said, "to not have people talking to you, pretending you don't even exist."
> Auggie started smiling.
> "Ya think?" he said sarcastically. "Welcome to my world!"[65]

Access intimacy is another disability habit of mind which extends from the family to the community. August transfers his access intimacy with his mother to Summer, his lunch friend at school. Mia Mingus writes, "Access intimacy is that elusive, hard to describe feeling when someone else 'gets' your access needs. The kind of eerie comfort that your disabled self feels with someone on a purely access level. . . . There is a good feeling after and while you are experiencing access intimacy. It is a freeing, light, loving feeling."[66] Food is one of August's access issues: both what he eats and with whom he eats. Because he has a hole in the roof of his mouth, he can only eat soft foods and chew with his front teeth. He feels uncomfortable eating in front of people. "I didn't even realize how this looked until I was at a birthday party once, and one of the kids told the mom of the birthday boy he didn't want to sit next to me because I was too messy with all the food crumbs shooting out of my mouth. . . . I eat like a tortoise, if you've ever seen a tortoise eating. Like some prehistoric swamp thing."[67] With his mother and then with Summer he has an access intimacy around food that translates into a more general comfort and ease.

Many of the novel's deepest conversations happen while August's mother is making the foods he can eat. While his mother is "cutting one of the apples we had just gotten at the farmer's market into teensy-weensy bites so I could eat it,"[68] he shares his worry that only five people from school are coming to his birthday party. While she is making him grilled cheese and chocolate milk, he tells her about being assaulted on the school camping trip.

> "I'm just so grateful you and Jack and Amos are fine. When I think about what could have happened . . . ," she trailed off, flipping the grilled cheese again.
> "My Montauk hoodie got totally shredded."
> "Well, that can be replaced," she answered. She lifted the grilled cheese onto a plate and put the plate in front of me on the counter. "Milk or white grape juice?"
> "Chocolate milk, please?" I started devouring the sandwich. "Oh, can you do it that special way you make it, with the froth?"[69]

Summer provides the kind of food access August needs at school: someone willing to eat with him. She is the one person who joins him at his empty lunch table on the first day. When another girl suggests she switch back to her old table away from Auggie, Summer stays put and regards Auggie quite matter-of-factly: "Summer looked at me, shrugged-smiled, and took another bite of her mac and cheese."[70] Summer meets August's access needs without a lot of pity, fuss, or self-congratulation. Their friendship builds with the same ease.

> I do admit August's face takes some getting used to. I've been sitting with him for two weeks now, and let's just say he's not the neatest eater in the world. But other than that, he's pretty nice. I should also say that I don't really feel sorry for him anymore. That might have been what made me sit down with him the first time, but it's not why I keep sitting down with him. I keep sitting down with him because he is fun. . . . He likes to play Four Square at recess, which I love to play, too.[71]

Just as intimacy develops between characters, this trove of twenty-first-century best sellers draws readers into a circle of intimacy. Readers' comfort with disabled characters shows how far we've come in forty years. As family and friends help Auggie rehearse his future roles in public, this crop of best sellers helps a large readership rehearse its future in a diverse world. Disability habits of mind like fierce advocacy, body humor, and access intimacy enter the public space of popular fiction.

However, the boom in young adult and middle-grade novels featuring main characters with disabilities also shows how far we still need to go toward full inclusion. With rare exceptions, these main characters all share the same personality profile: smart, charming, and quick with a comeback. Most of them can fit into the adult world exactly as it is, whereas real inclusion requires the hard work of daily adaptation and drastic reimagining. We need books that show young readers what that hard work looks like, so they can help do the work in the future. We need better education and work supports so that young people with intellectual disabilities, in fiction and in real life, have the opportunity to rehearse meaningful and assertive futures for themselves.

Seven

One Difference at a Time

Like *Wonder*, *Out of My Mind*, *Face*, and *The Absolutely True Diary of a Part-Time Indian* belong to the crop of twenty-first-century best sellers that re-enact the history of mainstreaming, sending a character with a disability to desegregate a general classroom for the first time. Through their protagonists, these young adult and middle-grade school stories also replicate the mixed history of halfway inclusion. As discussed in the previous chapter, novels for young readers, like schools themselves, accommodate some students and some disabilities better than others. I have already traced the narrow personality profile of the fictional heroes who get to join the protagonists' club. However, the protagonists' club has yet another strange criterion for admission: you can't be a person of color and have a disability. You have to check one identity at the schoolhouse door. When writers create a main character with a disability, they make the character white or erase all racial markers. When the main character is not white, the disability vanishes by the end of the book.

I focus here on the school stories of Sharon M. Draper, Sherman Alexie, and Benjamin Zephaniah because if any authors for young readers could portray the complexities of identity it would be these three. These gifted, prominent writers have dedicated their careers to telling stories about communities of color. All three have personal acquaintance with disability. However, even their disability-related novels present the same either/or choice between disability and race. Sharon Draper's *Out of My Mind* leaves the main character's race an open question. Benjamin Zephaniah's *Face* features the author's only white protagonist. Sherman Alexie's *The Absolutely True Diary of a Part-Time Indian* focuses on Native American identity, but the disability soon fades away. Nonetheless these novels retain a kind of coalition politics. If minority identity cannot be intersectional, at least disability and race can run on parallel tracks.

All three novelists express concern for young people who feel remote from print culture and rarely see themselves reflected in it. Benjamin Zephaniah recalls starting school in Birmingham, England, with "me and my sister being the only black kids there." Struggling with unaddressed dyslexia, he was excluded (expelled) at age thirteen. "My two big concerns are race and dyslexia. Things are better these days, but so much is dependent on individual teachers."[1] Why, then do all three writers deny young people of color with disabilities the opportunity to see themselves in fiction? They do so in order to pull off a tricky feat: getting a wide general audience to find a shared emotional reality with a character who has a very specific, stigmatized difference. Alexie's challenge, for example, is to get the reading public to identify with a poor Spokane Indian teenager at a white school because he and they share the common experience of loneliness.

> I spent most of my youth fairly lonely, and I think most of us do, and this book acknowledges that. And you know, it's a lot about race and class in the book, about feeling like an outsider, but what you realize when you talk to young people is that everybody feels like an outsider, everybody feels ostracized.[2]

Sharon M. Draper faces a similar challenge. She gets a wide audience to identify with a young woman who cannot speak, eat, or move much on her own through their shared experience of feeling voiceless. Draper says she tried not to give the book "any regional flavor." The book is free of ethnic flavor as well, to keep the focus on the emotional reality of voicelessness. The main character "represents everybody."

> Well, *Out of My Mind* is a story for everyone. And I tried real hard not to give it any regional flavor. It could appeal to children from Ohio as much as children from North Carolina, because Melody represents everybody. She is a representative of any child who doesn't have a voice, who can't talk, who can't communicate, who wants to communicate. And that could be anybody. That could be a child who can't hear, a child who can't see, a child who is the only Chinese child in the school. That child has no voice. That child who is different in some kind of

way from the rest of his peers and has no voice and feels silenced. So Melody, even though she has cerebral palsy, is kind of the voice for the voiceless. So she represents everybody.[3]

For audiences most familiar with white, able-bodied characters, disability pulls focus away from the main story line and so does racial difference. They both demand explanation; they can't just be. Therefore, a story about people of color has to be about race, and a story about people with disabilities has to be about disability. As Lennard Davis writes, disability disrupts "the economy of visual storytelling" in film. "The film has to be, in some sense, obsessed with disability. But if the roving eye of the camera takes its focus off of disability, then disability has to disappear, or it will create a buzz of interference in the storytelling."[4] Similarly, Benjamin Zephaniah has to dial down the buzz of interference from race in a story about facial disfigurement, and Sherman Alexie has to dial down the buzz of interference from disability in a story about the complexities of Native American identity.

Why do we need characters of color with disabilities in books for young readers? Intersectionality matters for many reasons. First, as I argued in chapter 1, kids don't just read stories; they live inside them. They need stories they can fit inside without having to contort themselves. Second, whenever we reinforce the link between disability and whiteness, we obscure the fact that disability disproportionately affects people of color. In so doing, we also obscure the stories specific to the interaction of disability and race. We may leave unexplored the high rates of depression and anxiety among the children of undocumented immigrants, or the common practice of referring African American students with autism and behavioral disabilities to the police when they commit minor infractions at school.

Finally, fiction helps readers imagine their own futures. *Out of My Mind*, *Face*, and *The Absolutely True Diary of a Part-Time Indian* are all stories where a young person with a disability makes a conspicuous entrance into a new school space and ultimately succeeds. Kapria Daniels writes that African American students with disabilities "have seen little evidence of people who are similar to them and for whom school has served as a path to a better life."[5] Novels about students of color with disabilities can help fill this gap and open up new vistas of experience for nonminority students as well.

What feeds people during hard times? As a teenager Sherman Alexie "read books about monsters and monstrous things, often written with monstrous language, because they taught me how to battle the real monsters in my life."[6] The characters in these three novels find unlikely sources of sustenance. Arnold Spirit, Alexie's main character, draws his fighting spirit from his disability. Black music sustains Benjamin Zephaniah's Martin Turner. Sharon Draper's Melody Brooks learns to talk back to oppressors by listening to the outspoken women in her life.

Face: Shifting Locations in the Same Locale

In Benjamin Zephaniah's novel *Face*, a white teenager named Martin Turner reenters his old high school with a face transfigured by a fiery car accident and multiple skin grafts. Walking with his two best friends at night through their East London neighborhood, Martin accepts a ride from gang members and ends up in a crash that burns and disfigures him. Martin shifts social locations within the same place. No longer the handsome joker-king of the school, he encounters pity, disgust, and rejection. His two best friends since primary school fade out of the picture, and his girlfriend trades him in for a bloke with a face as pretty as hers. However, Martin makes his way to a different social niche, the gymnastics team, through new alliances with black British culture and hip-hop music. Martin shifts social locations along with his changing face.

Face's author, Benjamin Zephaniah, is an outspoken critic of racial injustice, neocolonial war, and anti-immigrant prejudice. His novels other than *Face* feature British youth of Afro-Caribbean, South Asian, African, and Romany descent. While writing *Face* he was also composing the poems of *Too Black, Too Strong* and working with the London law firm claiming police misconduct in handling the racially motivated murder of Stephen Lawrence. When Zephaniah turns to disability, however, he chooses white main characters. While Zephaniah does not depict any disability communities of color, he does depict a growing alliance between black British and white disability subcultures. Martin draws on his diverse London neighborhood to survive and gain confidence. "White people who shift locations," bell hooks writes, "begin to see the world differently."[7] Martin joins the hip-hop community while his new Afro-Caribbean friends join his community with facial disabilities. When he reenters public life and meets rejection, black music saves him. As Zephaniah writes in a poem from *Too Black, Too Strong*, "De gleaming, joyful beats employed / Are here to help you to survive."[8]

"What are the similar, but not same, aspects of the lived experiences of people of color and people with disabilities?" asks Sami Schalk. To use Schalk's distinction, Martin does not identify *as a* member of black culture, but he identifies *with* it. To identify with is "to personally and politically align oneself with a group one may or may not belong to, but with which one feels a positive connection."[9] Martin gains epistemic privilege, the knowledge you can only get from minority identity. To a smarmy youth club worker Martin says, "Anything I could do before I can do now. There are some things I can do better now, like spotting the patronizer." He thinks to himself, "*It isn't just about me and how I cope with it, it's me learning to deal with other people's prejudices.*"[10] Martin acquires an epistemology of social justice.

Armed with his new cripistemology, Martin enters a new culture in his East London neighborhood. East Ham is a working-class area, predominantly Asian but racially mixed. Martin "picked out Chinese shops, African dress shops, a Filipino bookshop, shops that sold jellied eels, Jamaican breads and Somalian foods." He also notices racist graffiti and scorch marks from firebomb attacks.[11] He forges a strong link to the music of this place. As Zephaniah writes in the poem "The London Breed":

The music of the world is here
Dis city can play any song
They came to here from everywhere
Tis they that made dis city strong.[12]

In *Face*, it is hip-hop music that makes the city strong. Hip-hop started in the United States but is now global, and one might argue it is most vital and connected to the grass roots outside the United States. Benjamin Zephaniah often portrays hip-hop as an important source of selfhood, political awakening, and pride for black British culture. In his novel *Gangsta Rap*, hip-hop's "unsentimental and uncompromising" spirit becomes a guiding light for three East London musicians of color excluded from high school.[13] As Ray, one of the musicians, explains, "Rap isn't important, hip-hop is important. Hip-hop is a philosophy, hip-hop is about the way we live, it's about the way we see life. We are outsiders and we survive by creating new families for ourselves."[14] In *Face* Zephaniah makes analogies between racial and disability epistemologies, even if the two identities don't intersect. After his old friends reject him, Martin survives by creating a new hip-hop family for himself.

Chosen family is a concept widely discussed in queer culture that operates in other forms of minority consciousness as well. Martin's new family of friends includes Anthony, born with severe facial disfigurements, who helps ease Martin into his new life with support, honesty, and crip humor. Martin's new friends Marica, Teen, and Naz are dark-skinned girls he meets at the Dancemania hip-hop club. The three girls are perpetually decked out in Jamaican paraphernalia proclaiming their black British allegiances: "One had a T-shirt saying 'I Love Jamaica.' Another wore a T-shirt that was a Jamaican flag and the third just had a West Ham football shirt on, but she, like the others, was adorned with yellow, black, and green bangles, badges and necklaces."[15] Before the accident Martin is reluctant to visit the hip-hop club: "The place is gonna be full of blacks, they don't like us . . . OK, some like us but not in their clubs."[16] He finds, however, that his gymnastics background works well with hip-hop dance. He receives a warm welcome both before and after his accident.

> "We read about you in the *Echo*," Marica said. "It was bad news, man, but we know you're cool. So just stay cool, all right, brother?"
>
> "Yeah, I'm all right," Martin replied, now smiling like everyone else around him.[17]

Dancemania is the only public place where Martin finds warmth instead of meanness, and hip-hop music sustains him through his difficult reentry into school and other public spaces. As I said in chapter 1, hip-hop concerns itself with tests of strength, and at its tender core lie many stories about surviving post-traumatic depression. Hip-hop eases Martin through his stages of grief. When he first glimpses his face after the skin grafts, "His breathing quickened with anger. He put on his headphones and listened to music until he fell asleep."[18] After small children taunt him on the playground, music is the only thing that pulls him out of bed: "Martin put on his headphones and his pyjamas and began to pad around the house."[19] Hip-hop teaches him that strength and scars do not contradict each other.

Hip-hop guides Martin into a new social niche at his high school. He joins the school gymnastics squad and throws himself into choreographing a hip-hop routine for it. At the regional competition, Martin's new friends cheer him on as a mighty hip-hop beat shakes the gym. Anthony "pointed to Martin and shouted loudly, 'You see that man there? He is the man, he is the brother.' The Jamaican sistas shouted their approval and there were laughs throughout the gymnasium."[20] Martin's father is surprised to see not his old friends, but new friends "who seemed to him to speak another language."[21] The sharing of neighborhood, language, working-class identity, and hip-hop blends them into one tribe. As Zephaniah writes in *Too Black, Too Strong*:

> We just keep melting into one
> Just like the tribes before us did,

I love this concrete jungle still
With all its sirens and its speed
The people here united will
Create a kind of London breed.[22]

The Absolutely True Diary of a Part-Time Indian: Strategic Disembodiment

Sherman Alexie begins *The Absolutely True Diary of a Part-Time Indian* with an epic disability origin story. "I was born with water on the brain," says Arnold Spirit.[23] Arnold then recites the tragicomic saga of all the disabilities the hydrocephalus left in its wake. He has a lisp, a stutter, an enormous head, and a history of seizures. "My brain damage left me nearsighted in one eye and farsighted in the other, so my ugly glasses were all lopsided because my eyes were so lopsided. I get headaches because my eyes are, like, enemies, you know, like they used to be married to each other but now hate each other's guts."[24] Why do Arnold's disabilities vanish from the rest of the book when the first chapter focuses on nothing else?

Impairment fades away because *The Absolutely True Diary of a Part-Time Indian* puts race before disability and because it belongs to the genre of young adult novels that depict their characters headed for conventional success. Arnold fits the narrow personality profile of many disabled protagonists: book smart, charming, and quick with a comeback. The main dynamic of the story is the balancing act between tribal identity and individual success. The silencing of disability allows race to take over as the main form of embodiment and lets Arnold succeed on his own. The silencing of disability allows Arnold to become the conventional individualist hero of young adult novels who overcomes obstacles as he comes of age.

Alexie subordinates disability to the main story line of an ambitious Native American teenager struggling to reconcile his tribal identity with his choice to attend the white high school twenty-two miles from home. Arnold goes to extraordinary lengths to get himself to Reardan High School every day and endures the tribe's hatred for doing so. The effort would seem futile if he were incapable of succeeding there. We all have our own definitions of disability, and Alexie redefines it as an indomitable will that shapes the main character's decisions. *Absolutely True Diary* is an autobiographical novel reflecting the author's own youthful experiences. Alexie credits his disability with teaching him to fight harder.

It's strange, you know. You think about the brain damage that almost killed me. I think in order to survive it, it instilled in me this will to live that was stronger than most people's, this competitive instinct that was stronger than most people. I think my brain damage actually made me stronger, a sort of Nietzschean hydrocephalus, I guess.[25]

Alexie endows his main character with the same Nietzschean hydrocephalus. "I wept because I was the only one who was brave and crazy enough to leave the rez. I was the only one with enough arrogance."[26] In a sense, then, it is disability, redefined as fighting spirit, that impels Arnold off the reservation. It is a curiously disembodied form of disability, however. Each aspect of his growing success at the white school—book smarts, wit, and basketball—syncs up with the disappearance of a particular impairment.

Smarts and Wit

"First of all, I learned that I was smarter than most of the white kids. . . . And not just smart for an Indian, okay? I was smart, period."[27] Arnold struts his intellect in friendly competition with Gordy, the smartest guy in the school. In their banter, intelligence proves masculine potency. The boys agree that really good books give you a "metaphorical boner."[28] A voracious reader, Arnold confesses, "I am a book kisser. Maybe that's kind of perverted or maybe it's just romantic and highly *intelligent*."[29] Despite his visual impairment and chronic headaches, Arnold requires no adaptations to read: no large print, no audiobooks, no screen-reading software, no need to limit his reading time. His intellect also refutes his childhood encounters with the R-word, which licenses physical abuse.

And if you're fourteen years old, like me, and you're still stuttering and lisping, then you become the biggest retard in the world.
Everybody on the rez calls me a retard about twice a day. They call me retard when they are pantsing me or stuffing my head in the toilet or just smacking me upside the head.
I'm not even writing down this story the way I actually talk, because I'd have to fill it with stutters and lisps, and then you'd be wondering why you're reading a story written by *such a retard*.[30]

The narrator edits his stutters and lisps out of the story to reassure an imagined reader who may doubt his mental capacity. Alexie himself performs similar feats of strategic disembodiment. Arnold owes part of his success at Reardan to his skill with a comeback. Arnold's lisp and stutter move out of the way to spotlight his comic timing, which takes him from being the bullied kid on the reservation to a somewhat hip kid at Reardan. It is difficult to imagine Arnold's punch lines hitting home if delivered with a lisp and stutter.

The jokes not only serve the novel's ethic of success but also bring race to the fore while pushing disability to the back. Body humor may be a weapon of choice for kids with disabilities; here, however, the jokes take aim not at ableism but at racial difference. In this exchange with Gordy, Arnold succeeds by mocking the Caucasian cult of success. He contrasts the repression of the white kids at Reardan with his ex-best friend Rowdy's penchant for letting it all hang out. Furious at Arnold for leaving the reservation, Rowdy responds to Arnold's friendly email with a photo of his bare ass.

> The Reardan kids were so worried about grades and sports and their futures that they sometimes acted like repressed middle-aged business dudes with cell phones stuck in their small intestines.
>
> Rowdy was the opposite of repressed. He was exactly the kind of kid who would e-mail his bare ass (and bare everything else) to the world.
>
> "Hey," Gordy said. "Is that somebody's posterior?"
>
> Posterior! Did he just say "posterior"?
>
> "Gordy, my man," I said. "That is most definitely not a posterior. That is a stinky ass. You can smell the thing, even through the computer."[31]

Alexie twins individual success with conflicted racial identity. He suppresses the lisp and shutter to emphasize Arnold's wit and to shift attention from Arnold's body to the tribal bodies back home. Gordy, with his big words and love of everything British, compliments Arnold on his "singular wit."[32] Meanwhile, Rowdy's ass stares out from the computer screen. The material realities of Arnold's disability fade away, replaced by the material reality of Rowdy's body, left behind on the reservation. The urgency of race trumps the urgency of disability.

Basketball

Mainly, *Absolutely True Diary* writes disability out of the story so that Arnold can play varsity basketball. Arnold has to play varsity high school basketball because it is a principal arena of white-Native race relations in Alexie's work. Basketball becomes a central way the racial body eclipses the disabled body. Winning and losing, the names of teams and mascots, replay the entire legacy of racial conquest, stereotypes, and segregation. Ironically, the Reardan High School mascot is an Indian. Arnold is "the only *other* Indian in town," a twisted symbol of his isolation.[33] Arnold makes two amazing plays that help the Reardan Indians slaughter the reservation team, the Wellpinit Redskins. Magically and miraculously, he jumps high above Rowdy's head to steal the ball, then fakes him out to score the game's first three-pointer.[34]

Strategic disembodiment erases the kinds of adaptations Arnold would probably need in order to become a phenomenal shooter. Because his eyes don't work together, he would have to create strategies for eye-hand coordination, focusing on the basket, and identifying the lines on the court. For instance, visually impaired basketball players usually use a ball that jingles or beeps and a different color or surface for offsides and the center square of the backboard. I am not saying that Arnold couldn't possibly be a great athlete. Rather, I am arguing that Alexie could show us Junior's ingenuity at working around his impairments, just as the reader sees and respects Junior's ingenuity at working around his poverty: hitchhiking the twenty-two miles to school and wearing his father's "retro" polyester suit from the 1970s to the winter formal.

Arnold's physical vulnerabilities vanish on the basketball court because Alexie prefers to focus on the racial inequality and subsequent class differences underlying the reservation team's physical vulnerabilities. After the Indians beat the Redskins, Arnold is jubilant at first, then recognizes how that loss sums up the power differential between Reardan and Wellpinit. "All of the guys on our team had their own cars," while "two or three of those Indians might not have eaten breakfast that morning. No food in the house."[35]

Playing varsity ball for Reardan means something entirely different from playing for Wellpinit. At Reardan, being a good player awakens the possibility of college scholarships. "Coach was thinking I would be an all-state player in a few years. He was thinking maybe I'd play some small-college ball. It was crazy. How often does a reservation Indian kid hear that?"[36] At Wellpinit, being a good player may become a treasured memory, but it has nothing to do with college or a bright future: "I knew that none of them were going to college. Not one of them. And I knew that Rowdy's father was probably going to beat the crap out of him for losing the game."[37] Alexie mutes Arnold's challenges to play up the other Native players' physical vulnerability, especially Rowdy's, so that his basketball experiences convey the gap between his old peers and his new ones. The specter of Rowdy's beaten body hangs over Arnold's triumph.

Basketball serves as microcosm of all the novel's themes: conflicting loyalties, legacies of pain, individual success, power differences, and Arnold's indomitable will: "I will never quit playing hard. And I don't just mean in basketball."[38] Like his wit and intellect, basketball helps him change his social standing. "I'd always been the lowest Indian on the reservation totem pole—I wasn't expected to be good so I wasn't. But in Reardan, my coach and the other players wanted me to be good. They needed me to be good. They expected me to be good. And so I became good."[39] Arnold's basketball success story erases the risks his history of brain trauma presents. At the start of the novel Arnold mentions he gets headaches because his eyes don't work together.[40] However, hydrocephalus, headaches, and visual impairment never interfere with his fortunes on the court. When Rowdy fouls Arnold and gives him a concussion, Arnold's mother is distressed because his previous brain damage heightens his risk of seizures.[41] Neither Arnold nor his coach give this risk a moment's worry.

Even though Arnold has a heightened risk of brain trauma, he has to play basketball. The game expresses racial power imbalances and engineers individual success at the same time. With Arnold's physical challenges erased, Rowdy's material reality can take center stage: his prowess on the court, his bare ass on the computer screen, but also his father's constant beatings. The better Arnold does, the more we are aware of Rowdy's beaten, defeated body and his rage at his best friend for leaving him behind on the reservation. The author takes physicality away from Arnold and gives it to Rowdy, so that conflicted tribal loyalties trump the material reality of disability. This bait-and-switch also allows Arnold to appear as a conventional individualist hero who triumphs over his circumstances.

It is eminently possible that a teenager with visual impairment, brain damage, chronic headaches, speech impediments, and high seizure risk could be a successful and funny student athlete. I'd just like to see how he does it. To downplay Arnold's disability workarounds misses an opportunity to show the creativity of young people with disabilities, to redefine impairment as problem-solving, and to furnish young, disabled people of color with characters who live like them. Arnold succeeds in the strategic absence of his disability, rather than succeeding while his body stays with him the entire time. Furthermore, if we saw him having to make adaptations, we would also see the barriers he faces in his new school and the ways he needs to ask that social system to change rather than fitting into its existing form.

"Nietzschean hydrocephalus," Alexie's jocular term for the fighting spirit born of childhood disability, replaces disability's material reality. Strategic disembodiment—the magic trick of conjuring up disability only to make it disappear—gives a young Native American man the flexible body he needs to succeed in the neoliberal economy.[42] The strategic disembodiment of disability also cedes ground to the material reality of race. Arnold's flexible body stands in painful contrast to the inflexible bodies left behind on the reservation, which Alexie portrays as loving, resilient, yet stuck in place and stuck in pain. "And that's when I knew I was going to be okay. But it also reminded me of the people who were not going to be okay. It made me think of Rowdy. I missed him so much."[43] The disappearance of Arnold's vulnerable body ensures his individual success and allows Rowdy to take his place as the designated vulnerable body.

Most readers of *Absolutely True Diary* don't notice the disappearance of disability. Why? Every day we hear justifications that make it ordinary not to notice barriers. Most societies define accommodation as an individual rather than a collective problem, so people ignore a barrier unless it affects them personally. "It is, after all, ordinary to not notice what is taken to be irrelevant."[44] We also don't notice the disappearance of disability because it is a common feature of young adult fiction. Novels, films, and television shows often depict adolescence itself as a temporary disability shrugged off when adulthood nears. Julie Passanante Elman writes that "this rendering of 'normal' adolescence as a disability to be overcome" has become "the stuff of common sense."[45] Therefore, the disappearance of Arnold's disabilities feels natural in a young adult novel. This vanishing act paves the way to a satisfying ending and spurs the reader to root for Junior as he gains traction in his new school. We come to focus on his abilities rather than his disabilities and assume Arnold succeeds by doing the same thing. Strategic disembodiment also shifts the focus from disability to race in a literary culture that doesn't allow us to consider both at the same time.

Out of My Mind: An Embodied Politics of Inclusion

Sharon M. Draper's *Out of My Mind* has a more embodied politics of inclusion than *The Absolutely True Diary of a Part-Time Indian, Face*, and *Wonder*. Not by coincidence, Draper's heroine needs significant human and technological help to succeed in her new school setting. Solving her problems on her own won't work for her. The need for accommodations means the need to make demands, and the need to make demands sparks an ethic of resistance.

Unlike Arnold Spirit, Martin Turner, and August Pullman, Melody doesn't win the other kids over. The author has said, "I wanted to make this story real. You know, if Melody went to class and everything was perfect and everybody liked her and everybody accepted her, that would not be real."[46] *Out of My Mind*'s frank depictions of ableism and prosthetic community show the strategies real-life students with disabilities must employ to become successful.

Unable to speak, Melody Brooks acquires a voice computer in the fifth grade. Because this technological advance dovetails with the start of mainstreaming, Melody can suddenly do academic work. Like other protagonists in these school stories, she is brilliant: "I'm ridiculously smart, and I'm pretty sure I have a photographic memory."[47] For her genius to emerge in public, however, Melody requires both technology and people. She has a strong prosthetic community of adults, but her classmates refuse to become an accepting community with disabilities. The women in her life help her outface them, rehearsing her future as an assertive adult long before she acquires the ability to speak. Although the main character's race is indeterminate, the author draws from African American women's legacy of courage and leadership in portraying her ethic of resistance. Thus, *Out of My Mind* retains some kinship with the rich depictions of African American culture found in all of Sharon Draper's other books.

Sharon M. Draper is a five-time winner of the Coretta Scott King awards, "given annually to outstanding African American authors and illustrators of books for children and young adults that demonstrate an appreciation of African American culture and universal human values."[48] Her other novels make frequent references to African American culture. In *Ziggy and the Black Dinosaurs*, for instance, the character Rashawn suggests the name "Tuskegee" for the password to their secret clubhouse. He has a dog named Afrika and a father who belongs to the Black Heritage Club.[49] In *Panic*, Mercedes Ford's mother dresses "straight out of *Essence* magazine."[50] Readers need a certain degree of black cultural literacy to enter the worlds of Draper's other books.

By contrast, the characters in *Out of My Mind* lack racial specifics. We only know that Melody has short, dark, curly hair and dark brown eyes, her sister Penny is "copper-bright, just like her name," and their mother's hair "gets stringy and limp" in the rain.[51] The family could be any race where dark, coppery, curly, and limp hair are options. Nor are there cultural markers of race: Melody's parents listen to jazz, classical, and country music. Nearly all Draper's other book covers feature images of African American boys and girls. This one has a goldfish.

Draper dials down race so that a wide mainstream readership only has to accept disability in order to see itself in Melody Brooks. Readers can identify with the common childhood feeling of lacking a voice. Those unfamiliar with nonverbal people can learn to recognize their intelligence. Draper's strategy seems to have worked. Often taught in schools, *Out of My Mind* has meant a great deal to many readers. It spent several years on the *New York Times* best-seller list, won dozens of awards, and has been translated into twenty different languages.[52]

The problem with this strategy, at least in the white worlds of narrative, is that unmarked characters get read as white. If race is not mentioned, whiteness becomes the default mode. Readers lose the opportunity to see African American and disability cultures intersect. Nonetheless, Draper draws on the history of African American struggles, including the Civil Rights Movement's desegregation of schools, as a source of resilience for Melody's struggle against disability segregation.

Segregation and Inclusion

Like *Wonder*, *Out of My Mind* reenacts the history of mainstreaming: the main character desegregates a general classroom for the first time. While *Wonder* shows how able-bodied people gather a community around the child and come into a disability consciousness of their own, *Out of My Mind* critiques the unfinished business of inclusion. At the beginning of the book, special education students go to their local elementary school; however, an invisible wall of ableism wraps around Room H-5. "When the weather is bright and sunny, we sit outside the school. I like to watch the 'regular' kids as they play four-square while they wait for the bell to ring. They look like they're having so much fun. They ask one another to play, but no one's ever asked any of us."[53] The special education class takes place in the mainstream school, but remains socially segregated.

An invisible wall of low expectations also surrounds the special-ed kids. In Room H-5, the kids learn the exact same things they did last year. They listen to baby songs and look at baby murals on the walls. With her characteristic wit, Melody calls it "another long day in the happy-face room."[54] Even when mainstreaming begins, the revolution remains unfinished. Melody can do real schoolwork once she gets her computer, but she still sits alone at recess.[55] When she joins the quiz team and her genius secures them a spot in the national finals, a reporter asks her, "How will being on the winning team change your life at school?" Melody replies, "Maybe kids will talk to me more."[56] She has a rich prosthetic community of adults and acquires the technology to communicate, but she has yet to crack the glass wall of social inclusion—with painful consequences for herself and her team.

The Prosthetic Community

People usually think of prosthetics as inanimate technologies, but they only work in concert with people and money. Herself the mother of a young woman with cerebral palsy, Draper shows what the hard work of inclusion really looks like. The embodied politics of *Out of My Mind* foregrounds not only Melody's voice computer but the entire prosthetic community. Adults listen to Melody, respect her personhood and abilities, build ingenious things, slog through paperwork, find money, stay patient, and help her with the goals she sets. Inclusion requires decent public policy and public funding. Inclusion also requires many steps and stages that narratives about overcoming obstacles usually omit.

To answer the question "How does Melody end up on television in the regional quiz team competition?" we have to follow the whole trail of people, resources, things, and habits of mind that make up her prosthetic community. Melody has to be able to get places in her power wheelchair, so she is lucky to have a father who builds ramps and never patronizes her.[57] She also happens to live in a nation that mandates ramps on public buildings and curb cuts on sidewalks. Her school bus driver, Gus, is a patient man who understands families with disabilities. "Gus is really cool and often waits a few minutes as parents hustle to get their children out of their houses. It just takes us longer sometimes to get it together in the morning."[58] The school bus driver comes to the Brooks house because Melody has a right to that service under the Individuals with Disabilities Education Act.

Melody also needs paid caregivers and aides beyond the circle of her loving family. As disability studies scholar Alison Kafer argues, paid assistance is not only a key resource for families but also central to "the political realm of public policy." "Seeing attendant care as something best provided by a family member too easily perpetuates the idea that disability is a private problem concerning the family that has no place in the public sphere."[59] *Out of My Mind* showcases the importance of caregiving's wider circle. Melody Brooks learns and gains crucial things from paid helpers that are not the same things her family gives and teaches her. Mrs. V, her neighbor and paid caregiver, never underestimates her potential. She teaches Melody to roll over and later to read.[60] Mrs. Shannon, one of her teachers, pushes through "budget-bustin' paperwork" to find the money for Melody to get a one-on-one instructional aide, Catherine.[61] Catherine figures out that Melody is asking for a computer and helps her research "all kinds of electronic talking and communication devices that have been designed for people like me."[62] Then the circle of care returns back to the family: Melody's mother fills out the online application for the computer, requests a doctor's prescription, and submits and resubmits the extensive and frustrating paperwork the insurance company demands.[63] Her parents pay half the cost. Then they all wait.

When the Medi-Talker arrives, Mrs. V. types thousands of words into it. Catherine and Mrs. V. help Melody study for the quiz team qualifying test.[64] When the team shows up at the local TV station for the competition, Melody finds unexpected access intimacy with Paul, the stage manager. As it turns out, Paul knows how to adapt for her because he is part of a family with physical disabilities. Their easy conversation puts the genius protagonist in the wider context of other young wheelchair users who could not do what she's about to do.

> "And here, Miss Melody, is where you will sit. Right next to your team-mates. I have rigged a special answer board for you, so it's adjusted to the height of your wheelchair." He looks pretty proud of himself as he shows me the setup.
>
> "Wow!" I type. "This is perfect. How did you know?"
>
> "My son is in a wheelchair," he says with a shrug. "I build stuff for Rusty all the time, but there's no way he could do what you are about to do." He kneels down so he can look me in the eye. "Knock their socks off, champ! Rusty will be watching."[65]

Unfinished Revolution

Full inclusion, however, requires more than a dedicated circle of allies. It requires a larger community willing to change their attitudes and ways of doing things. The question "Why doesn't Melody go to the national quiz finals with the rest of the team?" exposes the failure of that wider world to become a community with disabilities. The quiz team coach, Mr. Dimming, is a human ball of microaggressions: "If Melody Brooks can win the first round, my questions must not be hard enough!"[66] Melody's peers don't want to be seen on television with a teammate who might drool or screech, and Mr. Dimming does nothing to check their ableism. Without the support and knowledge of mainstream educators, inclusion only goes so far.

The decisive lack, however, is access intimacy around food. Like August in *Wonder*, Melody needs a friend willing to eat with her, but none appears. She needs help to eat and dining companions who roll with her slow pace.

Melody avoids eating in front of her teammates until the celebratory dinner after the regional win. As her mother begins spooning pasta into her mouth, her teammates exchange looks. "Nobody said anything, but I saw them look down at their plates with way too much attention. It got quiet . . . Finally, even though my plate was still full, I pushed it away."[67] Ultimately, the lack of food access intimacy blocks Melody's access to the national competition. When she and her family arrive at the airport, the rest of the team has already left for Washington, DC. Mr. Dimming and the other students ate breakfast together, arrived at the airport early, and caught a morning flight before a storm grounded all the planes. Melody confronts them upon their return.

> At last I break the silence. I turn the volume up loud on my machine, then type out, "Why did you leave me?"
>
> Eventually Rose stands up. She looks directly at me and says, "We didn't plan to leave you, Melody. Honest."
>
> I look her dead in the eye and wait.
>
> I don't react at all.
>
> I just wait.
>
> She continues. "We all went out to breakfast early that morning—"
>
> I interrupt. "Nobody told me about that. How come?"
>
> None of them answer. Their silence says what their words cannot—it's better without me.
>
> I blink real fast.
>
> Clare finally stammers, "We figured you'd slow us down because you have to be fed and stuff."[68]

The circle of adults around Melody are not the only people who advocate for her. Melody herself asks the tough questions and outfaces antagonists with a level stare. Where does she get this courage under fire? She has rehearsed her future by listening to the assertive women in her life and talking like them when she gets the means to talk. From the time she was small, "My mother whispered her strength in my ear."[69] African American women's legacy of resistance equips Melody, a girl without a race.

The Legacy of African American Women

Although we can't tell the race of the assertive women in Melody's life, Draper draws their depictions from the spirit of African American women throughout history who have confronted oppression. Draper has written, "I'd like to sit down and have a conversation with women like Mary McLeod Bethune and Sojourner Truth and Harriet Tubman—women who fought for civil rights and women's rights. I'd like to thank them for their courage and leadership."[70] In her historical fiction about slavery and the Civil Rights Movement, Draper's women characters proceed with resolve, fierceness, and dignity, facing their challenges head on. In *Fire from the Rock*, Elizabeth Eckford walks toward Little Rock Central High School: "Down that long sidewalk in front of the school, up to the steps that led to the front door, she walked with her head held high, slowly, deliberately."[71] In *Copper Sun*, Amari, an escaped slave in the eighteenth-century Carolinas, is determined to flee south instead of north to Fort Mose in Florida, where the Spanish government has granted freedom to escaped slaves. She tells her companion Polly, "You want to go north? Go alone," and leads them surely as if by instinct in the right direction.[72] These role models proceed with courage and deliberate speed.

In *Out of My Mind* the women in Melody Brooks's life have a gift for straight talk. They speak with a ringing clarity that cuts through excuses. Before she gets her voice computer, Melody starts to bellow in special-ed class one day because she is sick and tired of learning the letter B for six years in a row. The school calls in her mother, who backs her up.

> "School started in August. You haven't gotten past the letter 'B' in six months?" Mom was balling and unballing her fists. I've never seen my mother hit anything, but when I see her doing that, I always wonder if she might.
> "Who are you to tell me how to run my class?" the teacher asked angrily.
> "And who are you to bore these children with mindless activities?" my mother snapped back.
> "How dare you!" the teacher gasped.
> "I dare anything for my daughter," Mom replied, her voice dangerous, "and for the rest of these children!"[73]

Melody's caregivers share her mother's daring. Mrs. V "has one of those voices that can make anybody shut up, turn, and listen."[74] Her aide Catherine asserts Melody's smarts to her teammates and her rights to Mr. Dimming: "By law, she cannot be excluded. You know that, sir."[75] From all these women

Melody learns to speak up. At the end of the book, the quiz team offers Melody the measly ninth-place trophy they won in her absence. She refuses their hypocrisy with class, grace, and blunt humor.

> I look at the ugly little statue, and I start to giggle. Then I crack up. Finally, I roll with laughter. My hand jerks out and hits the trophy—I'm not sure if it was an accident or not—and it falls to the floor, breaking into several pieces.
>
> The class stares at me in surprise. When they see that I'm not going to go ballistic on them, they finally start to laugh as well—a little. Even Rose sniffs and smiles.
>
> "I don't want it!" I finally type. Then, turning the volume as loud as it will go, I add, "You deserve it!"
>
> Still laughing, I click on the power to my chair, do a smooth turn, and roll myself out of the classroom.[76]

When Melody drops the mike and exits the stage, she leaves a final question behind: Will halfway inclusion ever become full inclusion? That question remains unanswered. Melody doesn't just rehearse the future. She challenges it.

Part Four

Fantasy

And so I get what my little brother has known for a while:
Sometimes an alternative world is much better than this one.
  —Meg Wolitzer, *Belzhar*[1]

Fig. 15. Lewis Carroll's drawing of Alice stuck upside down. Courtesy of The British Library Board, *Alice's Adventures Underground*, MS 46700.

Eight

Portkeys to Disability
in British Fantasy Literature

_____

Lewis Carroll illustrated and hand-lettered *Alice's Adventures Underground* as a Christmas gift for the Alice who inspired the story. Now nestled among the treasures of the British Library, this handmade book is the first draft of *Alice's Adventures in Wonderland.* One of Carroll's droll pictures shows Alice stuck upside down in a cramped rectangle, as if she's fallen head first down a chimney.[2] Carroll has drawn a box around the page, leaving a narrow border. Packed so tightly into this rectangle, Alice looks rectangular herself. Carroll has deleted her neck, hunched up her shoulders, and distorted the right side of her jawline so her head fits into the lower left corner of the box. In fetal position, she pulls on the fabric of her skirt as if to draw her body even closer. Her curly hair undulates across the bottom of the page like ocean waves. Despite the obvious discomfort of her position, Alice's face remains composed and serene. Her beautiful dark eyes look right into you.

Alice blames her predicament on her body size. She has spent the first two chapters shrinking and expanding, attempting to fit through the door "into the loveliest garden you ever saw."

> How she longed to get out of that dark hall, and wander about among those beds of bright flowers and those cool fountains, but she could not even get her head through the doorway, "and even if my head would go through," thought poor Alice, "it would be very little use without my shoulders. Oh, how I wish I could shut up like a telescope! If I only knew how to begin."[3]

We could interpret this picture of Alice in a world of ways. The oversized Alice could represent the constant bodily transformations of childhood, in which one's clothes and shoes and bed seem to become too small overnight. The drawing might also symbolize the dynamics of Lewis Carroll's own Victorian life: how his meticulous rules of conduct, love of formal logic, and Christian morals struggled to contain his nonsensical imagination and his powerful attraction to young girls. Here, however, I suggest that the picture represents Carroll's experiences of disability as a child and adult. The image neatly sums up the experience of misfitting. As Rosemarie Garland-Thomson writes, "A misfit occurs when world fails flesh in the environment one encounters."[4] We could redefine Alice's misfitting as a failure of space rather than the failure of Alice's body. British fantasy literature has long captured the emotional core of encounters between public space and young people with disabilities.

Misfitting creates political awareness because it reveals the hidden contours of exclusion. "Misfits can also be agents of recognition who by the very act of misfitting engage in challenging and rearranging environments to accommodate their entrance to and participation in public life as equal citizens."[5] The picture of Alice-in-a-box exposes the ludicrous things people with disabilities must do to fit the strictures of the normate world. In his social satire Lewis Carroll operates as an agent of recognition: he pushes a line of logic until it explodes into nonsense of its own accord. Michael Levy and Farah Mendlesohn call the *Alice* books "relentlessly, irresistibly destructive of the social order to the extent that they push societal and fantastic conceits to absurd extremes."[6] The self-possessed, contorted Alice represents people the social order fails to include.

This picture is one of many ways British fantasy fiction makes room for the experience of childhood disability through ingenious metaphors. It has done so for well over 150 years. The disability metaphors we find in nineteenth-century British fantasy writers like Lewis Carroll and Dinah Maria Mulock refute the idea of a progress narrative in which the Victorians misunderstood everything we enlightened twenty-first-century people grasp in full. Instead, we find an unbroken chain of like-minded writers across the centuries from Carroll and Mulock to J. K. Rowling. These three authors exemplify how British fantasy registers the entrance of disability into public space. Their writings convey the inner experience of disability, express the discomfort of misfitting, critique the existing social order, and record the emergence of new heroes. Readers identify strongly with these heroes and form another kind of public space: an imagined disability community of fans. In this chapter I consider the reading life of the first disabled person I ever knew, my mother. In the next chapter I assess *Harry Potter*'s importance for fans with disabilities, including myself.

Victorian Disability Fandom

Lewis Carroll was a disability insider. Carroll, known outside his fantasy fiction as the Reverend Charles Lutwidge Dodgson, had multiple disabilities. Like Alice in the picture, Dodgson was asymmetrical. One of his shoulders was higher than the other, and "His face presented the peculiarity of having two very different profiles; the shape of the eyes, and the corners of the mouth did not tally."[7] Carroll was deaf in his right ear, blind in his right eye, and walked with a jerky gait.[8] The disability that most affected his life, however, was his speech impediment.[9] He undertook speech therapy at least twice, at the ages of twenty-seven and forty, but his stammer remained.[10] Dodgson learned to work around his stammer. For instance, he found lecturing much easier than reading aloud: "The hesitation, from which I have suffered all my life, is always worse in *reading* (when I can *see* difficult words before they come) than in speaking."[11] For Alice Liddell, the original Alice, Dodgson's hesitation formed part of his storytelling magic. His "fantastical tales" changed and grew with the frequent interjections of his young listeners. "In this way the stories, slowly enunciated in his quiet voice with its curious stutter, were perfected."[12] His speech enabled a fantastic story.

Charles Dodgson already had a disability fandom for his writing when he was a child. He wrote poetry, stories, and puzzles to amuse his primary disability community, his ten brothers and sisters, most of whom shared his speech impediment as well as his love of whimsy and invention. While he may have felt like a misfit in boarding school and the world at large, he fit perfectly into his own family. His niece Menella recalled, "Several members of the family stammered slightly; nearly all shared Lewis Carroll's love of detail, and one especially his passion for inventing small devices."[13] At age thirteen Charles wrote the poem "Rules and Regulations," which lampooned prejudice against speech impediments and already displayed his gift for pushing a worldview until it explodes into nonsense. He wrote for an audience of insiders who knew how harshly outsiders could judge them.

Learn well your grammar,
And never stammer.
Write well and neatly,

And sing most sweetly.
Be enterprising,
Love early rising,
Go walks of six miles,
Have ready quick smiles . . .
Drink tea, not coffee;
Never eat toffy.
Eat bread with butter.
Once more, don't stutter.[14]

Charles's mockery takes aim at the rigid imagination of the rule-maker rather than the disability itself. "Rules and Regulations" bans stuttering and stammering as if they were voluntary. "Never stammer" and "don't stutter" join a list of increasingly fantastical pronouncements such as "Starve your canaries / Believe in fairies" and "Don't have a stable / With any mangers. / Be rude to strangers." The satire recasts a body's natural way of being as a deliberate misbehavior, like the Duchess's lullaby in *Alice* that urges parents to "Speak roughly to your little boy, / And beat him when he sneezes: / He only does it to annoy, / Because he knows it teases."[15] While the moral tacked on to the end of the poem is "Behave," the satire's underlying moral is "Change the rules, not the child." Charles's poem for his siblings shows how disability can prompt not only repression but also a tender complicity. At the age of thirteen he was already creating a literature in which he and his siblings could recognize themselves and poke fun at rules and regulations.

Disability Metaphors in Fantasy Literature

Let us return for a moment to the picture of Alice in a box. She misfits into a specific type of rectangle: the page of a storybook. We could interpret this image as a silent call for a literature that makes more room for children with disabilities. Alice shouldn't have to shut herself up like a telescope to fit on the page, or even wish she could shut herself up. Lewis Carroll was not alone among fantasy authors in his awareness. The British fantasy tradition welcomed and accommodated disabilities long before realist literature or public life did. Realist novels of the nineteenth and early twentieth centuries featured children with disabilities, but on one condition: they had to be cured by the end of the book. The contrast between genres appears dramatically in the work of a single author, Frances Hodgson Burnett. Her realist novel *The Secret Garden* (1911) and her romance *The Lost Prince* (1915) both feature a main character with an orthopedic impairment. In the realist story, however, the impairment vanishes and the character learns to walk; in the romance, the character gets to keep his disability. Both boys go on to claim leadership roles in their societies.

Why has disability found a home in British fantasy literature for so long? It may be a question of access. Given the high access barriers of previous centuries, perhaps realists could not imagine a happy ending for a disabled child in a world that resembled theirs. Fantasy, by contrast, devises magical forms of access through metaphors. These metaphors include structures of feeling, like the rhetoric of misfitting Lewis Carroll employs in *Alice*. They also include imaginary assistive devices, like the magical traveling cloak that serves as a power wheelchair in "The Little Lame Prince" and the Patronus charm that becomes a magical antidepressant in the *Harry Potter* books. Fantasy also personifies disability in the form of fantastic creatures or redefines it as an offshoot of supernatural powers. All these inventions turn bodymind disabilities into observable forces at work in the world. They also make virtual disability community possible when inaccessible in real life.

Along with visibility, fantasy metaphors have two other distinguishing features: tangibility and transport. Fantasy readers grasp abstract meaning through the tangible forms of objects or creatures. As Helen Cooper writes, fantasy treats "inward meaning as literal narrative."[16] Borrowing from J. K. Rowling, I propose the term "portkey" to describe fantasy metaphors. As Mr. Weasley explains in Rowling's fourth *Harry Potter* book, portkeys are "objects that are used to transport wizards from one spot to another at a prearranged time. You can do large groups at a time if you need to."[17] A portkey is a random thing, like a moldy-looking old boot or a trophy cup, magically altered into a form of public transport. When Harry Potter puts his forefinger on the boot or grasps the handle of the cup, he feels "as though a hook just behind his navel had been suddenly jerked irresistibly forward," and he finds himself speeding to a new location.[18] While portkeys in *Harry Potter* move people from place to place, the fantasy metaphors I am calling portkeys transport readers into new worlds of human histories and emotions. Portkeys are simple, easily grasped things, yet they open into vast symbolic terrains.

Portkeys convey disability experiences in the British fantasy fiction of Dinah Maria Mulock and J. K. Rowling, two authors who wrote more than a century apart. I explore what their stories might mean for readers who see their own disabilities reflected yet magically transformed. Fantasy is a crucial space of freedom, recognition, and solace. It operates both as an individual experience and an imagined community, especially in children's literature, where adults and children often read together and children base their games, and even their ethics and futures, on the stories they know. *Harry Potter* has inspired both virtual and real-world communities involving millions of fans worldwide, among them fans with disabilities. As Mr. Weasley says, port-keys can move "large groups at a time if you need to." First, however, I focus on a child reader of a previous generation: my late mother, Phyllis Huntley Wheeler, and her fondness for "The Little Lame Prince."

Lame

I have my mother's copy of *The Little Lame Prince and Other Stories*. It was one of her favorite books from childhood. This edition was published in 1927, when my mother was four. The cover shows a boy kneeling on the roof of a castle, his back to the viewer, conversing with a magpie. As a child I found "The Little Lame Prince" (1875) too quaint and slow-moving, but in reread-ing it now I find it surprisingly hip about disability, as have other scholars.[19] Granted, the author Dinah Maria Mulock does some Victorian moralizing that is neither useful nor instructive. For instance, the narrator frequently exhorts the lame prince to resist the temptation to rely on others. Most un-usually, however, he becomes king, impairment and all. The people of No-mansland clamor for Prince Dolor to take the throne: "Nobody remembered his lameness—or, if they did, they passed it over as a matter of no conse-quence."[20] King Dolor lives out a long, distinguished reign. "And such was the love his people bore him that they never heard the sound of his crutches on the marble palace-floors without a leap of the heart, for they knew that good was coming to them whenever he approached them."[21] In a Victorian society that locked people with disabilities in attics and institutions, a lame king rules the Nomansland of fantasy.

Mulock uses magic assistive devices to accommodate the prince's disabil-ity and facilitate his movement into public space. Prince Dolor's godmother gives him several supernatural gadgets, including his traveling cloak, gold spectacles, and silver ears. The prince cannot walk independently because his legs never developed. When he was a baby, a lady-in-waiting dropped him on the way to his christening, injuring his spine.[22] His godmother gives him the cloak, his first mobility device, when he is a school-age boy. "Outside it was the commonest-looking bundle imaginable—shabby and small," but as a fantasy motif it opens up a vast world of terrains and experiences.[23] The cloak gives Prince Dolor the unprecedented freedom to move as fast and far as he wants to go. His godmother adds the subsequent gifts of gold spectacles and silver ears, so the prince can "see every minute blade of grass" and hear all "the sounds of the visible world" even when flying high above the ground.[24]

> Slowly unfolding, it laid itself down on the carpet, as flat as if it had been ironed; the split joined with a little sharp crick-crack, and the rim turned up all around till it was breast-high; for meantime the cloak had grown and grown, and become quite large enough for one person to sit in it as comfortably as if in a boat. . . . The cloak rose, slowly and steadily, at first only a few inches, then gradually higher and higher, till it nearly touched the skylight . . . the minute the window was opened out it sailed—right out into the clear, fresh air, with nothing between it and the cloudless blue.
> Prince Dolor had never felt any such delicious sensation before.[25]

Awesome as they are, the cloak and its accessories represent much more than magical gadgets. The cloak is a portkey to disability. This seemingly humble object not only whisks the prince from place to place, but transports readers into many important features of the disability experience: social death, the movement into ever-expanding public spheres, and the journey from the jarring discovery of one's own limitations to the resolve to advocate for oneself and others.

Declared dead while still alive, Prince Dolor lives a social death many people with disabilities have endured. Exiled by the uncle who usurped his throne, Prince Dolor resides in the Hopeless Tower, "eighty feet from the ground, and as inaccessible as a rook's nest on the top of a tree," in the midst of a barren and forsaken plain.[26] His uncle obtains an order from the royal council to send the child away, supposedly for his health, then informs the public that Dolor died on the journey. "The country went into deep mourning for him, and then forgot him, and his uncle reigned in his stead."[27] There are many Hopeless Towers in disability history. Until recent decades US doctors used to tell the parents of a disabled infant, "Put him in an institution where they know how to take care of him, forget about him, and have another child." Subtler forms of social forgetting still hold sway over the lives of people with disabilities, from the refusal of Social Security benefits to preposterously long wait times for wheelchair repairs. And some families still hide their children at home.

The traveling cloak serves as Prince Dolor's portkey back into the public sphere. He ventures into one social world after another, working his way up the animacy hierarchy from inanimate nature to animals and people. At the same time, he undergoes the emotional changes of taking a disability public. Sailing over the barren plain, he discovers the joy of physical freedom previously denied him: "This was the happiness of the little lame Prince when he got out of Hopeless Tower, and found himself for the first time in the pure open air, with the sky above him and the earth below."[28] He next encounters landscape: trees, plants, and rivers. He glimpses a cataract in the river that goes "tumbling over and over, after a fashion that made the Prince—who had never seen water before, except in his bath or his drinking-cup—clap his hands with delight. 'It is so active, so alive! I like things active and alive!' cried he, and watched it shimmering and dancing, whirling and leaping."[29] In overcoming his separation from nature, he makes the connection between the resources he uses and their sources in the landscape.

Mulock welcomes the prince into the living world through his kinship with animals. Animal companionship and comparisons between humans and animals play roles here as important as the ones in the picture books I discussed in chapter 2. As in *Seal Surfer* and *Sosu's Call*, animals provide assistance, solace, and delight in ways that do not diminish the masculine independence of the young hero with a physical disability. Mulock compares and contrasts the movements of animals to the boy's movements. "Above all, the motion of the animals delighted him: cows walking, horses galloping, little lambs and calves running races across the meadows, were such a treat for him to watch—he that was always so quiet. But, these creatures having four legs, and he only two, the difference did not strike him painfully."[30] As with the landscape, the prince meets animals with joy.

Mulock frequently compares the prince's movements to those of frogs, flies, puppies, or monkeys. In early childhood the prince "learned to crawl like a fly, and to jump like a frog, and to run about on all-fours almost as fast as a puppy," and as he grows he develops "great sturdy shoulders, and muscular arms, upon which he could swing himself about like a monkey."[31] Despite the hateful history of comparing people with disabilities to animals, Mulock's comparisons never disparage the prince. On the contrary, they make the prince's ways of moving seem right and natural. "He had scarcely reached the floor, and was still sitting in the middle of his traveling-cloak—like a frog on a water-lily leaf, as his godmother had expressed it—when he heard his nurse's voice outside."[32] The prince belongs on his cloak just as a frog belongs on his lily pad. Like animals, Prince Dolor claims his place in nature.

While he greets air, landscape, and animals with joy, the prince hits more difficult feelings on entering the human world. He pays the emotional cost of learning about his physical differences and closed options. He has a compare-

and-despair moment when he observes a shepherd boy and his collie dog racing each other across the countryside. "They did not seem to have anything to run for—but as if they did it, both of them, for the mere pleasure of motion. And what a pleasure that seemed! To the dog of course, but scarcely less so to the boy. How he skimmed along over the ground—his cheeks glowing, and his hair flying, and his legs—oh, what a pair of legs he had!"[33] As the prince comes to understand what other boys can do, he sinks into bitter thoughts and the desire to retreat from the world.

> "I think I had rather not look at him again," said the poor little Prince, drawing himself back into the center of his cloak, and resuming his favorite posture, sitting like a Turk, with his arms wrapped round his feeble, useless legs.
>
> "You're no good to me," he said, patting them mournfully. "You never will be any good to me. I wonder why I had you at all; I wonder why I was born at all, since I was not to grow like other little boys. *Why* not?"[34]

Depression, dislike of one's own body, and existential questioning plague many young people, especially in adolescence, and a physical disability only intensifies this state of mind. Like many of his peers, the prince retreats from the world for a while. "After his last journey in the traveling-cloak, the journey which had given him so much pain, his desire to see the world had somehow faded away."[35] Because "The Little Lame Prince" is a work of fantasy, it sends magic to solve the problem. The magic appears through the consolations of the traveling cloak and a skylark, his godmother in animal guise. Remarkably, however, this magic comes not to cure the disability but to comfort the boy's grief and guide him toward acceptance of his limits.

> Then he fancied the cloak began to rock gently to and fro, with a soothing kind of motion, as if he were in somebody's arms; somebody who did not speak, but loved him and comforted him without need of words; not by deceiving him with false encouragement or hope, but by making him see the plain, hard truth in all its hardness, and thus letting him quietly face it, till it softened down, and did not seem nearly so dreadful after all.[36]

While the traveling cloak is comforting him, a singing skylark drops out of the sky, nestles into the prince's chest, and returns to the Hopeless Tower with him. "Whenever he listened for a moment, he heard it singing still. He went to sleep as happy as a king."[37] Through the prince's relationship to animals, Mulock suggests that the prince is equal to the shepherd boy even though their legs don't work the same way. Like the shepherd, the prince has an animal companion who delights him. The prince flies from place to place like the skylark, just as the shepherd runs like his dog. Comparisons between animal and human movements serve to render disability an ordinary part of childhood. As noted above, the author compares the prince's movements to those of a puppy, a frog, and a monkey. Similarly, the shepherd boy's actions resemble his dog's. "They started off together, boy and dog—barking and shouting, till it was doubtful which made the most noise or ran the fastest."[38] Comparing both boys to animals, Mulock makes different kinds of movements seem equally natural, even though one boy moves with his legs and the other moves with his arms and a flying cloak.

Prince Dolor completes his journey into the public sphere by acquiring a grasp of human society as a whole. Although this story was published in 1875, it follows a pathway from solitude and self-doubt to awareness and activism more typical of late twentieth- and twenty-first-century disability narratives. The prince channels his pain into the determination to fight for his own rights and the rights of others. Mulock portrays this bravery as the prince's arrival into manhood. His nursemaid, a convict who has been his only companion in the Hopeless Tower, finally defies official orders and explains to the prince that his uncle usurped the throne and he is the rightful king. She urges him to "get out into the world, and fight for your rights like a man. And fight for me also, my Prince, that I may not die in this desolate place." The prince decides to "go out into the world, no matter how it hurts me."[39] He asks his godmother to

> "show me whatever I ought to see—never mind what I like to see," as a sudden idea came into his mind that he might see many painful and disagreeable things. But this journey was not for pleasure—as before. He was not a baby now, to do nothing but play—big boys do not always play. Nor men neither—they work.[40]

His godmother sends the cloak above a great city, from its "grand public buildings" to its "miserable little back alleys."[41] Witnessing large groups of people for the first time, the prince expands his sense of justice beyond his own immediate concerns. The division between rich and poor shocks and baffles him. "One-half the people seemed so happy and busy—hurrying up and down the full streets, or driving lazily along the parks in their grand carriages, while the other half were so wretched and miserable. 'Can't the world be made a little more level? I would try to do it if I were the king.'"[42] He witnesses the horrors of the revolution that follows his uncle's death. His nurse spreads the word that he is still alive, and the people call for his ascension to the throne.

After he becomes King Dolor, the traveling cloak, golden spectacles, and silver ears change from personal assistive devices to instruments of kingship. They give him what a good ruler needs: a grasp of the country as a whole to fuel his analysis and decisions. As a ruler he uses the traveling cloak "less for his own pleasure and amusement than to see something or investigate something for the good of the country."[43] His magic godmother continues to transform into animal companions, but now they act as royal advisors rather than sources of comfort. In the form of a magpie his godmother is "intimately acquainted" with the court and "all the inhabitants of the city. I talk a good deal, but I always talk sense, and I daresay I should be exceedingly useful to a poor little ignorant boy like you."[44] His magic animals, along with his cloak, golden spectacles, and silver ears, serve as his eyes and ears around the kingdom.

Dinah Maria Mulock deepens the meaning of "The Little Lame Prince" by fusing two powerful motifs: the social death of people with disabilities and the heroic fantasy of the Fair Unknown. In her study of motifs in British romance, Helen Cooper defines the Fair Unknown as a hero "brought up in ignorance of his parentage. . . . Such heroes are brought up outside the court and only find their place within it in the course of the romance, but they have a claim to such belonging before they know it themselves."[45] This motif plays a major role in British fantasy literature from medieval King Arthur stories to the Harry Potter books. The Fair Unknown usually carries a trait or mark that proves his leadership even though no one in the halls of power knows him. For example, Arthur distinguishes himself as the true heir to the throne of England because he is the only one who can pull the enchanted sword from the stone.

Prince Dolor's kingly nature appears through the very thing that might be seen as disqualifying him: the way he carries his body. "His eyes glistened; he held himself erect. Lame as he was, anybody could see he was born to be a king."[46] His moral courage in confronting social injustice also distinguishes him. When he witnesses the disparity between rich and poor in the great city, "Prince Dolor had need to be a king—that is, a boy with a kingly nature—to be able to stand such a sight without being utterly overcome."[47] Like other young people with disabilities before and after him, the prince travels from social death to the supports needed for independence; from isolation to belonging in nature and human society; from the painful awareness of one's limitations to the resolve to seek justice for oneself and others. These are the goals of disability rights movements around the world. By redefining the disabled child as a king in hiding, Mulock invests this journey with the nobility and urgency it deserves. She makes it more difficult to take the social marginality of disabled children for granted, leading readers to ask, like the prince, if the world could be made a little more level. The emergence into the public sphere benefits not only the disabled child, but society as a whole. He has a hero's role to play, and his people need him.

My mother, Phyllis Wheeler, held on to her copy of *The Little Lame Prince and Other Stories* from childhood into her eighties and through more than twenty moves within and between seven different states. What did she take from "The Little Lame Prince"? I believe she carried with her the prince's moral courage and the way she used the word "lame" to describe her rheumatoid arthritis. She received her diagnosis at age thirty-six, shortly after I was born. She told me she left the doctor's office and leaned against a parked car, staggered by the news. In the course of my childhood the knuckles swelled on her hands, hands that made precise hospital corners on beds, sewed my clothes, sliced carrots and green onions for homemade soup, stroked my shoulders, and turned the pages of books. When her feet curved into the shape of a pair of parentheses, she never drew attention away from them; quite the opposite. She always wore open-toed sandals dripping with vibrant beads and rhinestones. She danced at parties, her bracelets, her tongue, and the beads on her sandals all clicking.

My mother used the word "lame" as an index of the work she could or could not do on a given day. For instance she would say, "I don't think I can have you and the kids over today, Bets. I was on my feet too long yesterday and today I'm awfully lame and moving slowly. I need to lie flat." Raised by two hardworking Methodist parents during the Depression, she was a brilliant student and a hard worker. At thirty-six, however, she started learning a new lesson: how to value herself for refraining from hard work. Her discernment resembled the little lame prince's: "He could only show his courage morally, not physically, by being afraid of nothing, and by doing boldly all that it was in his narrow powers to do. And I am not sure but that in this way he showed more real valor than if he had had six pairs of proper legs."[48] Her ability to judge her own lameness, her joie de vivre, her bold fashion choices, and her astonishing sense of humor all signaled her valor in the face of life's surprises.

Now that I have fibromyalgia, I understand how one day's activities become the measure of the next day's comfort. From different generations, my mother and I use different words to describe our daily inventory of mobility and energy. While she talked about lameness, my generation talks about "counting spoons," after Christine Miserandino's spoon theory: "When you are healthy you expect to have a never-ending supply of 'spoons.' But when you have to now plan your day, you need to know exactly how many 'spoons' you are starting with."[49] It bothers me when I hear people use the word "lame" to mean weak, inadequate, or worthy of ridicule. For my mother it meant not weakness but self-respect.

Fantasy as a Public Space

How is fantasy a public space? It envisions new human and natural orders within its pages and creates communities of readers outside them. British fantasy fiction has held a space open for disability communities that predates the communities' existence in real life. Fantasy invents metaphors that capture the emotional core of the encounter between young people with disabilities and public space. This emotional core includes the feeling of misfitting, the tender complicity among members of the same subculture, and the struggle to move from social death to leadership and justice. As we shall see in the next chapter, *Harry Potter* resembles "The Little Lame Prince" in bestowing on this journey the nobility and urgency it deserves.

Nine

Inside Your Head

Harry Potter's Pain and Disability Fandom

> "Of course it is happening inside your head, Harry,
> but why on earth should that mean that it is not real?"
> —Albus Dumbledore[1]

In the *Harry Potter* series J. K. Rowling creates supernatural analogues to real-world disabilities. Because they result from malevolent powers he ultimately defeats, Harry Potter doesn't keep his impairments. Along the way, however, the books offer insights into the experience of living with chronic pain. In the previous chapter I borrowed Rowling's word "portkey" as the name for a visible, tangible fantasy metaphor that transports the reader into a whole world of human histories and feelings. Portkeys give invisible disabilities visible form and turn them into characters in the story. One portkey, the creature called a dementor, transports readers into the experience of depression, while the pain in Harry's supernatural scar reveals the hidden world of chronic headache.

"It's all in your head" is a timeworn phrase used to dismiss pain or mood disorders as imaginary. Harry Potter literally has evil characters and traumatic memories in his head causing his disabilities, and their tangibility refutes the offhand dismissal of chronic pain. Even mental anguish never takes place only in one's head, and Rowling reveals the unity of body and mind in states like depression, headache, and post-traumatic stress disorder. Harry also has readers in his head. J. K. Rowling gives us unlimited access to his thoughts and feelings, embodying them in vivid, sensual metaphors. For many fans with disabilities, myself included, what goes on inside Harry's head closely resembles our own experiences and provides a virtual disability community.

To the millennial generation of fans who read each book as they were published, *Harry Potter* is synonymous with childhood. Millennial fans carry the students of Hogwarts around in their heads, turning to them as role models and sources of comfort even in adulthood. Disabled fans identify with characters who begin as targets of ridicule or cruelty and finish as heroes. The series satisfies the longing to move from misfitting into finding the world where you fit, a world that was ready for you even before you got there. It also provides a necessary break from the fatigue of chronic pain and the struggle against barriers. The pleasurable experience of reading fantasy allows disabled readers to join an imagined community available even at times when pain, anxiety, or lack of access precludes a social life with real people.

J. K. Rowling dignifies the experience of chronic pain and the challenges of social stigma, depicting them as wellsprings for ethical decision-making. In *Harry Potter* both headache and depression are political: they emerge from the presence, often the officially tolerated presence, of hatred and destruction at loose in the wizarding world. Harry's experience of chronic pain intertwines with his journey from social death to political struggle. His story moves from shame and isolation to awareness and activism, like many contemporary disability narratives. He begins as a despised character locked in a closet under the stairs and becomes a freedom fighter who navigates psychic and physical pain at the same time he fights evil. Harry can identify that evil long before others do precisely because of his chronic pain.

Rowling redefines chronic headache and depression as part of the hero's journey. She draws from the British medieval romance tradition to single Harry out as a Fair Unknown uniquely capable of leadership. Although Harry gets sick of people staring at the scar on his forehead, it becomes a symbol common in medieval romance, as Helen Cooper writes: "a sign visibly and demonstrably beyond everyday experience, such as raises the man who bears the mark of it beyond the common run of humanity."[2] Like the sword in the stone that marked Arthur as the next king and the regal bearing and courage that marked Prince Dolor, the lightning-shaped scar distinguishes Harry as the Chosen One uniquely capable of defeating evil. Even if a leader has the mark, however, his actions must confirm his worth. In British fantasy, the hero distinguishes himself through his "active readiness to engage with whatever comes, or even to seek it out . . . That willed acceptance is one of the driving forces of romance."[3] Harry seeks out Voldemort's evil despite the good advice of those who love him and shows that active readiness at every turn.

In this chapter I explore what *Harry Potter* means to fans with disabilities. J. K. Rowling's fantasy metaphors refute the stigmas surrounding invisible conditions and do justice to the ethical struggles at the core of chronic pain. As a *Harry Potter* fan who experiences fibromyalgia, chronic migraine, and depression, I trace how the books have kept me company on my journey with pain. Finally, I analyze the characteristics of *Harry Potter* disability fandom among the millennial generation who grew up with him. Fans have used the Potterverse as a laboratory for fashioning their own identities and exploring what it means to be part of a community. *Harry Potter* has provided an escape into another world, yet one resonant with the emotional truths of their own lives.

Dementors and Headaches: Making Pain Visible

Benefits flow from translating invisible disabilities into visible things and making them characters in the story. By changing inward experience into external forces, *Harry Potter* reveals the hidden workings of pain while avoiding triggering the readers' own. Fantasy lends nobility to the struggle with barriers and discomfort by recasting it as an epic battle between heroes and villains. Maria Nikolajeva argues that the children's fantasy genre as a whole empowers young readers through the act of translating internal forces into external ones.

> The spiritual growth of the protagonist can be presented more tangibly when depicted in terms of struggle with external magic forces than in terms of inner tension. In particular, fantasy can empower a child protagonist in a way that realistic prose is incapable of doing.[4]

Harry Potter has headaches because an external being lives inside his head. In one flash of green light, Lord Voldemort killed Harry's parents, left his own body, and forged a psychic link between himself and the infant Harry. Headmaster Albus Dumbledore explains, "Part of Voldemort lives inside Harry, and it is that which gives him the power of speech with snakes, and a connection with Lord Voldemort's mind that he has never understood."[5] The resulting scar on Harry's forehead causes headaches whenever Voldemort is near or feeling a strong emotion.[6] The scar has also made Harry famous as the only person ever to survive Voldemort's curse.[7]

Harry's supernatural disability shares many symptoms with chronic migraine, including severe pain, physical weakness, impaired vision, nausea, and vomiting.[8] By letting us into Harry's mind, Rowling reveals the unsung achievement of everyone with chronic migraine: having an inner dialogue with the pain while also trying to interact with daily tasks and other people. His headaches and depression have their root cause in the early childhood trauma of Voldemort's violence. In embodying post-traumatic conditions through physical forms and forces, Rowling's metaphors do justice to the actual experience of trauma, which lives on in the body as well as the mind. Psychiatrist and trauma expert Bessel van der Kolk explains, "Posttraumatic stress isn't 'all in one's head,' as some people [have] supposed . . . the symptoms have their origin in the entire body's response to trauma."[9] Fantasy portkeys convey the interconnection of body and mind that disability studies scholars call the bodymind.[10]

The tangibility and visibility of the portkeys in *Harry Potter* refute the common notion that invisible pain is exaggerated or unreal. Physicians inherit "a collective history of the medical system that trains doctors to view pain and people in pain as suspect," in Alyson Patsavas's words.[11] Because Harry's headaches come from an external source, another person in his head, they refute the suspicion that swirls around people with chronic migraine. The recent epidemic of opioid addiction in the United States has only heightened this suspicion. Neurologists often seem at a loss to treat migraine because they have to take the patient's word for it. Dr. Richard B. Lipton's study of clinical interactions concluded that "chronic migraine is underdiagnosed, undertreated, and disabling" because doctors don't know how to ask the right questions and listen to the patients' answers.[12] Researcher Dr. Joost Haan seeks an objective genetic test for migraine to avoid reliance on patient narratives: "The only reason we take it as true is because they are all telling the same story."[13] By contrast, readers cannot deny Harry Potter's headaches because we witness firsthand what happens inside his head.

It is easy for readers to identify with Harry because Rowling embodies his experiences so tangibly. We can feel the inner workings of his body and mind. Rowling conveys chronic pain through metaphors of touch that are timeless, ordinary, and easily understood across cultures. These metaphors draw from earthy compounds and properties: water, fire, heat, and metals. Like me, Harry touches his head when a headache starts, and his scar burns "beneath his fingers as though someone had just pressed a white-hot wire to his skin."[14] Rowling describes pain with the imagery of torture-by-metal-tools we migraineurs often use. The headache feels like a "white-hot poker . . . applied to his forehead," a spike driven through it, or a knife slicing into it.[15] These easily felt and understood metaphors bring home the interplay between body and mind. For instance, Harry feels the strength of Voldemort's emotions along with headache pain. While Harry battles Bellatrix Lestrange, "Pain seared across his forehead. His scar was on fire again, and he felt a surge of fury that was quite unconnected with his own rage."[16] In *Harry Potter* as in real life, depression has physical as well as emotional symptoms, and migraine is a mood disorder as well as a physical pain.

A portkey can transport you into the experience of pain, then whisk you back out again. By turning depression into a supernatural being, *Harry Potter* introduces readers to despair in an intense but controlled encounter. The hooded, skeletal creatures called dementors are metaphors for depression, and their character traits replicate its symptoms. "They represent the coldness and deadness of clinical depression," J. K. Rowling has said. "Anyone who has had it knows that feeling of emptiness."[17] Dementors "drain peace, hope, and happiness out of the air around them," Professor Lupin explains in *The Prisoner of Azkaban*. "If it can, the dementor will feed on you long enough to reduce you to something like itself . . . soulless and evil. You'll be left with nothing but the worst experiences of your life."[18] The dementors guard the prison of Azkaban, and Hagrid recounts their effects on him during his brief imprisonment there: "Yeh can't really remember who yeh are after a while. An' yeh can' see the point o' livin' at all. I used ter hope I'd jus' die in me sleep."[19] Rowling captures the lack of meaning and selfhood that separates depression from ordinary sadness.

I often find it hard to read realistic portrayals of depression for fear of triggering my own. By turning a mood disorder into a character, however, a fantasy author draws borders around the emptiness. Jacqueline Rose argues that fantasy provides a way of partially recognizing the memory of trauma without activating it. "But fantasy is also a way of re-elaborating and therefore of partly recognizing the memory which is struggling, against the psychic odds, to be heard."[20] Fantasy allows for partial recognition because magic has ground rules. As Brian Attebery writes, "The impossible in fantasy is generally codified. Magical operations are grouped into principles resembling natural law."[21] The rules of magic build a perimeter around the disability to contain it.

Turning depression into a character, Rowling gives the mood disorder a firm deadline. When the dementor goes away, the depression goes away. For example, in *The Prisoner of Azkaban* Harry is safe from dementors within Hogwarts castle because Albus Dumbledore bars them from entering as long as he is headmaster.[22] Harry recovers from his first encounter with dementors after the right dose of chocolate.[23] Rowling sets limits on the depressive episode by resolving it with the familiar treat of chocolate and by alternating scary moments with light, cozy, quirky ones. Associating a disability with a supernatural being helps draw a perimeter around physical pain as well. Harry's headache disappears with the death of Voldemort at the end of the series. "The scar had not pained Harry for nineteen years. All was well."[24] Fantasy is a crucial resource for young people surviving rough times. The partial recognition of pain lets them escape to another world, yet one with the emotional veracity of real life.

The Stigma of Invisible Disabilities

While fantasy literature allows a controlled and partial recognition of pain itself, it fosters full recognition of pain's social stigma. J. K. Rowling and Harry Potter both serve as agents of recognition, leading readers to identify and critique stereotypes of invisible disabilities. Rowling has been a vocal critic of the shame surrounding depression and AIDS. The author herself thought about suicide during an episode of depression in her midtwenties. "I have never been remotely ashamed of having been depressed. Never," Rowling said in an interview. "What's to be ashamed of? I went through a really rough time and I am quite proud that I got out of that."[25] Her dislike of stigma also impels her compassionate portrayal of Professor Remus Lupin, whose disability, like Harry's headaches, consists of a beast inside him. In a background sketch of the character, Rowling writes, "Lupin's condition of lycanthropy (being a werewolf) was a metaphor for those illnesses that carry a stigma, like HIV and AIDS. . . . The wizarding community is as prone to hysteria and prejudice as the Muggle one, and the character of Lupin gave me a chance to examine those attitudes."[26] By turning depression and chronic headache into visible, tangible beings, Rowling challenges misconceptions that these disabilities are signs of weakness, danger, or mental instability.

The media and the government discredit Harry by exploiting the stereotypes of invisible illness. Minister of Magic Cornelius Fudge finds it "preposterous" that Voldemort has returned and that Harry's headaches give him a view into Voldemort's mind.[27] Fudge calls Harry's visions "hallucinations" and accuses him of lying.[28] "For heaven's sake, Dumbledore—the boy was full of some crackpot story at the end of last year too—his tales are getting taller, and you're still swallowing them."[29] Under the headline "Harry Potter: 'Disturbed and Dangerous,'" the *Daily Prophet* newspaper runs Rita Skeeter's story suggesting that Harry is simultaneously confused, unstable, and dangerous and is making the whole thing up to get attention.

On Monday last, midway through a Divination lesson, your *Daily Prophet* reporter witnessed Potter storming from the class, claiming that his scar was hurting too badly to continue studying. It is possible, say top experts at St. Mungo's Hospital for Magical Maladies and Injuries, that Potter's brain was affected by the attack inflicted upon him by You-Know-Who, and that his insistence that the scar is still hurting is an expression of his deep-seated confusion.

"He might even be pretending," said one specialist. "This could be a plea for attention."[30]

Rowling underlines, however, that the people who distrust Harry are untrustworthy themselves. Fudge's cowardice and Skeeter's duplicity become objects of Rowling's satire, while two of Harry's most trusted mentors, Albus Dumbledore and Minerva McGonagall, believe him immediately.[31] Furthermore, Voldemort's return is a verifiable fact everyone eventually accepts. In a different context Harry asks Dumbledore, "Is this real? Or has this been happening inside my head?" Dumbledore replies, "Of course it is happening inside your head, Harry, but why on earth should that mean that it is not real?"[32] In fantasy, something can be inside your head and independently observable at the same time. Voldemort is literally in Harry's head. It's not that Harry is crazy, lying, or confused.

The literal nature of the dementors similarly allows Rowling to counter the stigma of depression. Dementors are three-dimensional creatures, not an intangible state one experiences alone that others can dismiss or misunderstand. Even Harry's obtuse, deplorable nonmagical aunt and cousin acknowledge the reality of dementors.[33] However, Harry has a much more profound reaction to the dementors than other Hogwarts students, which allows Rowling to go deeper in addressing the shame surrounding mental illness. Some people experience depression, while others do not, and those who do not can mistake it for weakness or melodrama. The dementors incapacitate Harry, while his peers experience only a transitory change of mood. After the dementors' first appearance, "He felt weak and shivery, as though he were recovering from a bad bout of flu; he also felt the beginnings of shame. Why had he gone to pieces like that, when no one else had?"[34] Harry's sworn enemy Draco Malfoy and his pals mock and bully Harry by pretending to swoon and by dressing up as dementors.[35] Harry wonders if there's something wrong with him, if he's weaker than others. "Harry felt sick and humiliated every time he thought of them. Everyone said dementors were horrible, but no one else collapsed every time they went near one. No one else heard echoes in their head of their dying parents."[36]

Professor Lupin, who also meets with stigma because of his disability, helps Harry understand that he reacts more strongly to the dementors because he's been through harder times in his life. "'It has nothing to do with weakness,' said Professor Lupin sharply, as though he had read Harry's mind. 'The dementors affect you worse than the others because there are horrors in your past that the others don't have.'"[37] Lupin redefines Harry as a kind of war veteran whose experience deserves respect. He also teaches Harry how to wield the most powerful antidepressant of them all: the Patronus charm.[38] The Patronus is yet another animal companion who establishes a hero's strength and worth. Under Lupin's tutelage Harry acquires mastery of the Patronus, which places him among the elite of wizards. "Harry, I can't believe it," exclaims Hermione. "You conjured up a Patronus that drove away all those dementors! That's very, *very* advanced magic."[39] Harry's mastery demonstrates that he is not weaker than others, but in fact more skilled.

Each wizard's Patronus takes a different form, and the form of Harry's Patronus underlines his strength and worth. The silvery creature emerging from Harry's wand is a stag, an animal associated with nobility and powerful masculinity, the same animal into whom his father could transform. The stag Patronus is one of several ways Harry asserts masculinity by continuing the male line of his family. Like Voldemort, the stag Patronus lives in Harry's mind, but to help rather than harm him. In Harry's final showdown with Voldemort and his followers, "The fact of his own survival burned inside him, a talisman against them, as though his father's stag kept guardian in his heart."[40] A wizard summons a Patronus by mustering his happiest memories to counter the despair, like a magically enhanced version of cognitive-behavioral therapy. Unlike a prescription antidepressant with its risks of side effects, the Patronus is natural to the wizard, emerging from one's truest self and deepest resources. Unlike the snake inside Harry or the werewolf inside Lupin, the Patronus animal confirms rather than challenges human identity. The Patronus becomes one of Harry's best weapons in fighting evil. He can save others as well as himself from dementors, and he teaches it to everyone in Dumbledore's Army, the underground student resistance movement against Voldemort.[41] Like Prince Dolor, Harry uses his increasing knowledge to serve a justice far beyond his own immediate concerns.

The Beast in Me

Harry has a beast inside him. When he gets a headache, he enters the death-loving and death-dealing viewpoint of Lord Voldemort or Voldemort's snake Nagini. The headaches emerge from Voldemort's strongest emotions. In those moments of hatred and rage Rowling shows how the physical pain of headache fuses with emotional pain. This bodymind fusion leads to ethical dilemmas.

> At once, Harry's scar burned white-hot, as though the old wound had burst open again—and unbidden, unwanted, but terrifyingly strong, there rose within Harry a hatred so powerful he felt, for that instant, that he would like nothing better than to strike—to bite—to sink his fangs into the man before him—[42]

Harry grapples with the ethics of feeling the drive to kill and destroy. He isn't just watching the snake kill; he's doing the killing. "What if those fangs (Harry tried hard not to think 'my fangs') had been poisonous?"[43] Having a beast inside one's head muddles the distinctions between self and other, human and animal, body and mind, good and evil. After one such vision Harry feels "dirty, contaminated, as though he were carrying some deadly germ . . . he had not merely seen the snake, he had been the snake."[44] In the final showdown against Voldemort in *The Order of the Phoenix*, Harry feels as if he and the snake are "fused together, bound by pain."[45] This rendering of pain as another creature inside one's head captures the way pain moves between bodies, affecting more than the person who originally feels it. As Alyson Patsavas writes, "My experience of living with pain leaks onto those around me in a way that cannot be contained by the boundary of my body or my experience."[46] Because it signals Voldemort's return, the source of Harry's pain affects the well-being of everyone in his world. The beast in him threatens them all, so his disability is not an isolated, individual problem.

The beast is death-loving in every way. Through Harry's mouth it urges not only murder but suicide and the inevitability of death. In these moments, headache acts like depression.

> And when the creature spoke, it used Harry's mouth, so that in his agony he felt his jaw move. . . .
> *"Kill me now, Dumbledore. . . ."*

Blinded and dying, every part of him screaming for release, Harry felt the creature use him again. . . .

"*If death is nothing, Dumbledore, kill the boy.* . . ."

Let the pain stop, thought Harry. *Let him kill us.* . . . *End it, Dumbledore.* . . . *Death is nothing compared to this.*[47]

I have had a beast in me. In the depths of depression the beast sends me pictures of myself slicing my wrists open. It offers helpful suggestions like "Everything you touch turns to shit." The chronic migraine has felt like a savage beast, too. When the children were small, I had one continuous headache for about eight months. Every day the migraine clawed at my brain. When I woke up in the morning, I had a quiet minute or two before I felt it stirring. My neurologist and I were working our way through all the standard medications—Imitrex, Topamax, Maxalt, Zonegran, DHE—but nothing worked. I started to picture suicide. I didn't want to kill myself but couldn't think of any other way to stop the pain. One day I was driving home and heard Johnny Cash's remarkable version of Nick Lowe's song "The Beast in Me" play on the radio. I thought, that's exactly how the headache makes me feel, as if it might attack me at any moment.

> The beast in me
> Is caged by frail and fragile bars
> Restless by day
> And by night rants and rages at the stars
> God help the beast in me.[48]

When I left the car and came inside the house, both kids were napping and Jordan was reading in the living room. I sat down on the couch with her. Excited, I told her the song captured exactly how I felt about the migraine. Jordan replied, "Yes, you do hurt us sometimes when the headache is bad. It comes out of nowhere, like a beast." Her reaction shocked me. I thought, she really doesn't understand me. I am not the beast, hurting other people; the headache is the beast, hurting me. Yet with hindsight I know the beast spoke through my mouth often in those days, especially when I was on Zonegran. One Saturday we had an afternoon babysitter. I decided to take a nap before Jordan and I went out for an early dinner date. I lay in our bed in the sunny afternoon. Instead of sleeping I was nursing a grievance against Jordan. I don't remember what it was. The anger escalated until I rose out of bed and went to tell her what she did wrong. I found her in the backyard, using her precious free time to water and weed the flower garden. She turned, and her face lit up with the pleasure of seeing me. As I launched into a tirade the smile melted away from her face.

I ruined many fine moments back then. Jordan later told me that she had to shield her heart from me in those years but didn't blame me for my savage tongue. Instead she blamed the migraine, the meds, the beast. A year later I went all the way to Chicago to find the right doctor who started me on a preventative drug that began to work. This isn't a cure narrative, though. Three years ago, the migraine came roaring back after several years of remission. The beast has remained relatively tame, however, perhaps because I have learned to recognize its cycles. I am now a skilled wizard who can conjure a Patronus. I know depression will surface in November, so I up my antidepressants in October. I know I'm most likely to say cruel things at the start of a migraine, so if possible I go lie down alone before the pain fully strikes.

In the dark bedroom, between the knowledge of the headache and the onset of the pain, I hear the beast's invitation. My rational mind knows I can minimize the pain if I remain calm, do my relaxation breathing, and think positive. At the same time, though, I feel a voluptuous desire to let the beast in, to rant and scream with rage and self-pity, to let the rest of the family feel the force and reality of this animal so I won't be alone with it. Despair and fury can seem as inevitable as pain, and I identify with Harry's desire to open up his mind to the beast. Even though his friend Hermione chides him about the danger of his connection to Voldemort, Harry still succumbs to the temptation.

> "[Dumbledore] thought the connection was dangerous—Voldemort can *use* it, Harry! What good is it to watch him kill and torture, how can it help?"
>
> "Because it means I know what he's doing," said Harry. ". . . I hate it, I hate the fact that he can get inside me, that I have to watch him when he's most dangerous. But I'm going to use it."[49]

Harry retains control over his own ethical choices, using his psychic connection not to fuse with the beast but to halt its path of destruction. Like Harry, I know I have a choice whether to let the beast in or not. The goal is not to kill it but to assess its threat level and acquire the skills to handle it. In *Fantastic Beasts and Where to Find Them*, J. K. Rowling, writing as magizoologist Newt Scamander, notes that the Ministry of Magic divides beasts into five categories of threat level:

xxxxx	Known wizard killer / impossible to domesticate
xxxx	Dangerous / requires specialist knowledge
xxx	Competent wizard should cope
xx	Harmless / may be domesticated
x	Boring[50]

At this point I would assess my own beast-handling skills somewhere between "specialist knowledge" and "Competent wizard should cope." I know this beast can hurt people other than me. I've identified when it usually rears its head, and I don't underestimate my vulnerability to the threat. I know when and how to get help, whether professional expertise or asking Jordan to do my chores. I've learned that Jordan would much rather take on extra tasks that have me overstrain myself and then collapse in a heap of pain and emotions. I have also learned that I have many states of being inside myself which are deeply foreign to each other.

Right now, for instance, I have returned to my preventative migraine medication and feel confident it's working. This confident state of mind is a completely different one from the terrifying, vulnerable times when almost anything can trigger a headache. Right now I can think without pain and plan my workweek with some assurance. This state sits much closer to able-bodied privilege than the other mind-set. The difference between the two helps me clarify my politics. It helps me understand my other privileges, such as whiteness and affluence, and discern privilege and lack of privilege at work in the society around me.

Holly Batty argues that Harry's movement between human and animal consciousness is political, too. It helps readers think about social power and leads us to question the binary that divides humans from animals and ranks one above the other. She argues that "the series forces us to acknowledge both humans and animals as embodied creatures that change and suffer, calling into question the validity of a hierarchical system that ranks those bodies."[51] Newt Scamander might concur. Scamander points out that "the definition of a beast has caused controversy for centuries" and that the wizarding world has long grappled with the difficulty of distinguishing a beast from a being, "a creature worthy of legal rights and a voice in the governance of the magical world."[52] The many fond portrayals of beasts in the *Harry Potter* series also prompt questions about the animacy hierarchy.

I read the *Harry Potter* books as they were published, and his chronic headaches escalated at the same pace as mine. Harry and I learned at the same pace how to pause and consider when the pain hits: Do we throw ourselves into the rage and despair or do we cultivate calm and detachment? This ability to make a conscious choice came to both of us after we were spent and battle-weary.

> His scar burned, but he was master of the pain; he felt it, yet was apart from it. He had learned control at last, learned to shut his mind to Voldemort, the very thing Dumbledore had wanted him to learn.[53]

I will never really master the pain, and apparently neither will Harry. In the 2016 play *Harry Potter and the Cursed Child*, a thirty-seven-year-old Harry feels his scar hurting again.[54] Both of us would prefer the pain to go away and stay away. We also know, however, that our beastly states represent not a false consciousness but simply a different state of mind, beyond human yet also humane. For Harry and for me, the struggle with chronic pain has become a wellspring for ethical decision-making.

Harry Potter's Disability Fandom

What characterizes *Harry Potter*'s disability fandom? First of all, we tend to be a literal bunch, translating fantasy metaphors back into our material reality. This literal way of reading has also characterized disability studies scholarship at least since Sharon Snyder and David Mitchell wrote about "the materiality of metaphor."[55] Tom Felton, who played Draco Malfoy in the *Potter* films, interviewed a fan named J. D. who told him the series helped her out of depression by precisely mirroring a state of mind she felt ashamed to talk about. She said, "I've never read such an accurate description of what it feels like, like the dementors were sucking the life out of you, basically." Felton responded with surprise: "I'd never realized that something like the dementors could be taken so literally. It's hard to imagine that people watching those scenes can be so deeply affected."[56]

Fans' strong response to Harry's struggle with dementors shows how hungry we are for portkeys that reflect the truth of our experiences. Fans who struggle with depression easily imagine themselves into the story because Rowling had depression in mind when creating this metaphor. By contrast, *Harry Potter*'s queer fandom has to interpolate same-sex pairings into the Potterverse through slash fan fiction because there are no queer romances in the original stories. Similarly, fan artists have stocked the internet with portraits of the main characters transformed into people of color.

Many young adults of the millennial generation, particularly white cis-women like J. K. Rowling and myself, have written about the ways *Harry Potter* bolstered them while growing up with a disability. One common thread among their writings is the feeling of kinship with characters who see what others can't see. Karin Hitselberger has learning disabilities and grew up listening to the Harry Potter audiobooks. "The magic of Harry Potter's world meant everything to me, because it showed the immense value in being different and seeing what no one else can seem to see."[57] This ability takes on an ethical cast, since Harry and his friends see and resist evil while the leaders of their world are lost in complacency and denial. Through depression and chronic headache Harry gains heightened awareness of the threats Voldemort and the dementors pose, and he and his allies become the wizarding world's first line of defense.

Like "The Little Lame Prince," *Harry Potter* takes what others regard as weaknesses and redefines them as part of the hero's journey. Fans with disabilities also identify with other Potterverse characters dismissed as crazy, inept, irrational, anxious, confused, or ugly who nonetheless become heroes in the fight against evil. Bethany Rose Lamont writes, "I hated reading until *Harry Potter* came to me as a traumatized ten-year-old. In between bouts of psychosis and extreme suicidal ideation I would read, and read, and read."[58] The character of Luna Lovegood became "one of my teen idols." With her "distinct dottiness," Luna allowed Lamont to be a normal fangirl like the other kids her age while also seeing her personality disorder mirrored in children's popular culture. "Yes, her eccentricities are dismissed as 'loony,' but they belong to a heroic character in possession of creativity, wit, intellect—and, of course, unique style. (A necklace made out of butterbeer corks, anyone?)"[59] Lamont also identified with the prophetic Sybill Trelawney, who sees what others don't see. "Who would believe a mad woman? But who but a mad woman can see the truth in a chaotic world?"[60] Lamont could identify with Rowling's affectionate and lighthearted portrayals of Luna and Professor Trelawney because they didn't reinforce the same old pop culture stigma of the fearsome madwoman. Through pop culture fandom itself, Lamont found a way to claim an identity as a girl of her generation without the barrier of stigma getting in the way.

Both Carrie Mathews and Amelia Tait turned to *Harry Potter* during their depressions in the rocky transition from school to adulthood. What identities did they construct for themselves out of fantasy fiction? Through the character Neville Longbottom, Carrie Mathews redefined herself as persistent rather than stuck. Depression hit when she was unemployed and discouraged by a failed attempt at community college. When she enrolled again six years later she felt sheer terror, so she fixed her mind on Neville. "Throughout the series, I watched this boy with very low self-esteem slowly grow into the courageous young man he becomes in *Deathly Hallows* . . . he begins to stand up for himself and perseveres through being the target of many bullies. Neville never stops trying even when he is completely terrified."[61] He was a role model not because he vanquished his fears but because he acted anyway. "I began to think that starting over wasn't such an impossible thing, and maybe, just maybe, I am smarter than I think I am." She finished her first term of community college with a 3.5 average.[62]

Amelia Tait drew on her childhood attachment to the Potterverse during a severe depression. However, the books' importance had nothing to do with role models. *Harry Potter* did not cure her and did not offer optimistic messages. Tait's sarcasm offers a bracing challenge to the self-help discourses of role models, positive thinking, and overcoming narratives.

> When we talk of Harry Potter and depression—which we do, a lot—we imagine that the lessons of the book can teach us, in a *Don't let the Dementors get you down!* way, to not be depressed anymore. What do you mean you want to kill yourself? Banish that beast to Azkaban with your silvery kitty cat Patronus![63]

Instead, *Harry Potter*'s helpful qualities were inventive world-building and compelling storytelling.[64] After she graduated from university and was saving money for further training, Tait found herself living with her parents and working four menial jobs "in between sobbing in the disabled toilets."[65] *Harry Potter* was the only thing compelling enough to provide respite from "constant crying, and knowing-the-exact-number-of-storeys-you-have-to-jump-from-to-ensure-you-die."[66] The *Harry Potter* series' "episodic and addictive structure meant I couldn't put it down even when I knew what happened next. I couldn't enjoy anything at that time, and I'm not even sure I 'enjoyed' *Harry*. But the books were a total and complete distraction."[67] The usefulness of Rowling's books lay in their sheer narrative pleasure. Tait benefited from the fantasy genre's ability to allow partial recognition of pain while also placing limits on it. Filling her head with the happenings at Hogwarts, the immersive reading experience pushed the pain to the back of Tait's mind rather than intensifying it. For an hour or two a day, the books reminded

Tait of the child she used to be before life got so complicated. "It was something ordinary in a world where everything had changed."[68] The books didn't cure her, but they aided her self-care, reminded her she had other selves, and helped her ride the depression out.

Cal Montgomery's attachment to *Harry Potter* also has nothing to do with particular characters, but rather with the wizarding world as a public space. By contemplating the social order of the Potterverse, Montgomery defines disability as a political and collective matter and defines herself as an activist devoted to the exhausting work of social change. She also clarifies the relationships among fantasy, disability community, and the fight for inclusion.

Montgomery identifies the allure at the heart of the Potterverse: the discovery that you don't have to feel like a misfit because it turns out there is another world where you actually do fit. "Like Harry, and probably every other kid on the planet, I spent a significant amount of my childhood and adolescence not fitting in, knowing damn well I didn't fit in, and fantasizing about a world in which I 'really' belonged."[69] *Harry Potter* satisfies the longing to find a better fit between self and world. As a wheelchair and communication device user on the autism spectrum, Montgomery maneuvers through a world designed for people who walk, speak, and agree on certain norms. "I do my best to absorb the constant, unthinking grinding down that comes with running headfirst into barriers that could so easily be addressed, but somehow never are."[70] Her misfitting is a more intense version of the misfitting any child understands. She wants a world that is ready for her before she gets there, just as the wizarding world is ready for Harry before he finds it.

Montgomery identifies the ethical problem with the childhood fantasy "of a small and intimate world in which every mismatch between anyone else and me was resolved in my favor."[71] The Potterverse is fundamentally a "separatist fantasy" that favors a different elite instead of making the whole world more inclusive. "The topsy-turvy world is no freer of injustice than the one we have now: it's only that the injustice rains down on different people . . . I'm not interested in changing myself into the sort of person society automatically enables; I'm interested in changing society so that it enables all its members."[72] If *Harry Potter* fails to offer a world more inclusive than our own, what is the fantasy good for?

The Potterverse matters because it reproduces the delicious and relaxing sensation of finding yourself in disability community. You don't have to explain yourself. The people around you share your goals and frustrations, see and appreciate your efforts, and find the same things funny or infuriating. The feeling Montgomery gets when she drops into the fantasy world "is like the feeling that I get when I can finally spend a couple of hours with a couple of friends, talking about everyday frustrations and absurdities; it'll soothe me for a while and then it'll motivate me to get back up and try again."[73] The community hands back to you the energy and strength that the big world saps. It provides a respite from the hard work of misfitting and fighting for change.[74] "The disability rights community gives me strength. Partly by just existing. Partly by direct contact with people who respect what I'm trying to do and who understand why. Partly by the incremental gains that are being made. Partly by the angry resistance to the losses."[75] Separatism is not a permanent place to live, but it provides a necessary break from the grind.

Why turn to fantasy fiction, then, when disability community can give Montgomery the break she needs? *Harry Potter* books and movies are available any time, while multiple access barriers limit the time she can spend with disabled friends. These barriers include communication, money, transport, and fatigue. "I have too little time with too few friends and colleagues; we don't live near enough to one another, we don't have the time or the money or the stamina or the transportation access to get together, we hit access conflicts when we try to talk and type to one another, we're just overwhelmed."[76] When the barriers to real-life community loom too high, Harry and his friends provide relief from the "crushing isolation." Montgomery will start a *Harry Potter* movie, "turn on the captions and go through slowly, backing up when I'm pretty sure I've missed something."[77] Captioning and audiobooks provide access to fans who cannot grasp the stories through conventional reading and viewing practices.

HandiLand, that place where we don't have to struggle so hard to fit, that place ready for us before we get there, flickers intermittently. It appears briefly in the real world, at a school, on a trampoline, among a group of friends, then it disappears. In the meantime, while we work and wait, we have fantasy.

Ten

Runoff

Afroaquanauts in Landscapes of Sacrifice

———

Fantasy's cousin science fiction also envisions how young people with disabilities encounter public space. One of science fiction's gifts is the fashioning of future worlds. Earlier in this book I have discussed how children with disabilities rehearse their futures as assertive adults and challenge the future to turn partial inclusion into full inclusion. This chapter turns to Afrofuturism, an art form practiced by science fiction writers, musicians, and visual artists in Africa and across the African diaspora. Afrofuturism reflects the viewpoint of people immersed in risk and aware of historical atrocities who persist in envisioning and engineering a survivable future, and do so with panache.

This viewpoint arises from black history but also swims close to a disability epistemology. In chapter 6 I discussed how young people with intellectual disabilities navigate the problem of the future, but this worldview also reflects the experience of people exposed to environmental illness—many of whom are also people of color. In neighborhoods across the United States, African American children have disabilities because lead has poisoned the water in their taps and the paint on their walls. There is nothing wrong with having a disability. However, people in power do wrong when they create disabilities, then deny communities the means to care for themselves. Afrofuturist science fiction bears witness to such injustice. Just as the portkeys of British fantasy literature open up real worlds of human histories and feelings, the metaphors of Afrofuturist science fiction make the risks of environmental illness visible and tangible.

Sherri L. Smith's 2013 young adult dystopia *Orleans* imagines a blood-borne illness in the New Orleans of 2056 after multiple massive hurricanes. When the Delta Fever threatens to spread outside the Gulf region, the federal government declares it no longer part of the United States, cuts off all services, and erects a heavily policed quarantine wall. To survive in this abandoned society returning to swampy nature, people hunt and fish, barter and battle, form themselves into tribes based on blood type, and try to relieve the fever's pain by stealing cleaner blood. Fen de la Guerre, the teenage main character of *Orleans*, carries the disease, but her O-positive blood gives her some protection. She braves toxic and debilitating waters to secure a better life for the next generation. The novel follows her adventures as she evades blood hunters and tries to save an O-positive newborn baby from contracting the fever. Eventually they meet the scientist Daniel, who sneaks into Orleans with hopes of curing the Delta Fever and joins them in their quest.

Many observers draw parallels between the imaginary worlds of Afrofuturism and the realities of black life. What, then, is the relationship between science fiction and real life? It is not a one-on-one correspondence, but rather a set of metaphors opening the doors of insight. We might call these metaphors "significant distortions," following Samuel R. Delany. A reigning elder of Afrofuturist fiction, Delany explains that "in science fiction the future is only a writerly convention that allows the SF writer to indulge in a significant distortion of the present that sets up a rich and complex dialogue with the reader's here and now."[1] Afrofuturism takes science fiction tropes of interplanetary travel and alien species and retrofits them to black history and experience. However, *Orleans* features significant distortions different from outer space Afrofuturist tropes. Instead, its metaphors of disease and oppression spark a dialogue with our own watery planet. This chapter will focus on four significant distortions in *Orleans*: the quarantine wall, the toxic economy, runoff, and the Afroaquanaut. These metaphors unveil the surreal logic of environmental racism and the acts of imagination necessary to oppose it.

The metaphors of *Orleans* face down the contemporary politics of environmental illness for African American youth in urban landscapes of sacrifice across the United States. Afrofuturism has two poles, negative and positive. Positive Afrofuturism insists upon a better future, while negative Afrofuturism constructs dystopias that warn of a bleak future if we don't enact racial and environmental justice now. In its negative Afrofuturism, Smith's anarchic and authoritarian future city draws inspiration from severe and repeated flooding in the era of climate change and the abandonment of African Americans with disabilities during Hurricane Katrina (2005).

In its positive Afrofuturism, *Orleans* gives us a heroine dedicated to creating a decent survival niche for her people. With Afrofuturist panache, Fen is so adept at survival she seems to walk on water. She joins the bloodline of young black geniuses in African American science fiction who battle the forces militating against their survival.[2] Afronauts have a long tradition in Afrofuturism's interplanetary dreamscapes. We might call Fen de la Guerre an Afroaquanaut, who wades through alien landscapes here on Earth. In the words of redoubtable Afroaquanauts Parliament-Funkadelic, Fen attempts to "dance underwater and not get wet."[3] In the face of a government neglecting its basic duties, the teenage Fen embodies the bravery and self-sacrifice a real leader should have.

While astronauts wear space suits, Fen continually assesses and musters her own bodily forms of protection. These forms of protection include her sharp hearing, light tread, scarred arms to ward off blood hunters, and command of the local dialect. Elizabeth C. Hamilton calls such protective factors "technologies of survival" and writes that Afronaut figures in the arts "speak to the sustained feeling of isolation and otherness that people of color feel when traversing white spaces. The environments are sometimes hostile; so, the technologies that they wear are a necessity."[4] Thus, Fen's prowess speaks to positive Afrofuturism, her role as capable hero, but also to negative Afrofuturism, her body under threat. Her vulnerability matters as much as her strength.

Unlike Harry Potter, Fen won't discover one day that the pain is gone and all is well. As the scars on her arms attest, Fen has little chance of surviving whole. She will pay for her heroism with her life. Negative Afrofuturism, which Tiffany Barber calls "transgressive disfigurement," insists that we confront "the ruptured black body."[5] Like space explorers, young African Americans need life support systems like clean water, access to health care and disability services, and an end to state violence. Real-life Afroaquanauts struggle to survive the low-oxygen atmosphere of police brutality. "I can't breathe," said Eric Garner to the police officers choking him. Freddie Gray, who had asthma, asked officers for his inhaler but did not get it. He stopped breathing in the police van. Earth itself can be a toxic and alien planet.

The protagonist of *Orleans* who meets with state violence is female. In this Fen de la Guerre stands in for young African American women across the United States. Although media coverage focuses on black men, police brutality visits black women just as often. According to Andrea J. Ritchie, the evidence shows that "young women of color experience every form and context of police violence" that young men do, and at the same rates.[6] For example, "Racial profiling studies analyzing the experiences of women of color separately from those of men of color conclude that there is an *identical pattern of racial disparities in police stops for both men and women*."[7] The significant distortions of Afrofuturism reveal commonalities of oppression and resistance in young men's and women's lives across varied landscapes of environmental sacrifice.

Afrofuturism reveals kinships among locales and struggles that might seem very different from each other at first glance. To demonstrate this point I apply the four significant distortions from *Orleans* not to Hurricane Katrina—the obvious and intended real-life parallel—but to the lead-poisoning crises in Baltimore and Flint. *Orleans* holds up an Afrofuturist mirror to the young women and girls who protested the lead-poisoning crisis in Flint, Michigan, and to the life of Freddie Gray, who had learning and physical disabilities from childhood lead exposure. For Gray, Fen de la Guerre, and many young people of color with environmental illness, disability has served as a primary trigger of state surveillance and harm.[8] Exposure to toxic runoff leads to running off from police.

Four Significant Distortions

The Quarantine Wall

Orleans transforms the invisible boundaries of race and disease into the literal metaphor of the quarantine wall. As Isiah Lavender III writes, "SF's ability to literalize metaphor heightens what is often in our societies submerged as invisible and yet trenchantly remains, like divisive racial boundaries, a strong feature in the histories of race and disease."[9] For example, *Orleans* does not portray differential environmental risk as hard to track or easy to deny. Instead, it seals off the high-risk zone with a militarized quarantine wall and declares the Gulf Coast region no longer part of the "The Outer States of America." This negative Afrofuturism displays the consequences of current segregation if left unchecked.

The term "quarantine wall" signifies more than a necessary and temporary medical isolation. It declares a group no longer part of the larger society. In *Orleans*, the wall shields the rest of the country not only from disease but also from the responsibility of caring for those locked inside it. Armed troops man a wall twenty to thirty feet high and thick surrounded by protective moats and swamps and equipped with drones that can sniff out Delta Fever.[10]

The novel makes literal the invisible walls that surround many communities of color.

In *Orleans*'s commentary on climate change, the Gulf region has endured a series of ever-stronger hurricanes, beginning with Katrina in 2005 and culminating in Hurricane Jesus in 2019. Pollution of the Delta water results in mass epidemics. Delta Fever symptoms include fatigue, yellow skin, mobility problems, cramps, and hallucinations, but in the book's present, most people live with the symptoms rather than dying from them.[11] Among the worst affected, people with the AB blood type "shoot, swallow, and smoke anything to forget the pain of living with, but not dying from, the Fever."[12] Walled off from medical care, Delta residents endure the fever the best they can. They numb the pain with their own toxic technologies of survival. The quarantine wall echoes the medical model of disability: If you cannot be cured, you are consigned to social death. It also echoes the psychic pain of racial segregation.

The Gulf region survives in its own ingenious ways, yet also dies every day for want of the things the Outer States of America could provide. The Outer States withholds help in healing the environment, treating the fever, and providing disability services. Small-scale Gulf enterprises, such as shellfish beds and hydroponic greenhouses, demonstrate the power of nature to filter the water and help the Delta heal itself.[13] However, the devastated region needs outside help for large-scale environmental cleanup. Orleans scientists never conducted research to heal or treat the fever. Instead, they encouraged tribalism in the postapocalyptic society and studied its effects. *Orleans* likens their research to the US Public Health Service's infamous Tuskegee syphilis study, which tracked 399 poor African American men with syphilis for forty years but never treated any of them with penicillin.[14] Daniel exclaims, "It's like Tuskegee all over again. They never wanted a cure."[15] Smith extends medical abuse into future centuries to demonstrate that scientific racism will continue unless people deliberately interrupt it.

The Outer States also fails to assist people with disabilities. Smith underscores how chronic conditions become fatal in the absence of care. After the storms, "The list of no-longer-treatable diseases grew: diabetes, asthma, cancer."[16] Fen de la Guerre describes the abandonment after Hurricane Jesus to her new companion Daniel: "The Government give up, say everybody evacuate. But can't everybody fit on a road out of town at the same time. Some people can't even get up outta they beds, so what *they* gonna do? No gas for the cars, and the roads be clogged, and people be needing they medicine and whatnot. . . . The Government say they can't save us. There ain't enough of us left to bother."[17] The States consigns Orleans to social death.

The author knows firsthand how a lagging disaster response endangers people with disabilities. Her diabetic mother, Joan Marie Smith, was stranded in New Orleans after Hurricane Katrina with a dwindling insulin supply. Smith recalled in an interview, "It was devastating and while she was down there I was on the internet doing research trying to figure out how to get her out. Which actually worked; we got her out."[18] In the novel's acknowledgments Smith thanks "the Coast Guard for listening when no one else would, and helping evacuate my mother from New Orleans five days after the storm, three days after the levee broke, and the day before her insulin ran out."[19] Equipped with fewer resources, nearly everyone left behind seems to be black or mixed race in the postflood world of *Orleans*.[20] Smith evokes the surreal abandonment of the Lower Ninth Ward's low-income, primarily African American residents during Hurricane Katrina.

While the blood tribes improvise their technologies of survival, a scientist coming in from the Outer States has the luxury of a high-tech space suit. The containment suit symbolizes the differential risks of climate change for those inside and outside the wall. Daniel, a young scientist who sneaks into Orleans with hopes of curing the Delta Fever that killed his brother, wears this thick, impermeable wetsuit. He trades off narrating the story with Fen de la Guerre, who comes from Orleans and already carries the disease. Smith states, "Like an umbilical cord, [the suit] also processed bodily water, sweat, and other secretions into pouches, breaking solids into fluids, and distilled fluids into drinking water."[21] Daniel is a healthy ecology of one. Unlike the people of Orleans, his wearable wastewater treatment system protects him from disease. Daniel can even cause harm while remaining immune from it. Aiming to conduct medical research, he carries vials of ultrarefined Delta Fever virus that could wipe out the region's entire population.[22] He accidentally loses the vials in the course of the novel's adventures, and Fen watches him cry with guilt: "Daniel blink and I hear the tears in his eyes being sucked away into drinking water by his suit. I just can't bring myself to care."[23] Immersed in risk, Fen cannot afford the luxury of tears over scientific arrogance.

Smith contrasts Daniel's technology and formal education with Fen's deep knowledge of place and risk. While Daniel is a typical science fiction scientist-hero, Fen de la Guerre joins a long line of Afrofuturist "young black geniuses battling oppressive forces on behalf of themselves, their friends, and their various communities."[24] Instead of an immunity suit, she has a genius for hiding from danger. As a child her educated parents taught her how to "talk tribe," a close cognate of Black English, to conceal her naivete from Orleans's many predators. Talking tribe is like being a chameleon, hiding in plain sight "so no one can find me—and I'll be safe from owls and hawks."[25] Fen embodies an ethic of care. As she climbs up trees and across cars and rooftops, her body compensates for the extra weight of the newborn girl left in her protection. "This'd be easier without a baby strapped to my chest, but a lot of things be easier without that."[26] In the weight of the baby Fen feels the imbalance of differential environmental risk. She has seven days to protect Baby Girl "before the Fever take hold in a newborn."[27] Baby Girl counters the negative Afrofuturism of dystopia with positive Afrofuturism: she represents Fen's hope for a future generation to escape unharmed.

The trope of the quarantine wall illuminates the lead-poisoning crises in Flint, Michigan, and the Sandtown neighborhood of Baltimore. In both cities, racial segregation, postindustrial capital, and government malfeasance threw up walls no less real for being invisible. The quarantine walls shielded the (ir)responsible parties not only from environmental risk but from the obligation to care for those trapped inside. Lead exposure, common in postindustrial and low-income neighborhoods, creates disabilities in children. "Lead is a potent neurotoxin, and childhood lead poisoning has an impact on many developmental and biological processes, most notably intelligence, behavior, and overall life achievement," explains Dr. Mona Hanna-Attisha, pediatrician and public health researcher at Hurley Children's Hospital / Michigan State University Medical Center in Flint.[28] A soluble metal, lead leaches into drinking water via pipes or connectors. Infants bathe in the toxic water and drink it in their formula. Landlords have a legal obligation to remove lead-based paint. If they do not, toddlers like Freddie Gray and his siblings eat lead paint flakes, which taste as sweet as candy.

The story of lead poisoning in Flint and Baltimore's Sandtown neighborhood begins with racial segregation followed by the flight of capital. For more than a century, Sandtown has served as a containment zone for black people; however, under legal segregation at least they had jobs. African American steelworkers lived there because it had the closest housing open to them, so Sandtown declined when the steel mills closed.[29] By 1982 Baltimore's working-class economy had collapsed, losing half its jobs in primary metals, shipbuilding repair, and transportation assembly.[30] The people who stayed in Sandtown were the ones who could not afford to get out, and slumlording replaced homeownership. Thus the quarantine zone of poverty and lead poisoning replaced the containment zone of legal segregation. No concrete wall kept them in Sandtown, but poverty, industrial decline, and the old Jim Crow boundary lines did the job just as well.

Flint is also a quarantine zone. State officials poisoned the city because they no longer saw it as part of the state. Like Daniel in his encounter suit, they could harm Flint without harming themselves. Flint lives under emergency management laws that require austerity measures to balance the budget. These austerity measures came at the expense of clean water. After the cash-strapped Detroit Water and Sewage Department jacked up its prices, a series of Flint emergency managers made and executed the decision to use the Flint River as an interim water source.[31] They began drawing water from the postindustrial river in April 2014 without corrosion controls to prevent lead in old plumbing connections from leaching into the water supply. Elevated blood lead levels in young children soared, more so in African American children. In neglecting corrosion controls, emergency managers violated the basic principles of Infrastructure Engineering 101. This neglect could only happen because state officials saw Flint as a foreign planet whose resident aliens did not have the same bodily needs as humans. No wonder Afroaquanauts experience feelings of isolation and otherness.

Like Baltimore, Flint has weathered racial segregation and the flight of capital. The birthplace of General Motors and the United Auto Workers, Flint used to have a very high standard of living. As GM closed plants between 1980 and 2005, Flint lost 41 percent of its jobs.[32] By 2009, "The Flint area had lost more than 70,000 GM jobs since peak employment in 1968."[33] General Motors withdrew the jobs but left the polluted river behind. Past housing discrimination had left now-unemployed African Americans stranded in the central city just as the state of Michigan began to build a quarantine wall around it. Michigan's economic planning failed to imagine a future for black workers. The state focused infrastructure development on the white suburbs and left the central city to fend for itself, which "lessened the potential for new private investment" and "led to economic disinvestment and central city job loss."[34] Refused the technologies to support productive lives, Flint residents watched their city turn into an Afrofuturist dystopia.

Michigan evicted Flint from the larger democracy through emergency management, which opened the door to environmental racism. Since the collapse of the auto industry in the 1980s, appointed emergency managers govern impoverished Michigan cities rather than elected mayors and city councils. Emergency managers have a free hand at making decisions. This loss of local control overwhelmingly affects African Americans.

A startling 51% of African Americans residing in Michigan have been under the governance of emergency management laws at some point since 2008. . . . Even more shocking, in a state that is majority non-Hispanic White (76.6%), only 2.4% of Whites statewide were ever directly under the governance of an emergency manager during the same time period.[35]

Problems with the Flint River water began as soon as the switch in water sources. According to Marc Lamont Hill, "Had the authorities actually listened to Flint's residents, the crisis could have ended after a few weeks."[36] Instead, state agencies and officials denied and covered up these problems for more than a year and a half. The damage will now cost years and hundreds of millions of dollars to fix.

In Flint as in Sandtown, differential environmental risk correlates with both race and poverty. Dr. Hanna-Attisha and her colleagues conducted the Flint lead-poisoning study that exposed the problem to the public. Their study established correlations among race, poverty, and contamination. Flint's entire population is 70.6 percent African American, and the proportion of children under five with elevated blood lead levels rose from 2.4 percent to 4.9 percent after the switch to Flint River water. However, the areas of Flint with high lead levels were the poorest and were also 78.8 percent African American, and there the elevated blood levels rose from 4 percent to 10.6 percent.[37] After analyzing the government's slow response to the health issues of poor African Americans, an independent inquiry concluded, "The facts of the Flint water crisis lead us to the inescapable conclusion that this is a case of environmental injustice."[38] While poor black neighborhoods may not have a wall around them, elevated blood lead levels revealed their invisible boundaries.

The quarantine wall around Orleans shields the rest of the country not only from disease but also from the responsibility of caring for those locked inside it. The quarantine wall around Flint shielded state officials not only from environmental risk but from the responsibility of caring for Flint residents. The emails of Dennis Muchmore, chief of staff to Michigan governor Rick Snyder, reveal the depth of official denial. Muchmore knew and yet he did not know; he cared and yet he did not care. The governor's chief aide expressed concerns about water contamination long before the story broke in the press in September 2015. He had emailed his colleagues, "If GM refuses to use the water in their plant and our own agencies are warning people not to drink it . . . we look pretty stupid hiding behind some financial statement."[39] Muchmore did nothing, however, because no one in state government was willing to pay to fix the problem. Michigan's money was not Flint's money, just as Flint's problem was not the state's problem, even though Flint was under state emergency control.

After the scandal broke, Muchmore helped the governor erect a wall of denial. In September 2015, Muchmore emailed the governor, "It's really the city's water system that needs to deal with it. . . . I can't figure out why the state is responsible."[40] Muchmore had urged his colleagues, "Since we're in charge, we can hardly ignore the people of Flint." Nonetheless, that's exactly what they did: ignore the people of Flint while in charge of them. A quarantine wall permits power to seize control while denying care and responsibility. An Afroaquanaut musters her own resources as she looks trouble in the face. A state official on the other side of the wall can afford to look the other way.

The Toxic Economy

A toxic landscape becomes a toxic economy: people survive by harming themselves and others. This economy depends on the circulation of water, blood, and chemicals but also the liquidity of capital. Clean blood is the principal commodity in the toxic economy of Orleans. With its stark portrait of economic exploitation, *Orleans* like other science fiction "can help us overcome the obstacles to our full understanding of capital's role in environmental crisis."[41] Blood hunters assess and threaten the bodies of Fen and Baby Girl according to the market value of their O-positive blood type: "The Fever be in us, but it ain't eating O blood up from the inside like it do other types. So O types got to be extra careful of hunters and the farms where they be taking they kidnapped victims to drain them alive."[42] Blood hunters would love to capture a prize like Baby Girl. As Fen states, "Baby Girl brand-new. Cleanest blood there is. She ain't got the Fever in her yet, and won't if I be careful, don't give her Orleans water, or cuts to taint her blood."[43] Baby Girl puts the future in Afrofuturism: she has a chance to survive.

Orleans paints the toxic economy as violence against African American women. Fen refers to it as "blood whoring" and "blood slavery."[44] The sexual violence of the blood farm parallels the sexualized violence of police brutality African American women face in real life. Andrea J. Ritchie points out "the pervasive sexualization of young women of color during police stops, sexual intimidation, and extortion of sexual favors in exchange for their freedom."[45] On her own behalf and on Baby Girl's, Fen de la Guerre engages in feminist resistance against capitalist patriarchy. When Fen was nine years old, hunters and bloodhounds captured her and took her to a blood farm, a literal metaphor for child prostitution and the female experience of slavery. The madam took her to the outbuildings behind the big house and told her a gentleman wanted "a virgin, untouched by needle or knife."[46] Smith describes the theft of blood as if it were rape: "When he enter me, it be through the skin. First a swift wipe of a cold cotton pad, then a needle, sharp and hot, into the biggest vein of my right arm."[47] Like nineteenth-century slavery, the blood slavery of the twenty-first century relies on the rape and rupture of black bodies.

Orleans blends this negative Afrofuturism with the positive Afrofuturism of heroics. Her options limited, Fen resists patriarchy through self-harm. After the "gentleman" buys her outright, Fen wraps her arms around a hot stew pot and burns her arms "near to the bone." "Burn marks so thick, ain't nobody ever gonna get a needle in the easy way."[48] Fen also protects Baby Girl from patriarchy. She leaves Baby Girl in the care of Father John, whom she knows and trusts, only to find him with a dialysis machine preparing to drain off Baby Girl's blood. He sings the hymn "There Is Power in the Blood" while looking for an infant-sized needle.[49] When Fen returns, she "tackled him, sweeping a hand across the tray of instruments. Needles, scalpels, knives, she cut her own flesh gathering them into her fist, and she thrust them with one angry, desperate motion into the priest's heart."[50] She can only save Baby Girl by harming herself and others, using medical tools already co-opted from care into exploitation.

The toxic economy of Sandtown depends on the flow of capital and the circulation of water, lead, paint, and blood. These two kinds of liquidity cycle together, create disability, and turn young black bodies into countable commodities. Ruth Ann Norton is the executive director of the Coalition to End Childhood Lead Poisoning. In 1993, when Freddie Gray was a child, Norton would walk down the streets of Sandtown and "parents could tell me their kids' lead level right off the bat, before they could tell me the name of their child's school or their teacher."[51] Out of medical necessity, the children's blood had become quantifiable data.

The numbers for environmental risk correlate with both race and poverty. Sandtown is 97 percent black. Saul Kerpelman, a Baltimore attorney who has represented clients in more than four thousand lead-poisoning lawsuits over three decades, says that "nearly 99.9 percent of my clients were black. . . . That's the sad fact to life in the ghetto that the only living conditions people can afford will likely poison their kids."[52] Lack of decent, affordable housing creates a quarantine wall, trapping families within the lead-poisoning zone and subjecting them to the toxic economy of slumlording. Blood hunters track Fen and Baby Girl because their O-positive blood type has a high market value. In Sandtown, blood lead levels and Maryland judiciary lawsuit case files track the grisly economics of slumlording and environmental racism.

Sandtown residents live off the toxic economy through the drug trade and the lead checks they receive from lawsuits. Nonresidents profit from the toxic economy of Sandtown through slumlording, predatory finance, legal fees, policing, and electoral politics. Freddie Gray's family won a lead exposure settlement from their landlord Stanley Rochkind in 2008, but Rochkind's investment in substandard housing extended far beyond the Gray's apartment building. Between 2001 and 2015 hundreds of tenants sued Rochkind for lead paint exposure.[53] In 2001 the State of Maryland Department of Environmental Quality reached a lead abatement settlement regarding 1,250 rental properties with 87 separate entities in which Rochkind had a controlling interest.[54] Predatory finance companies also profit from lead poisoning. Access Funding, for instance, visits young people with lead-derived cognitive impairments in their Baltimore homes and offers to buy their structured settlements for cents on the dollar. Freddie Gray sold $146,000 of his settlement for $18,300.[55] In *Orleans*, Father John co-opts medical tools from care into exploitation, preying upon a child. In Sandtown, finance companies co-opt lead checks from redress into exploitation, preying upon young adults with intellectual disabilities.

In Gray's Baltimore, police promotions and electoral politics depend on collecting and counting black bodies. David Simon, former *Baltimore Sun* reporter and author of *The Wire* and *The Corner*, says that Baltimore police officers' "rounding up bodies for street dealing, drug possession, loitering and such—the easiest and most self-evident arrests a cop can make—is nonetheless the path to enlightenment and promotion and some additional pay."[56] Police and politicians hunt stats for their own professional advancement, and African American bodies supply the numbers.

In a few decades, Sandtown went from the old Jim Crow of residential segregation to the new Jim Crow of mass incarceration. The War on Drugs of the 1980s and 1990s opened the door to arrests without probable cause. Then Martin O'Malley, Baltimore mayor from 1999 to 2007, rewarded police solely on number of arrests, seeking good crime statistics to bolster his ambitions for higher political office.[57] Neill Franklin, a former Baltimore police officer, says, "And in these searches, we were stopping and searching anyone who might look like they fit the bill of a drug user . . . officers did whatever they had to do to lock up as many people as they could to satisfy police headquarters."[58] Often for petty crimes or no crime at all, arrests reached a high of a hundred thousand in a single year, and the excessive policing continues.[59] Like the blood farm, Sandtown serves as a profitable holding tank for black bodies.

Runoff

In landscapes of environmental sacrifice, runoff leads to running off from troops or police. Unchecked pollutions cause disabilities, and the state responds with quarantine and excessive policing instead of a prosthetic community. *Orleans*'s police state reflects the African American millennial generation's painful understanding of law enforcement since the War on Drugs. The Anti-Drug Abuse Acts of 1986 and 1988 and the 1994 crime bill led to people of color's mass incarceration for drug offenses. "As law enforcement budgets exploded, so did prison and jail populations . . . [by 1991] one fourth of young African American men were now under the control of the criminal justice system."[60] Not only individuals but entire zones find themselves under such control, which replaces care and prevention for young people with disabilities.

Escape seems the only healthy option. At the conclusion of *Orleans*, Fen braves the armed troops on the quarantine wall to help Baby Girl escape from Delta Fever. First running and then wading toward the guards through waist-high muddy water, Fen creates a distraction so Daniel can smuggle Baby Girl into the Outer States through a crack in the wall.[61] As the spotlights converge on Fen and ignore Daniel, he uses his immunity to save a young life. Physical courage, local knowledge, technology, and science come together to prevent environmental illness. Fen cradles a bundled-up coat as if it were an infant, believing the soldiers won't shoot a woman carrying a baby.[62] She is wrong:

> Her arms were raised, her face turned up, the bundle held high in the air. She rotated in a slow circle as the rain washed the mud from her skin.
> For an instant, she looked at him. The moment hung in the air, Fen's mouth curving into a smile, seeing Daniel and the baby almost there. Almost there. She turned away.
> A shot rang out. The bundle fell from her hands.[63]

This moment seals the pact between runoff and running off from state violence. Polluted Delta water covers Fen as the rain falls and she splashes through the mud. The slow violence of toxic water leads to sudden death from a gun. The Afroaquanaut succumbs, but in service to Afrofuturist ideals. She releases Baby Girl, now named Enola after East New Orleans, into the care of an unknown but safer planet in the Outer States.

While an act of heroism, Fen's death also embodies a toxic economy in which care of others requires hurting oneself. As Therí Pickens writes, the intersection of blackness, womanhood, and disability forecloses the possibility of an overcoming narrative. Pickens declares, "For those who have difficulty imagining disability as triumphant or as an advantage, the victories (where they occur) appear meager at best."[64] While Fen is a strong black woman, her vulnerability to violence and disease underlies her heroism as much as her courage. She matters in her totality.

Freddie Gray also found that runoff led to running off from police. Right before his last arrest, "He ran, like a lot of black men do when we see cops, because for our generation, police officers have been the most consistent terrorists in our neighborhoods," writes D. Watkins. He adds, "Almost every black person I know from a poor neighborhood can give you a collection of nightmare stories about the BCPD."[65] Under the best of circumstances it is difficult for young adults with intellectual disabilities to make the transition from school to work. In Sandtown, it is nearly impossible. For young people with impairments from lead poisoning, the missing safety net includes education, job supports, and service plans tailored to their needs. Ruth Ann Norton reports that "a child who was poisoned with lead is seven times more likely to drop out of school and six times more likely to end up in the juvenile justice system."[66] The criminal justice system steps in as the only sorry substitute for disability services.

For Gray the slow violence of environmental illness culminated in the sudden violence of police brutality. He died at the hands of Baltimore police after his April 12, 2015, arrest for "running unprovoked." As officers folded him awkwardly into the back of a police van, his leg seemed injured. The officers drove Gray around without a seat belt, making four stops while ignoring his pleas for medical attention. When they arrived at the police station half an hour later, Gray could not breathe. He died a week later from an 80 percent severed spine. All the officers were acquitted of wrongdoing in the case. The criminal justice system harmed him then denied him the means of care, operating in the same ethical void as the environmental racism that caused his disabilities in the first place.

Throughout this book I have used the term *prosthetic community* to describe the cluster of people, money, education, and job supports necessary to secure a decent future for young adults with disabilities. In *Orleans*, Fen and Daniel serve as a prosthetic community who furnish the technologies of survival Baby Girl needs. With a strong prosthetic community in place, it might have been possible for Freddie Gray to live a long, fulfilling life instead of dying in police custody at twenty-five. In the absence of a prosthetic community, the Baltimore police stepped in as a sorry substitute. "Poverty, injustice, and reading comprehension issues go hand in hand, like white cops and innocent verdicts," writes D. Watkins, who also grew up in poor black Baltimore.[67] Disability, injustice, and poverty live together in one house.

Freddie Gray is one of many men and women of color with disabilities killed by US police in recent years. In their study for the Ruderman Family Foundation, Lawrence Carter-Long and David M. Perry found that "disabled individuals make up a third to half of all people killed by law enforcement officers. Disabled individuals make up the majority of those killed in use-of-force cases that attract widespread attention."[68] Disability and police brutality go hand in hand. Young adults with lead-induced disabilities deserve the positive Afrofuturism of gleaming prosthetics and brand-new facilities. Instead, they get racial profiling.

By all accounts Gray lived off his lead checks, family help, and his own small part in the toxic economy of drug dealing. "In Freddie's case, there were some learning issues," said his lawyer, Creston Smith. "He had some learning disabilities from lead paint exposure. He didn't read or write perfectly, and that causes a person to seek economic independence other ways."[69] What was Freddie Gray doing when he could have been learning to read, write, and master a trade? He was running away from the police. As a sophomore he went to a Department of Juvenile Services facility and never returned to special education at his regular high school.[70]

Gray's time in juvie gives him something in common with many other Sandtown kids as well as African American students with disabilities across the country. A quarter of Sandtown children between the ages of ten and seventeen have spent time in a juvenile facility.[71] There isn't much else to do besides getting arrested: there is no swimming pool, no recreation center, and no police athletic league.[72] Across the United States, young African Americans with disabilities find themselves in the pipeline from special education to prison. In fact, "There is a profound racial dimension regarding the youth with disabilities who wind up incarcerated. Ultimately, compared to white students with disabilities, Black students with disabilities are four times as likely to be educated in a correctional facility."[73] We could see the justice system as a scattershot version of Orleans, confining young black men and women with disabilities.

Caught in the Baltimore Police Department's cycle of catch and release, Gray was a defendant in twenty-three cases between the ages of eighteen and twenty-five. As Nicolás Medina Mora reports:

> Most of the criminal cases brought against Gray did not result in a conviction . . .
> Court records show that Gray was arrested over and over again, for everything from possessing drugs to playing dice in a public housing development where he didn't live. Over and over again, records show his family and friends accrued debts with bail agents to keep him out of jail. Over and over again, overworked prosecutors dropped all charges.[74]

Gray spent most of his twenty-third year in jail without being charged. His family devoted their time and at least $29,000 to bailing him out rather than helping him enter the world of work.[75] The only job training Gray received was behind bars. *Washington Post* reporter Terrence McCoy writes:

> There, he learned brick masonry and harbored ambitions of getting into the trade. But even that seemed a stretch to some. "I don't know much about brick masonry because I am not very handy myself, but, you know, is he someone that I would want to plan my walkway?" said psychologist Neil Hoffman, who interviewed Gray as part of the lead-poisoning lawsuit. "No."[76]

Freddie Gray had a future, just as Sandtown has a future despite its toxic economy. We do not know what Freddie Gray's life could have been if he had experienced a strong prosthetic community instead of excessive policing. The toxic consequences of lead paint and runoff gave way to the toxic consequences of running off from the police. His death helped inspire the rise of the Black Lives Matter movement, staking a claim to a better future.

The Afroaquanaut

Fen de la Guerre, survivor of relentless floods, is an Afroaquanaut who renegotiates the physical laws of life on Earth. Despite the gravity of her situation she floats when she steps, like Neil Armstrong on the moon. She always marks the impact of her tread on risky ground, aware of her footprints on a fragile earth. She picks her way swiftly across Rooftops, a grassland of houses buried under silt and mud. "Aw, hell.' I start to run before the sinkhole take me with it. The ground be too damn soft here to be messing around like this. So I keep moving, watching my feet, and finally the soft fall of sod stop behind me."[77] The Afroaquanaut moves so fluently it seems miraculous to the outsider Daniel. Fen seems to walk on water.

> And then she stepped out onto the water and walked away, barely disturbing the surface as she strode toward the open arms of the statue in the middle of the lake.
>
> It take him a full half minute to pick his jaw up again. That boy be so blind sometimes, I don't know how he make it on his own. "Stay there," I call back to him. "You too heavy to be following me."
>
> Beneath my feet, the hard top of a car shift enough to make me glad he be listening and stay on the wall. I clutch Baby Girl to me and catch my balance.[78]

The young people of Flint are Afroaquanauts with the optimism to "dance underwater and not get wet" and the strength to push for change. Poetry is one of their technologies of survival. The slam poetry team of Flint's RAISE IT UP! Youth Arts and Awareness engage in the negative Afrofuturism of social critique and the positive Afrofuturism of staking a claim for their own survival. "Poetry is a way to let the world know that we are here and we aren't going anywhere,"[79] says Destiny Monet, eighteen. The team's collective poem "Flint" reflects the political priorities of African American youth in a landscape of environmental sacrifice. On February 28, 2016, the team performed "Flint" for a local audience who responded with cheers. Danielle Horton, nineteen, wants to counter the notion that Flint's young people deserve anything less than the best. "No, when you go out of town people pity you. They have all of these negative connotations of Flint and they don't even know us."[80] It's hard for outsiders to imagine the vibrant life inside quarantine walls.

Rejecting pity, the poets take a certain disability pride in their Flint identity while critiquing the injustice that created it. The chorus of "Flint" goes, "Pay for your poison / the girls and boys and / the city can't drink / lead altering the way we think."[81] Rather than distancing themselves from their city's toxic legacy, they claim it. The poets speak to the people outside the quarantine wall, informing them that Flint holds fast to its hope for the future. Insider's knowledge of the city comes with a cost, but its area code beats through them and keeps them going. "You ain't from the Fli? / You ain't familiar with famine, / The 810 in my pulse is all I need to keep standing."[82] Like lead, the city runs through their veins. Immersed in risk and aware of injustice, these Afroaquanauts persist in envisioning a survivable future, and do so with panache.

The Flint poets critique the toxic cycle of liquidity and hold state officials accountable for compromising their futures. They portray Flint as a woman with a blood disability denied care by Michigan governor Rick Snyder. Water filtration, like dialysis, could save her life. "I heard her holler as homeboy hung her out to dry, a drained cry. Never dialyzed the river that is her blood line . . . got mucked up." The poets and the city itself form a disability community denied decent care, like the blood tribes of *Orleans*. On the other side of the quarantine wall, Snyder "relaxes in his Ann Arbor home passing bills for the exact crime he committed in Flint." Politicians have turned Flint into a blood farm: "Policy always tried to pimp her out." Even though lead poisoning is "altering the way we think / futures gone in a blink," the RAISE IT UP! poets nonetheless rehearse a future for themselves. "If I ain't got it today . . . Trust I'mma have it tomorrow."[83] Like Afrofuturism, Flint poets trust that the future holds promise for young African Americans with environmental disabilities.

The young women of Flint raise their voices loud enough for people on the other side of the quarantine wall to hear them. President Obama visited Flint seven months after the crisis broke because an eight-year-old girl wrote him a letter and asked him to come. Amariyanna Copeny, who reigned as Little Miss Flint 2016, wrote the president, "I am one of the children that is effected by this water, and I've been doing my best to march in protest and to speak out for all the kids that live here in Flint."[84] The White House announced plans for President Obama's April 27, 2016, visit by posting online his letter to Miss Copeny accepting her invitation. Appearing at rallies in her beauty queen sash and tiara, Mari Copeny had rashes and dried skin on her arms from the poisoned water.[85] Whether meeting with the president or traveling to Washington, DC, to hear Governor Rick Snyder testify before Congress, Little Miss Flint asserted the beauty, activism, and future of Flint youth.

Like Jennifer Keelan twenty-six years before her, Amariyanna Copeny is another eight-year-old protester whose image circulated across the nation. In an Associated Press photograph, Little Miss Flint stands alone in a limitless field of snow, an Afroaquanaut floating in the frozen toxic water of

Fig. 16. Amariyanna Copeny, the reigning Little Miss Flint, at a protest on March 6, 2016. Jake May / *The Flint Journal–MLive.com* via AP Photo.

environmental sacrifice. Staring calmly at the camera, Copeny holds a sign reading "#Justice for Flint." While immersed in risk, the Afroaquanaut musters her considerable resources and insists on a survivable future. Among her resources are her warm winter clothes, her sash and tiara, and her ability to look trouble in the face.

Life Supports

The metaphors of Afrofuturism distort present reality just enough to help readers recognize the significant contours of environmental injustice across different contexts. These significant distortions offer working models for the interactions of race and disability. *Orleans* also gives us Fen de la Guerre, a teenage hero with disabilities who shows us what leadership ought to look like. In its heroism and adventure, *Orleans* allows readers to grasp the ethics at work in landscapes of sacrifice. Like Freddie Gray and many other African Americans, Fen de la Guerre finds that society regards her very existence as a threat. Her devotion to the next generation's survival makes her willing to meet that threat head on. Although constraints on her life abound, she strains against them. She runs up against the boundaries, "swirling through the water, spinning like the wheel that turns the world."[86]

Young life strives and deserves to live. Its survival depends greatly on its own initiative, and also greatly on the healthy or toxic ground from which it eats and drinks. Like Orleans, Sandtown and Flint survive in their own ingenious ways, yet also die every day for want of the things the Outer States of America could provide. Across a galaxy of American cities, Afroaquanauts navigate risky terrain. They could travel further and last longer on this planet with better life supports.

Conclusion

Tomorrowland

Kids with disabilities grow up into adults with disabilities. I conclude with some thoughts about prosthetic community, intersectionality, and disability community in the transition to the Tomorrowland of adulthood. Throughout this book I have argued that young people with disabilities need a flourishing prosthetic community in order to thrive. I have pointed to obvious resources like wheelchairs, service dogs, and reduced stigmas, but less obvious resources, too, like clean air and water, living wages for families and care workers, and an end to police brutality, mass incarceration, animal cruelty, and climate change. These resources don't come cheap, but they are necessary for real equality. Chief goals for the transition to adulthood include the greatest possible independence and a disability community of peers. However, independence and peer networks also rely on an ample prosthetic community.

Take, for example, one marker of adulthood: sex. Even sex, which might seem a private and individual activity, requires the public sphere of the prosthetic community. Lacking the right supports, young adults with disabilities cannot achieve healthy sexual relationships and sovereignty over their own bodies. As Russell Shuttleworth writes, sexual intimacy relies on "cultivating supportive and communal contexts" like "the Disability Rights Movement, disability-related work environments and peer support from other disabled people in general."[1] Healthy sex requires disability community, and disability community requires prosthetic community.

Disability studies scholarship on sex tends to focus on eliminating barriers to sexual access and dismantling the stereotype that people with disabilities are all asexual. However, we can't talk about freedom of sexual choice without talking about freedom from sexual assault. Young adults with disabilities need both kinds of freedom to achieve full sexual agency. And disabled youth experience sexual violence with horrific frequency. Children and teenagers with certain disabilities, intellectual disability among them, bear the greatest risk. Few researchers venture into this area; however, one comprehensive study of six nations concluded that minors with intellectual disabilities face a risk of sexual violence 4.6 times higher than nondisabled minors.[2]

While all young people with disabilities face significant challenges, there is a spectrum of sexual privilege dependent on type of disability but also on race, income, parenting, and access to prosthetic community. Young adults on the fortunate end of the spectrum have involved and loving parents, middle-class comforts, white privilege, and strong prosthetic communities. They stand a higher chance of healthy sexual relationships. On the least privileged end of the spectrum we find young adults with greater racial diversity, intellectual, behavioral, and communicative disabilities, low income, no parents or abusive parents, and a weak prosthetic community. The chance of sexual assault is much higher on this end of the spectrum. Two young adult novels from the United States illustrate the contrast between the two ends of the spectrum. *Girls Like Us* and *The Fault in Our Stars* demonstrate that full sexual agency requires disability community and prosthetic community, whether we are talking about recovery from sexual assault or the expression of sexual desire.

Girls Like Us

Girls Like Us features two narrators, Biddy and Quincy, who come from the less privileged end of the spectrum. They are young women from Texas, one white and one black, both wards of the state. One of the few young adult novels featuring narrators with intellectual disabilities, *Girls Like Us* chronicles their transition from high school to work. Neither has experienced much support in the past. Biddy grew up with a verbally abusive grandmother. Quincy grew up in a series of foster homes, some of which "treated me worse than a dog."[3] A sufficient prosthetic community for the first time in their lives makes disability community possible. Gradually they form a bond close enough to tell the truth about sexual abuse. They also bring their boss, a woman with a physical disability, into their alliance. Communication makes all the difference. For Biddy and Quincy, words mean the difference between safety and danger. In unsafe spaces, words license harm and then ostracize the person harmed. In safe spaces, words console and rectify.

In their new prosthetic community several assets bolster their independence. Ms. Delamino, their new job counselor, practices what professionals call person-centered advocacy. She matches them with jobs that suit their interests and talents in the home of a decent and trustworthy employer. The new service plan calls for Biddy to clean and care for Elizabeth, a widow in her sixties who uses a walker, while Quincy works at a supermarket deli. They share the apartment over the garage at the widow's home. Ms. Delamino is astute enough to place the two young women together, thinking their strengths and weaknesses will balance each other out.[4] Sure enough, Biddy's kindness balances Quincy's mistrust, while Quincy's practicality balances Biddy's fear and naivete. Quincy teaches Biddy to cook, while Biddy teaches Quincy "to be nice to people who never hurt me."[5] Ms. Evans, their last Living Skills teacher, gives them an important parting gift: voice recorders to serve as their journals because writing is difficult for Quincy and Biddy can't write. These recorders prove an important medium for telling their stories of sexual assault.

Men's violence has reshaped both young women's bodyminds. When Quincy was six her mother's boyfriend hit her in the head with a brick: "They's still a big ole dent in my head, and one of my eyes is push down."[6] After Biddy was gang-raped in seventh grade, she made herself fat from junk food to avoid boys' attention. Both Biddy and Quincy contemplate what makes a space safe or unsafe. For Quincy the presence of any man constitutes a risk because "Sometimes people get hurt from other people's men hanging around."[7] For Biddy, certain words go together with harm: "One whole calendar page since we moved here. That means it's been one calendar page since somebody called me bad names. It's been that long since some boy said nasty things to me."[8] Their quiet new home provides a respite from the hostilities of public space.

In unsafe spaces, certain words make it okay to hurt girls with intellectual disabilities. The R-word plays several roles in *Girls Like Us*. First, it lets readers know how they should and should not think about intellectual disability. The novel begins, "My name is Biddy. Some call me other names. Granny calls me Retard."[9] Biddy adds, "Granny shouldn't call me Retard. I know that. It ain't nice. It hurts my feelings."[10] Biddy's use of the R-word brings readers to her side. By invoking the R-word right away then rejecting it, the novel defuses readers' possible doubts about trusting narrators with intellectual disabilities. The R-word performs another function as well: name calling ushers in violence.

Sexual assault acts as a violent strain of ableism, meant to punish Biddy and Quincy for their disabilities as well as their womanhood. Because the same cycle of insults and violence affects two very different women, it becomes clear that abuse serves a larger system of dominance. Boys and men hurl gendered insults like "bitch," "slut," and "ho" before committing rape. Afterward girls and women use the same insults to blame and ostracize survivors. After her rape, Biddy "told Granny what those boys done. She slapped me cross my face and called me Slut."[11] The other girls in Biddy's class, including Quincy, make the same assumption: "Everybody know Biddy be a ho."[12] Boys target Biddy for attack because her intellectual disability makes her more vulnerable; then the rape and its aftermath target her as a woman. The cycle of verbal and physical abuse continues partly because other women reinforce it.

Quincy faces the challenge of entering the working world with a visible disability. As we have seen in previous chapters, public space can be challenging for people with obvious facial differences. While Biddy works at Elizabeth's home, sheltered from public eyes, Quincy has to face strangers in her transition to work. At the supermarket a bagger named Robert remarks, "They shore hiring 'em ugly lately."[13] When Quincy speaks up for herself, his rough words and actions escalate. Quincy hears the same insults directed at her that have followed Biddy around since seventh grade. Under scrutiny from her new coworkers, she rethinks her harsh judgments of Biddy. "My mind was boiling. These people don't know me and they do know Robert and they know he's no count, but they still be looking at me . . . well, like people look at Biddy."[14] When Robert rapes Quincy he uses the same gendered insults Biddy has heard for years. "You deserve this, bitch. No ho gonna dis me."[15] Like Biddy's rape, this intersectional assault begins with Quincy's disability and concludes with her womanhood.

The only good thing to come out of the assault is the stronger bond between Quincy and Biddy as they form a disability community together. Quincy starts to recognize their shared experiences as disabled women, whereas in the past she saw only their differences of race and temperament. However, they both still accept a main tenet of social death: they believe they must remain silent about rape because they are intellectually disabled women. The laws that protect others don't apply to them. One symptom of social death is the temptation to deaden oneself, in this case the deadening effect of silence. Biddy tells Quincy, "Police or nobody else care what happen to girls like us."[16] Biddy also counsels her not to tell Elizabeth, their employer: "Peoples change when they hear about this kind of evil doing."[17] Unfortunately, Biddy speaks from direct experience of victim blaming.

Words can license harm, but words can also console and tell the truth. Men's violence reshapes Quincy's body in yet another way: one of the rapists carves the word "ho" in her stomach. However, Biddy immediately contests that word with her own decisive words: "It ain't true. Don't you never go thinking it's true."[18] Biddy believes that language can help reduce the post-traumatic effects of rape. "You got to tell me about it. If you don't, you won't never be able to think of nothing else." When Quincy replies, "I can't look at you and tell you what they done," Biddy comes up with the solution of voice recorders.[19] They both record their stories of sexual assault, and the transcripts of the recordings are the first time the reader hears either story in full. Just as Biddy and Quincy have enough intimacy now to share their worst stories, the reader finally knows them well enough to be privy to such knowledge.

Like the assaults, the consolation begins with words then moves to physical actions. After she hears Biddy's story, Quincy puts her hand on Biddy's hand. "I don't like touching nobody, but I put my hand on Biddy's like Lizabeth do."[20] Biddy bandages Quincy's wounds and hugs her until she can get to "a different crying. The kind that feel good."[21] Despite her fear of going out in public, Biddy starts walking Quincy to and from work every day.[22] Biddy's bravery melts Quincy's heart. "That cold, hard feeling I always had inside me felt like it be slipping a bit sideways. Biddy is plumb scared to come out into the world, and she was coming here to protect me from Robert."[23] For each other and with each other, two women with intellectual disabilities brave public space.

Quincy's ethic of care for both the women with disabilities in her life leads her to tell her employer Elizabeth about the rape. She tells the truth "'cause I feel wrong, letting Robert be out there, watching you and Biddy, without you knowing that he could hurt you."[24] Elizabeth doesn't blame the victim or call her names. Instead she says, "Oh, Quincy, what can I do to help you?"[25] When Quincy decides to press charges, Biddy and Elizabeth "sat by me and hold my hand while that policeman made a tape of what I said about Robert."[26] Two words from the policeman, her formal name, persuade Quincy the law might protect someone like her. "Maybe folks like Biddy and me not different. He done call me Ms. Ford."[27] Reporting a rape can be a risky and traumatic business. By pressing charges, however, Quincy rejects social death and claims her place in the body public. With the right supports, two young women with intellectual disabilities can draw strength from each other to assert that they matter.

The Fault in Our Stars

The teenagers in *The Fault in Our Stars* are scarcely awash in privilege. They lose organs, limbs, and eventually their lives to cancer. Hazel Lancaster and Augustus Waters only get to have sex once before the disease intervenes. Nonetheless, they sit on the privileged end of the sexual spectrum. *The Fault in Our Stars* pairs sex with romance and never with assault. When Augustus first meets Hazel and asks her to come watch a movie, she says, "I hardly know you, Augustus Waters. You could be an ax murderer."[28] However, the novel's banter quickly and lightly dismisses any risk of male violence. The characters face literal death but not social death.

Their prosthetic community supports a disability community of teenagers that yields a resplendent love story. *The Fault in Our Stars* asserts that three seventeen-year-olds with bodies disabled by cancer have the same romantic and sexual desires they had before cancer, even if the world at large sees them as asexual. Talking on the phone to Hazel, Augustus complains that it's difficult to get laid once you've had your leg removed.

> "Hazel Grace," he said, "do you have a pen and a piece of paper?" I said I did. "Okay, please draw a circle." I did. "Now draw a smaller circle within the circle." I did. "The larger circle is virgins. The smaller circle is seventeen-year-old guys with one leg."[29]

Augustus and Hazel achieve the goal of losing their virginity thanks to the novel's rich prosthetic and disability communities. The Lancasters may be in debt from the cost of Hazel's medications, but they still provide her with an ample prosthetic community. She has loving, educated, and protective parents. Her mother doesn't have a job because "she had taken on the full-time profession of Hovering Over Me."[30] "My mom knew more about differentiated thyroid carcinoma in adolescents than most oncologists."[31] Hazel has access to the trials of an experimental drug that halts the growth of her lung tumors, which does not remove her cancer but does buy her a future of indeterminate length.[32] She and her friends who have cancer come from white, two-parent, middle-class families in single-family suburban homes. They have the equipment they need, from Augustus's prosthetic leg to Hazel's rolling oxygen tanks. Most relevantly to their love story, the community has a support group for teenagers with cancer. When Hazel becomes depressed, her mother makes sure she gets out of the house to the support group.

As in *Girls Like Us*, words matter here. They spark romance, mock cancer clichés, and let teenagers bond. With their wit and intelligence Hazel and Augustus not only meet but surpass the standards of the young adult fiction personality profile: smart, charming, and quick with a comeback. They indulge in erudite and philosophical flirting. The night they meet at support group, Augustus says he fears oblivion. Hazel replies, "And if the inevitability of oblivion worries you, I urge you to ignore it. God knows that's what everyone else does." Augustus responds with a smile "too big for his face." "'Goddamn,' Augustus said quietly. 'Aren't you something else.'"[33] Augustus also wields big words to romantic effect. As Hazel listens to his story about the last time he played basketball before his leg amputation, she thinks, "I really, really, really liked him . . . I liked that he took *existentially fraught* free throws."[34] Hazel is much more interested in a guy who can talk than a guy who can shoot hoops.

Many people who get cancer do not die from it immediately. Living with cancer over the years endows the bearer with a disability identity, what Hazel calls "our cancer selves."[35] *The Fault in Our Stars* is rich with cancer kid culture. Hazel and Augustus understand each other's cancer selves in ways no outsider could understand. They speak their own subcultural languages to each other. Hazel finds she has little common ground with her old high school friends. "I felt a certain unbridgeable distance between us. I think my school friends wanted to help me through my cancer, but they eventually found out that they couldn't. For one thing, there was no *through*."[36] Her old friends feel equipped for a short-term overcoming narrative with a happy ending, but they can't fathom a condition without cure and a permanently changed identity. By contrast, Hazel and Augustus swap their insider knowledge of cancer kid culture. Hazel teases Augustus about his bad driving by claiming his license must have been a Cancer Perk. "Cancer Perks are little things cancer kids get that regular kids don't: basketballs signed by sports heroes, free passes on late homework, unearned driver's licenses, etc."[37] Augustus teases Hazel for wasting her Make A Wish wish on Disney World.[38] Things that make outsiders feel solemn and respectful make insiders laugh.

Hazel, Augustus, and their friend Isaac constitute a disability community of three. Their shared sensibility gives them some relief from the cancer clichés that insist on a fortitude and determination no one could embody in real life. At the support group Hazel and Isaac communicate through sighs to mock the new age miracle cures that surround cancer. They get away with it because they have their own wordless language. "Each time someone discussed anticancer diets or snorting ground-up shark fin or whatever, he'd glance over at me and sigh ever so slightly. I'd shake my head microscopically and exhale in response."[39] When Augustus talks to Hazel in the language of inspiration porn, she answers back in the same language without missing a beat.

> "Like, you are familiar with the trope of the stoic and determined cancer victim who heroically fights her cancer with inhuman strength and never complains or stops smiling even at the very end, etcetera?"
>
> "Indeed," I said. "They are kindhearted and generous souls whose every breath is an Inspiration to Us All. They're so strong! We admire them so!"[40]

The three of them also share a sensibility when one of them is in pain. Augustus and Hazel react with appropriate nurturing and outrage when Isaac's able-bodied girlfriend dumps him right before the surgery to remove his second cancerous eye. "'She said she couldn't handle it,' he told me. 'I'm about to lose my eyesight and *she* can't handle it.'"[41] Augustus and Hazel don't expect Isaac to be stoic. Concluding that Isaac needs to smash something breakable, Augustus offers up his trophies from his former life as a basketball star. Isaac's need to vent his rage matters much more to Augustus than the remnants of his glory days.

> "I've been looking for a way to tell my father that I actually sort of hate basketball, and I think we've found it." The trophies came down one after the other, and Isaac stomped on them and screamed while Augustus and I stood a few feet away, bearing witness to the madness. The poor, mangled bodies of plastic basketballers littered the carpeted ground: here, a ball palmed by a disembodied hand; there, two torsoless legs caught midjump.[42]

Isaac does to the tiny ball players what cancer has done to the three teenagers: amputated limbs, mangled bodies, and removed them from the social context that once gave them meaning. This moment crystallizes the unsentimental and wry approach all three of them take to cancer. In the Supercrip version of his life, the postamputation Augustus would have become a wheelchair basketball star. Instead, he accepts that he is not the person he used to be and wastes no time mourning his former self. His cancer self finds different sources of meaning in life, including Isaac and Hazel.

It stands to reason, then, that Hazel and Augustus's physical intimacy will differ from the sexuality of precancer selves. Hazel takes in their first kiss with her whole body, cancer and all. "The space around us evaporated, and for a weird moment I really liked my body; this cancer-ruined thing I'd spent years dragging around suddenly seemed worth the struggle, worth the chest tubes and the PICC lines and the ceaseless bodily betrayal of the tumors."[43] The kiss does not whisk her away from the struggle with cancer but sheds a new and warmer light on it. Their first and only lovemaking is crip sex, what Hazel later calls "a quantum entanglement of tubes and bodies."[44] Scars and medical equipment intertwine with the wonder and ease of a first great love. Augustus hesitates on their way to his bed, then finally says, "It's above my knee and it just tapers a little and then it's just skin. There's a nasty scar, but it just looks like—" Hazel's reply? "Oh, get over yourself."[45] Her oxygen tube interferes with the removal of clothes but not with their closeness or erotic discovery.

> We crawled into the bed, my freedom circumscribed some by the oxygen, but even so I could get on top of him and take his shirt off and taste the sweat on the skin below his collarbone as I whispered into his skin, "I love you, Augustus Waters," his body relaxing beneath mine as he heard me say it. He reached down and tried to pull my shirt off, but it got tangled in the tube. I laughed.
>
> "How do you do this every day?" he asked as I disentangled my shirt from the tubes.[46]

The fumbling is part of sex's human comedy. Hazel leaves Augustus a funny love letter: a Venn diagram with a circle marked "virgins" and a very small circle mostly but not entirely inside the big circle marked "17-year-old guys with one leg."[47] Nothing can guarantee a first time of good humor and true regard like this one. However, many factors helped tip the balance in this direction for Hazel and Augustus. These factors include attentive parents, the right medications, driver's licenses and access to cars, white privilege, and even the cheesy teen support group.

Absent these protective factors, young people with disabilities stand a higher chance of a first time more like Biddy's and Quincy's. The lack of decent parents and class privilege has left them more vulnerable to sexual predators. It takes public money and deliberate community-building—in other words, it takes all of us—to give Biddy and Quincy a better chance at a voluntary and pleasurable first time instead of hate speech and violation. Even when sexual assault happens, as it does in every social level, a good prosthetic community provides medical care, recourse to justice, and a safe place to tell the truth.

Ready Before They Get Here

Young people with disabilities on the less privileged end of the spectrum, including those in poor countries, need well-financed public supports to raise their odds of success not just in relationships but in all aspects of the transition to adulthood. Here are more specifications for the builders of Handi-Land as young people enter the Tomorrowland of adulthood:

Everyone has the same access regardless of race, nation, class, or type of disability. Everyone's first sexual experience is voluntary, and while we're at it, relatively happy. Adapted and affordable college and trade training await. No one has to beg for a living. Your work makes the most of your talents. Those who cannot work have a safe and interesting place to be during the day. Everyone who needs government benefits gets them on the first try, and no one makes you feel guilty for taking public money. You can afford and obtain your equipment, medications, and care workers. It is easy to find peers and trustworthy mentors who understand your experiences. Slurs and insults disappear from our vocabularies. All the creative output of young adults with disabilities, all the screenplays, comics, poems, songs, and paintings, come out of obscurity and get published, shown, or produced instead of mocked. There are no cages, no institutions, and no one who preys or profits on other's vulnerabilities. No teenagers contemplate killing or otherwise deadening themselves.

Whether young adults fail or succeed in entering public life, whether they enter with laughter and ease or bafflement and anger, depends a great deal on the resources adults have prepared for them before they arrive. I wrote above that words license actions, for good or for ill. Children's and young adult literature licenses the building of HandiLands. Another genre of words, disability rights laws, has licensed the movement of people with disabilities into public space. In nations around the world, however, justice rests on one or two fragile laws at most. We need to extend legal and social benefits to the people who have not yet enjoyed them, and we need to protect the laws we have. Like Prince Dolor flying over many landscapes in his traveling cloak, we have come a long way and still have a long way to go in creating a fair and safe world for young people with disabilities. It would be a waste to travel backward along the ground we've already gained. HandiLand is a possible dream, but it takes hard work and cold cash to turn words into actions.

Notes

Introduction

1. Welch, "Disabled Climb Capitol Steps."
2. Shapiro, *No Pity*, 133.
3. Keelan, "Climbing the Capitol Steps for ADA."
4. Sygall, "Community Conversation."
5. Draper, *Out of My Mind*, 292.
6. Kim, Losen, and Hewitt, *School to Prison Pipeline*, 51.
7. Tomlinson, "Race and Special Education," 83.
8. Tomlinson, 82–3.
9. Finnerty, interview with the author.
10. Finnerty.
11. Not until halfway through writing *HandiLand* did I realize I had used the map of Disneyland as a blueprint. The homage happened at an entirely subconscious level (blame a Southern California childhood). While my adult self understands that the Magic Kingdom hardly represents an ideal world open to all, apparently my inner five-year-old disagrees.
12. Garland-Thomson, "Misfits," 603.
13. Crenshaw, "Mapping the Margins," 1242.
14. Reyes, "A Letter to Writers about Autism."
15. Giles, *Girls Like Us*, 211.
16. Higashida, *Reason I Jump*, 85.
17. Higashida, 111.
18. Reyes.
19. Chen, *Animacies*, 13.
20. Yoon, *Everything, Everything*, 263.
21. Siebers, *Disability Theory*, 106; see also Davis, *Enabling Acts*, 196.

Chapter One

1. Garland-Thomson, "Feminist Materialist Disability Concept," 594.
2. Biondo, *Once Upon a Playground*, xix-xx.

3. Ray, *Ecological Other*, 41.
4. Solomon, *American Playgrounds*, 84.
5. Addams, *Spirit of Youth*, 4.
6. MacLeod, *Age of the Child*, 71.
7. Gulick, "Play and Democracy," 483.
8. Arkin, email to the author.
9. Skinner, diary excerpt quoted on interpretive sign.
10. Eugene Parks and Open Space, *Eugene Outdoors! Spring 2004*, 2.
11. Brooks, "Race, Politics, and Denial," 736.
12. Paley, *Storytelling in the Classroom*, 6.
13. E, "Disney's *Frozen* and Autism."
14. Lindsey, "Reflected in Ice: An Aspergers Review of *Frozen*."
15. Buck and Lee, directors, *Frozen*.
16. Bascom, "Quiet Hands."
17. Bascom.
18. Zare, "An Autistic's Reflection on Disney's *Frozen*."
19. Zare.
20. E.
21. E.
22. Lindsey.
23. Lindsey.
24. Bednar, director, *The Story of Frozen: Making a Disney Animated Classic*.
25. Bednar.
26. Bednar.
27. Bednar.
28. Gray, "Let it Go (Autism Version)."
29. McCloskey, "To See Ourselves through Visuals," 2–3.
30. McCloskey, 5.
31. McCloskey, 3.
32. McCloskey, 4–5.
33. Cottin and Faría, *Black Book of Colors*.
34. Von Ravensberg, conversation with the author.
35. Cottin and Faría.
36. Charlton, *Nothing about Us without Us*, 3, 39; "Minister Tshililo Michael Masutha," Department of Justice and Constitutional Development.
37. Pickens, "Aesthetics of the Novel," 172.
38. Tricia Rose, *Hip Hop Wars*, 1–2.
39. Trust, and Caulfield, "Eminem Marks Sales."
40. Eminem, "Cleanin' Out My Closet."
41. Haze, "Cleaning Out My Closet."
42. Haze.
43. Tettenborn, "Melancholia as Resistance," 116.
44. Makarechi, "Angel Haze's 'Cleaning Out My Closet.'"
45. Berne, "Disability Justice—a Working Draft."

46. Black et al., *The National Intimate Partner and Sexual Violence Survey*, 20.
47. Black et al., 62.

Chapter Two

1. Christou, email interview with the author.
2. Wendell, *The Rejected Body*, 55–6.
3. Cooper, personal interview with the author.
4. Odom, "Preschool Inclusion," 20–2.
5. Christou.
6. Siebers, 54.
7. Lalvani and Hale, 33–4.
8. Cooper.
9. Early Childhood CARES, "Circle of Friends."
10. Cooper.
11. Puar, "Queer Times, Queer Assemblages," 121–2.
12. Crenshaw, "Mapping the Margins," 1242.
13. Hames-Garcia, *Identity Complex*, xi.
14. Kane, "Parents' Responses to Children's Gender Nonconformity," 153.
15. Kane, 167.
16. Martin, "Becoming a Gendered Body," 510.
17. Martin, 498.
18. Martin, 498.
19. Eng, *Racial Castration*, 2.
20. Ayrault, *Beyond a Physical Disability*, 70.
21. Shuttleworth, "Adverse Context of Disability and Desirability," 116–7.

Chapter Three

1. Young, "It's Not My Fault I'm Obsessed with Toilets."
2. Plaskow, "Role of Toilets in Struggles for Social Justice," 58.
3. Kafer, *Feminist, Queer, Crip*, 157.
4. Morrell, telephone interview with the author.
5. Morrell.
6. Titchkosky, *Question of Access*, 70.
7. Yozzo and Yozzo, personal interview with the author.
8. Garland-Thomson, "Misfits," 597.
9. Chess et al., "Calling All Bathroom Revolutionaries," 216; Hollmann and Kotis, "It's a Privilege to Pee."
10. Mateik and Spade, *Toilet Training*.

Chapter Four

1. "About Us," Ghana Federation of Disability Organizations; "Constitutional History of Ghana," International IDEA.

2. Rose, "Disabled People Took to the Streets."

3. Quayson, *Aesthetic Nervousness*, 205; Anthony, "Disability in Ghana," 1073.

4. Thind, "Understanding the Equality Act."

5. "Rights of Persons with Disabilities," United Nations, ch. 4, sec. 15.

6. Howard, *Colonialism and Underdevelopment in Ghana*, 17–23, 59–90.

7. Hediger, "Crossing Over," 323.

8. Taylor, "Disability Studies and Animal Rights," 201.

9. Singer, *Practical Ethics*, 118, 171.

10. Wolfe, *Animal Rites*, 34, 37, 69.

11. Haraway, *Companion Species Manifesto*, 3.

12. Derrida, *Animal That Therefore I Am*, 79.

13. Hearne, *Calling Animals by Name*, 42.

14. Chen, *Animacies*, 89.

15. Blackford, "*Raw Shok* and Modern Method," 288.

16. Brittain, "Portrayal of Deaf Characters."

17. Taylor, *Beasts of Burden*, 103.

18. Taylor, 104.

19. Taylor, 146.

20. Friedrich, "Eggs from Caged Hens."

21. Larsson, "Out of Sight."

22. Hadjimatheou, "Disabled Children Locked Up."

23. Chen, 90, 129.

24. Chen, 129.

25. Melson, "Human-Companion Animal Bond," 37.

26. Osofsky, *My Buddy*.

27. Spitz, *Inside Picture Books*, 189.

28. Osofsky.

29. Shin-Wheeler, conversation with the author.

30. Hughes, "Seeing Blindness in Children's Picturebooks," 47.

31. Haraway; Halberstam, *Queer Art of Failure*, 80.

32. Chen, 104.

33. Osofsky.

34. Melson, 32.

35. Bastian et al., "When Closing the Human-Animal Divide Expands Moral Concern," 427.

36. Carey, "Michael Foreman"; "Walker Contributors: Michael Foreman."

37. McReynolds, "Animal and Alien Bodies as Prostheses," 118.

38. Nodelman, *Words about Pictures*, 150.

39. Foreman, *Seal Surfer*.

40. Foreman.

41. Nodelman, 136.

42. Foreman.

43. Jordan, "Troubling Companions," 272.

44. Foreman.

45. Foreman.
46. Foreman.
47. Gray, "An African Century."
48. Quayson, 205; Anthony, 1073.
49. Yaghr, email to the author.
50. Alhassan, "Implementation of Inclusive Education," 116.
51. Yaghr.
52. Yaghr.
53. Quayson, 206.
54. Asare, *Sosu's Call*, 6, 10, 16.
55. Asare, 7.
56. Asare, 3.
57. Asare, 9.
58. "In Their Own Words," EDIN and the National Bureau for Students with Disabilities.
59. Anonymous interview subject quoted by Anthony, 1078.
60. Yenika-Agbaw, *Representing Africa in Children's Literature*, 114–6.
61. Asare, 7.
62. Asare, 17.
63. Asare, 19.
64. Asare, 21.
65. Asare, 21.
66. Kuusisto, "Ann Coulter and the R Word Ride Again!"
67. Asare, 22.
68. Asare, 23.
69. Asare, 27.
70. Asare, 33.
71. Yenika-Agbaw, 34.
72. Yenika-Agbaw, 50.
73. Quayson, 207.
74. Many thanks to Mary E. Wood for suggesting this idea.

Chapter Five

1. Haraway, *Companion Species Manifesto*; Hearne, *Calling Animals by Name*.
2. Elliott; Emily.
3. Brosh, *Hyperbole and a Half*, 354.
4. Brosh, 20.
5. Brosh, 80.
6. Brosh 19, 26; "Effects of the Word," *R-Word: Spread the Word to End the Word*.
7. Trachtenberg, "Social Media Embraced Allie Brosh's Book"; National Public Radio, "Hyperbole and a Half."
8. Brosh 165, 167.

9. American College Health Association 14.

10. Reetz et al., "The Association for University and College Counseling Center Directors Annual Survey," 15.

11. Alexander and Black, "Darker Side of the Sorting Hat," 214.

12. Brosh, "Contact," *Hyperbole and a Half* (blog).

13. Maron, *WTF with Mark Maron: Allie Brosh*.

14. Maron.

15. Bessler, "It's Hyperbole, and a Little More"; Schmitz, Fillippone, and Edelman, "Representations of Attention Deficit / Hyperactivity Disorder," 383–406.

16. Lakoff, "Adaptive Will," 151.

17. Danforth and Kim, "Tracing the Metaphors of ADHD," 50; "Laws Pertaining to ADHD Diagnosed Children," WGBH Educational Foundation.

18. Diller, "The Run on Ritalin," 12.

19. Danforth and Kim; Whitt and Danforth, "Reclaiming the Power of Address," 143–64; Graham, "ADHD and Schooling," 1–6; Graham, "Teaching ADHD?," 1–20.

20. Ravitch, *Great American School System*, 95.

21. Au, *Unequal by Design*, 53.

22. Ravitch, 15.

23. Lakoff, 157, 161, 166.

24. Whitt and Danforth, 162.

25. Brosh, *Hyperbole and a Half*, 269.

26. Emerald and Carpenter, "Politics of School Recognition," 106–7.

27. Brosh, 54–75, 345–69.

28. Brosh, "FAQ," *Hyperbole and a Half* (blog).

29. Greenblatt, *Will in the World*, 323–4.

30. Halberstam, *Queer Art of Failure*, 3.

31. Chute, *Graphic Women*, 4, 5.

32. Brosh, *Hyperbole and a Half*, 219.

33. Brosh, 220.

34. Brosh, 221.

35. Brosh, 223.

36. Brosh, 223.

37. Brosh, 224, 227.

38. Literally Media Ltd., "X all the Y"; Brosh, "I Am Allie Brosh."

39. Brosh, *Hyperbole and a Half*, 4.

40. Brosh, 15.

41. Brosh, 16.

42. Brosh, 16.

43. Brosh, 16.

44. Brosh, 16.

45. Braitman, *Animal Madness*, 3.

46. Brosh, 19.

47. Brosh, 19.

48. Brosh, 20.

49. Brosh, 25.
50. Brosh, 27–8.
51. Brosh, 28–29.
52. Brosh, 29–32.
53. Brosh, 20.
54. Brosh, 19.
55. Brosh, 32.
56. Brosh, 76.
57. Brosh, 80.
58. Brosh, 78.
59. Brosh, 85.
60. Brosh, 171.
61. Brosh, 254.
62. Brosh, 267.
63. Brosh, 81.
64. Brosh, 86–7.
65. Brosh, 90.
66. Brosh, 88.
67. Brosh, 95.
68. Brosh, 96–7.
69. Brosh, 96–7.
70. Brosh, 4.
71. Brosh, 90.
72. Brosh, 98.
73. Brosh, 270.
74. Brosh, 269.
75. Brosh, 269, 277.
76. Brosh, 282.
77. Brosh, 283.
78. Brosh, 275.
79. Brosh, 275.
80. Brosh, 94.
81. Brosh, 281.
82. Brosh, 282.
83. Brosh, 270.
84. Brosh, 283.
85. Brosh, 284, 286.
86. Brosh, 282.
87. Brosh, 283.

Chapter Six

1. Draper, *Out of My Mind*, 29.
2. Barcott, "Off the Rez."
3. Shapiro, *No Pity*, 69.

4. US Department of Education, "Individuals with Disabilities Education Act."

5. Shah and Priestley, *Disability and Social Change*, 40, 99, 105.

6. Taylor and Taylor, *Tell Me the Number before Infinity*, 62.

7. Quayson, *Aesthetic Nervousness*, 30.

8. Yoon, *Everything, Everything*, 1.

9. Haddon, *Curious Incident*, 44.

10. Palacio, *Wonder*, 285.

11. Draper, 13.

12. Meyer, "'But She's Not Retarded,'" 273–4.

13. Carey, *On the Margins of Citizenship*, 189.

14. SABE, quoted in Carey, 189.

15. "Rosa's Law," US Government Publishing Office, 1.

16. Kuusisto, "Ann Coulter and the R Word Ride Again!"

17. Trueman, *Stuck in Neutral*, 4, 11.

18. Zimmer, *Reaching for Sun*, 75.

19. Haddon, 43.

20. Haddon, 44.

21. Haddon, 26.

22. Haddon, 6.

23. Palacio, 218.

24. Bérubé, *Secret Life of Stories*, 63, 116.

25. Bogard, personal interview with the author.

26. Unfried, transcript of audio recording for "Life Stories" theater class.

27. Adams, "My Son Has Down Syndrome."

28. Solomon, *Far From the Tree*, 177.

29. Leiter, *Their Time Has Come*, 112.

30. Institute for Community Inclusion, Think College! College Options for People with Intellectual Disabilities, University of Massachusetts, Boston.

31. Leiter, 109.

32. Roulstone and Prideaux, *Understanding Disability Policy*, 14, 74.

33. Anderson, *Speak*, 52.

34. Brooks, *Bobos in Paradise*, 14, 37.

35. Palacio, 3.

36. Review of *Wonder* by R. J. Palacio, *Publishers Weekly*; *New York Times* best-seller list, "Best Sellers: Children's Middle Grade Hardcover," April 28, 2013, and July 31, 2016.

37. Hodson, "Interview with R.J. Palacio."

38. Kit and Ford, "Julia Roberts to Play Jacob Tremblay's Mother in 'Wonder.'"

39. Thanks to Priya Lalvani, who shared this idea with me.

40. Palacio, 304.

41. Palacio, 306.

42. Dunn, *Disabling Characters*, 14.

43. Palacio, 3.

44. Snyder and Mitchell, "Geo-Politics of Disability," 117.
45. Palacio, 163.
46. Palacio, 99, 211.
47. Palacio, 48.
48. Young, "A Fate Worse than Death?"
49. "Home," Mothers from Hell 2.
50. Trapp, conversation with the author.
51. Palacio, 190.
52. Palacio, 10.
53. Palacio, 13–4.
54. Palacio, 30.
55. Garland-Thomson, *Staring: How We Look*, 87, 94.
56. Palacio, 63–4.
57. Garland-Thomson, 58.
58. Bakhtin, *Rabelais and His World*, 336.
59. Palacio, 64.
60. Palacio, 274.
61. Palacio, 266.
62. Palacio, 85.
63. Palacio, 77.
64. Simplican, *Capacity Contract*, 124.
65. Palacio, 176.
66. Mingus, "Access Intimacy."
67. Palacio, 50.
68. Palacio, 67.
69. Palacio, 278.
70. Palacio, 51.
71. Palacio, 120.

Chapter Seven

1. Zephaniah, quoted in Staff Blogger, "Does Skool Suck?"
2. Alexie, "Conversations at KCTS-9."
3. Draper, "Sharon Draper, Out of My Mind."
4. Davis, "Disability in the Media," 37.
5. Daniels, "What Teachers Never Taught."
6. Alexie, "Best Kids Books Are Written in Blood."
7. hooks, "Whiteness in the Black Imagination," 177.
8. Zephaniah, *Too Black, Too Strong*, 82.
9. Schalk, "Coming to Claim Crip."
10. Zephaniah, 150–1.
11. Zephaniah, 28.
12. Zephaniah, 84.
13. Zephaniah, *Gangsta Rap*, 131, 158.

14. Zephaniah, 225.

15. Zephaniah, *Face*, 25.

16. Zephaniah, 32.

17. Zephaniah, 169.

18. Zephaniah, 105.

19. Zephaniah, 183.

20. Zephaniah, 199.

21. Zephaniah, 205.

22. Zephaniah, *Too Black, Too Strong*, 84.

23. Alexie, *Part-Time Indian*, 1.

24. Alexie, 3.

25. Alexie, "Conversations at KCTS-9."

26. Alexie, *Part-Time Indian*, 217.

27. Alexie, 84.

28. Alexie, 97.

29. Alexie, 31.

30. Alexie, 4.

31. Alexie, 131.

32. Alexie, 93.

33. Alexie, 56.

34. Alexie, 192–3.

35. Alexie, 195.

36. Alexie, 180.

37. Alexie, 195.

38. Alexie, 186.

39. Alexie, 180.

40. Alexie, 3.

41. Alexie, 147.

42. Martin, *Flexible Bodies*.

43. Alexie, 217.

44. Titchkosky, *Question of Access*, 87.

45. Elman, *Chronic Youth*, 2.

46. Draper.

47. Draper, *Out of My Mind*, 13.

48. "Coretta Scott King Book Awards," American Library Association.

49. Draper, *Ziggy and the Black Dinosaurs #1*, 7, 14, 25.

50. Draper, *Panic*, 99.

51. Draper, *Out of My Mind*, 3–4, 75, 273.

52. Draper, "Biography"; *New York Times* best-seller list, September 17, 2017.

53. Draper, 28.

54. Draper, 51.

55. Draper, 145.

56. Draper, 226.

57. Draper, 11, 41.

58. Draper, 271.
59. Kafer, 62.
60. Draper, 42–7.
61. Draper, 104.
62. Draper, 124–8.
63. Draper, 131.
64. Draper, 161–5.
65. Draper, 201–2.
66. Draper, 155.
67. Draper, 235–6.
68. Draper, 289–90.
69. Draper, 3.
70. Draper, "Sharon Draper, Out of My Mind."
71. Draper, *Fire From the Rock*, 211.
72. Draper, *Copper Sun*, 208, 247.
73. Draper, *Out of My Mind*, 57.
74. Draper, 40.
75. Draper, 179.
76. Draper, 292.

Chapter Eight

1. Wolitzer, 8.
2. Carroll, *Alice's Adventures Underground*, 37.
3. Carroll, 6–7.
4. Garland-Thomson, "Misfits," 600.
5. Garland-Thomson, 603.
6. Levy and Mendlesohn, *Children's Fantasy Literature*, 36.
7. Rowell, "He Was Mr. Dodgson," 131; Shute, "Well Worth the Cricks," 56.
8. Cohen, *Lewis Carroll: A Biography*, 8; Carroll, *Diaries of Lewis Carroll*, vol. 1, 73; Bowman, "Inner Life of a Famous Man," 90.
9. Jaques, "Conversation with Dodgson's Niece," 27.
10. Cohen, 76; Carroll, vol. 2, 311.
11. Quoted in Cohen, 533.
12. Cohen, 86.
13. Dodgson, "Do You Believe in Fairies?," 15.
14. Quoted in Cohen, 332.
15. Carroll, *Alice's Adventures in Wonderland*, 83.
16. Cooper, *English Romance in Time*, 101.
17. Rowling, *Goblet of Fire*, 70.
18. Rowling, 73.
19. Miller, "Rethinking Care," 5; Stemp, "Devices and Desires."
20. Mulock, *Little Lame Prince*, 119.
21. Mulock, 129.

22. Mulock, 13, 20.
23. Mulock, 46.
24. Mulock, 68, 80.
25. Mulock, 60–62.
26. Mulock, 34, 32.
27. Mulock, 31.
28. Mulock, 62.
29. Mulock, 78.
30. Mulock, 81.
31. Mulock, 37, 92.
32. Mulock, 64.
33. Mulock, 84.
34. Mulock, 85.
35. Mulock, 91.
36. Mulock, 86.
37. Mulock, 89.
38. Mulock, 84.
39. Mulock, 95.
40. Mulock, 97.
41. Mulock, 98.
42. Mulock, 101.
43. Mulock, 128.
44. Mulock, 99–100.
45. Cooper, 55.
46. Mulock, 95–6.
47. Mulock, 98–9.
48. Mulock, 60.
49. Miserandino, "The Spoon Theory."

Chapter Nine

1. Rowling, *Deathly Hallows*, 723.
2. Cooper, *English Romance in Time*, 324.
3. Cooper, 52–3.
4. Nikolajeva, "The Development of Children's Fantasy," 61.
5. Rowling, *Deathly Hallows*, 686.
6. Rowling, *Goblet of Fire*, 600.
7. Rowling, *Sorcerer's Stone*, 55.
8. Rowling, *Sorcerer's Stone*, 256; Rowling, *Goblet of Fire*, 639, 672; Rowling, *Order of the Phoenix*, 463.
9. van der Kolk, *Body Keeps the Score*, 11.
10. Price, "Bodymind Problem," 269.
11. Patsavas, "Recovering a Cripistemology of Pain," 215.
12. Tucker, "Communication Lacking in Chronic Migraine Encounters."

13. Haan, quoted in Honeyman, *Child Pain, Migraine, and Invisible Disability*, 97.

14. Rowling, *Goblet of Fire*, 16.

15. Rowling, *Order of the Phoenix*, 463, 541; Rowling, *Deathly Hallows*, 655.

16. Rowling, *Order of the Phoenix*, 811.

17. Miller, "'Harry Potter' Casts a Spell."

18. Rowling, *Prisoner of Azkaban*, 187.

19. Rowling, 221.

20. Rose, *States of Fantasy*.

21. Attebery, *Strategies of Fantasy*, 55.

22. Rowling, *Prisoner of Azkaban*, 166.

23. Rowling, 86.

24. Rowling, *Deathly Hallows*, 759.

25. Johnson, "J.K. Rowling Contemplated Suicide."

26. Rowling, "Remus Lupin."

27. Rowling, *Goblet of Fire*, 707.

28. Rowling, 705.

29. Rowling, 706.

30. Rowling, 611–12.

31. Rowling, *Goblet of Fire*, 706; Rowling, *Order of the Phoenix*, 465; Rowling, *Deathly Hallows*, 84.

32. Rowling, *Deathly Hallows*, 723.

33. Rowling, *Order of the Phoenix*, 31–2.

34. Rowling, *Prisoner of Azkaban*, 86.

35. Rowling, 96, 263.

36. Rowling, 184.

37. Rowling, 187.

38. Rowling, 237.

39. Rowling, 412.

40. Rowling, *Deathly Hallows*, 728.

41. Rowling, *Prisoner of Azkaban*, 411; Rowling, *Order of the Phoenix*, 606–7.

42. Rowling, *Order of the Phoenix*, 474–5.

43. Rowling, 466.

44. Rowling, 435.

45. Rowling, 816.

46. Patsavas, 214.

47. Rowling, 816.

48. Lowe, music and lyrics, "The Beast in Me."

49. Rowling, *Deathly Hallows*, 234.

50. Scamander (J.K. Rowling), *Fantastic Beasts*, xxxv.

51. Batty, "(Post)human Animal Body," 27.

52. Scamander, xviii, xix.

53. Rowling, 478.

54. Thorne, Rowling, and Tiffany, *Cursed Child*, 48.

55. Snyder and Mitchell, *Narrative Prosthesis*, 47.
56. Felton, "'Harry Potter' Helped This Fangirl's Battle."
57. Hitselberger, "Harry Potter and the Inaccessible Book."
58. Lamont, "*Harry Potter's* 'Mad Women.'"
59. Lamont.
60. Lamont.
61. Mathews, "My Harry Potter Story," 183–4.
62. Mathews, 184.
63. Tait, "*Harry Potter* Didn't Cure My Depression."
64. Tait.
65. Tait.
66. Tait.
67. Tait.
68. Tait.
69. Montgomery, "Allure of Separatism."
70. Montgomery.
71. Montgomery.
72. Montgomery.
73. Montgomery.
74. Montgomery.
75. Montgomery.
76. Montgomery.
77. Montgomery.

Chapter Ten

1. Delany, "Dichtung und Science Fiction," 147.
2. Yaszek, "The Bannekerade," 22.
3. Collins et al., "Aqua Boogie."
4. Hamilton, "Afrofuturism and the Technologies of Survival," 22.
5. Barber, "Cyborg Grammar," 4, 14.
6. Ritchie, *Invisible No More*, 87.
7. Ritchie, 10.
8. Ritchie, 91.
9. Lavender, "Digging Deep," 66.
10. Smith, *Orleans*, 321.
11. Smith, 21–2.
12. Smith, 39.
13. Smith, 143, 250.
14. "Syphilis Study at Tuskegee," Centers for Disease Control and Prevention.
15. Smith, 207.
16. Smith.
17. Smith, 172–3.
18. "Interview with Sherri L. Smith," WETA Television, Washington, DC.

19. Smith.
20. Smith, 77.
21. Smith, 53.
22. Smith, 46, 111.
23. Smith, 266.
24. Yaszek, "The Bannekerade," 22.
25. Smith, 189.
26. Smith, 68.
27. Smith, 61.
28. Smith, 283.
29. Singer, "Why Baltimore Burns"; Allam, "Baltimore's Sandtown-Winchester."
30. Levine, "Downtown Redevelopment," 107.
31. Fonger, "Ex-Emergency Manager Says He's Not to Blame."
32. Jacobs, "Impacts of Variations," 351, 354–5.
33. Young, "Plumbers Volunteer to Help in Flint," 2.
34. Jacobs, 359.
35. Lee et al., "Racial Inequality and the Implementation of Emergency Management," 5.
36. Hill, *Nobody*, 160.
37. Hanna-Attisha et al., "Elevated Blood Lead Levels," 285.
38. Bosman, "Flint Water Crisis Inquiry."
39. Livengood, "Flint Water Warnings."
40. Chan, "5 Most Important Flint Water Crisis Emails."
41. Otto, *Green Speculations*, 121.
42. Smith, 16.
43. Smith, 61.
44. Smith, 257, 17.
45. Ritchie, 86.
46. Smith, 95.
47. Smith, 96.
48. Smith, 98, 17.
49. Smith, 308, 313.
50. Smith, 314.
51. Rentz, "Freddie Gray Remembered as a Jokester."
52. McCoy, "Freddie Gray's Life a Study on the Effects of Lead Paint."
53. "Stanley Rochkind," Maryland Judiciary.
54. "480 Baltimore City Dwellings," Maryland Department of the Environment.
55. McCoy, "Companies Make Millions."
56. Keller, "David Simon on Baltimore's Anguish."
57. Keller.
58. Lowery, "They Can't Kill Us All," 138.
59. Lowery, 137–9.

60. Alexander, *New Jim Crow*, 53, 56.
61. Smith, 322.
62. Smith, 320.
63. Smith, 323.
64. Pickens, "Aesthetics of the Novel," 171, 176.
65. Watkins, *Beast Side*, 123–4, 142.
66. McCoy, "Freddie Gray's Life a Study on the Effects of Lead Paint."
67. Watkins, xxi.
68. Carter-Long and Perry, "Law Enforcement Use of Force and Disability," 1.
69. Rentz.
70. Rentz.
71. Ross, "What Happened in Freddie Gray's Life."
72. Allam; Lowery, 138.
73. Kim, Losen, and Hewitt, *School to Prison Pipeline*, 51.
74. Mora, "Short, Hard Life of Freddie Gray."
75. Mora.
76. McCoy.
77. Smith, 228.
78. Smith, 243.
79. Segal, "More to Flint than a Water Crisis."
80. Segal.
81. Segal.
82. Segal.
83. Segal.
84. *Los Angeles Times* Staff, "Read the Letter from 'Little Miss Flint.'"
85. Acosta, "Letter That Brought President Obama"; Acosta, "Meet the Girl."
86. Smith, 323.

Conclusion

1. Shuttleworth, 116.
2. Jones et al., 904.
3. Giles, *Girls Like Us*, 177.
4. Giles, 143.
5. Giles, 285.
6. Giles, 4–5.
7. Giles, 88.
8. Giles, 211.
9. Giles, 1.
10. Giles, 2.
11. Giles, 254.
12. Giles, 12.
13. Giles, 113.
14. Giles, 115.

15. Giles, 247.
16. Giles, 251.
17. Giles, 238.
18. Giles, 242.
19. Giles, 239–40.
20. Giles, 256.
21. Giles, 260.
22. Giles, 275.
23. Giles, 282.
24. Giles, 323.
25. Giles, 322.
26. Giles, 339.
27. Giles, 340.
28. Green, *Fault*, 17.
29. Green, 119.
30. Green, 79.
31. Green, 92.
32. Green, 25
33. Green, 13.
34. Green, 31.
35. Green, 96.
36. Green, 45.
37. Green, 23.
38. Green, 80.
39. Green, 6.
40. Green, 173.
41. Green, 60.
42. Green, 63.
43. Green, 203.
44. Green, 237.
45. Green, 206.
46. Green, 206–7.
47. Green, 208.

Appendix A

Picture Books Featuring Children with Disabilities and Animals

Asare, Meshack. *Sosu's Call*. Accra, Ghana: Sub-Saharan Publishers, 1997.

Davis, Patricia A. *Brian's Bird*. Illustrated by Layne Johnson. Morton Grove, IL: Albert Whitman, 2000.

Foreman, Michael. *Seal Surfer*. San Diego: Harcourt Brace, 1997.

Harter, Debbie, illustrator. *The Animal Boogie*. Vocals on accompanying CD by Fred Penner. Cambridge, MA: Barefoot Books, 2000.

Kluth, Paula, and Patrick Schwarz. *Pedro's Whale*. Illustrated by Justin Canha. Baltimore: Paul H. Brookes, 2010.

Herrera, Juan Felipe. *Featherless/Desplumado*. Illustrated by Ernesto Cuevas Jr. San Francisco: Children's Book Press / Editorial Libros para Niños, 2004.

Hudson, Charlotte. *Dan and Diesel*. London: Red Fox, 2006.

Lears, Laurie. *Waiting for Mr. Goose*. Illustrated by Karen Ritz. Morton Grove, IL: Albert Whitman, 1999.

Martin, Bill, Jr., and John Archambault. *Knots on a Counting Rope*. Illustrated by Ted Rand. New York: Henry Holt, 1987.

Osofsky, Audrey. *My Buddy*. Illustrated by Ted Rand. New York: Square Fish / Henry Holt, 1992.

Peete, Holly Robinson, and Ryan Elizabeth Peete. *My Brother Charlie*. New York: Scholastic, 2010.

Rabinowitz, Alan. *A Boy and His Jaguar*. Illustrated by Cátia Chien. Boston: Houghton Mifflin Harcourt, 2014.

Senisi, Ellen B. *All Kinds of Friends, Even Green!* Bethesda, MD: Woodbine House, 2002.

Stockham, Jess. *Having Fun! Just Like Us!* Auburn, ME: Child's Play, 2008.

Stryer, Andrea Stenn. *Kami and the Yaks*. Illustrated by Bert Dodson. Palo Alto, CA: Bay Otter Press, 2007.

Bibliography

Acosta, Roberto. "Little Miss Flint and the Letter That Brought President Obama." *MLive Media Group*, May 4, 2016. https://www.mlive.com/news/flint/index. ssf/2016/05/how_little_miss_flint_brought.html

Acosta, Roberto. "Meet the Girl Whose Letter on the Water Crisis Brought Obama to Flint." *MLive Media Group*, April 28, 2016. http://www.mlive.com/news/flint/index.ssf /2016/04/meet_the_girl_whose_letter_on.html

Adams, Rachel E. "My Son Has Down Syndrome—Stop Telling Me He Has No Future." *Pacific Standard*, April 25, 2016. https://psmag.com/news/my-son-has -down-syndrome-stop-telling-me-he-has-no-future

Addams, Jane. *The Spirit of Youth and the City Streets*. New York: Macmillan, 1909.

Alexander, Jonathan, and Rebecca Black. "The Darker Side of the Sorting Hat: Representations of Educational Testing in Dystopian Young Adult Fiction." *Children's Literature: Annual of the Children's Literature Association and the Modern Language Association Division on Children's Literature* 43 (2015): 208–34.

Alexander, Michelle. *The New Jim Crow: Mass Incarceration in the Age of Colorblindness*. New York: New Press, 2012.

Alexie, Sherman. *The Absolutely True Diary of a Part-Time Indian*. Boston: Little, Brown, 2007.

Alexie, Sherman. "Conversations at KCTS-9." Interview by Enrique Cerna. *KCTS-9 Seattle*, November 12, 2008. https://www.youtube.com/watch?v=Io9vRHYMiFM

Alexie, Sherman. "Why the Best Kids Books Are Written in Blood." Speakeasy, *Wall Street Journal*, June 9, 2011. https://blogs.wsj.com/speakeasy/2011/06/09 / why-the-best-kids-books-are-written-in-blood/

Alhassan, Awal Mohammed. "Teachers' Implementation of Inclusive Education in Ghanaian Primary Schools: An Insight into Government Policy and Practices." *Advances in Social Science Research Journal* 1, no. 2 (March 2009): 115–29. http:// doi.org/10.14738/assrj.12.124

Allam, Hannah. "In Baltimore's Sandtown-Winchester, Every Day Is an Ongoing Katrina." *McClatchy DC*, May 5, 2015. http://www.mcclatchydc.com/news/ crime/article24784570.html

American College Health Association. *National College Health Assessment II: Reference Group Executive Summary Spring 2014.* Hanover, MD: American College Health Association, 2014.

American Library Association. "The Coretta Scott King Book Awards." http://www.ala.org/rt/emiert/cskbookawards

Anderson, Laurie Halse. *Speak.* New York: First Square Fish, 1999.

Anderson, Reynaldo, and Charles E. Jones. "Introduction: The Rise of Astro-Blackness." In *Afrofuturism 2.0: The Rise of Astro-Blackness,* edited by Reynaldo Anderson and Charles E. Jones, vii–xviii. Lanham, MD: Lexington Books, 2016.

Anthony, Jane. "Conceptualising Disability in Ghana: Implications for EFA and Inclusive Education." *International Journal of Inclusive Education* 15, no. 10 (December 2011): 1073–86. https://doi.org/10.1080/13603116.2011.555062

Arkin, Dan. Email to the author. August 21, 2006.

Asare, Meshack. *Sosu's Call.* Accra, Ghana: Sub-Saharan Publishers, 1997.

Attebery, Brian. *Strategies of Fantasy.* Bloomington: Indiana Univ. Press, 1992.

Au, Wayne. *Unequal by Design: High-Stakes Testing and the Standardization of Inequality.* New York: Routledge, 2009.

Ayrault, Evelyn West. *Beyond a Physical Disability: The Person Within. A Practical Guide.* New York: Continuum, 2001.

Bakhtin, Mikhail. *Rabelais and His World.* 1965. Translated by Helene Iswolsky. Bloomington: Indiana Univ. Press, 1984.

Barcott, Bruce. "Off the Rez." Review of *The Absolutely True Diary of a Part-Time Indian,* by Sherman Alexie. *New York Times,* November 11, 2007. http://www.nytimes.com/2007/11/11/books/review/Barcott3-t.html

Barber, Tiffany E. "Cyborg Grammar? Reading Wangechi Mutu's *Non je ne regrette rien* through *Kindred.*" In *Afrofuturism 2.0: The Rise of Astro-Blackness,* edited by Reynaldo Anderson and Charles E. Jones, 3–26. Lanham, MD: Lexington Books, 2016.

Bascom, Julia. "Quiet Hands." *Just Stimming* (blog). *WordPress,* October 5, 2011. https://juststimming.wordpress.com/2011/10/05/quiet-hands/

Bastian, Brock, Kimberly Costello, Steve Loughnan, and Gordon Hodson. "When Closing the Human-Animal Divide Expands Moral Concern: The Importance of Framing." *Social Psychological and Personality Science* 3, no. 4 (2012): 421–9.

Batty, Holly. "Harry Potter and the (Post)human Animal Body." *Bookbird: A Journal of International Children's Literature* 53, no. 1 (2015): 24–37. http://doi.org/10.1353/bkb.2015.0020

Bednar, Rudy, director. *The Story of Frozen: Making a Disney Animated Classic.* ABC Television, 2014. http://abcnews.go.com/Entertainment/fullpage/story-frozen-making-disney-animated-classic-movie-25150046

Berne, Patty. "Disability Justice—a Working Draft." *Sins Invalid: An Unshamed Claim to Beauty* (blog), June 10, 2015.

Bérubé, Michael. *The Secret Life of Stories: From Don Quixote to Harry Potter, How Understanding Intellectual Disability Transforms the Way We Read.* New York: NYU Press, 2016.

Bessler, Chris. "It's Hyperbole, and a Little More." *Sandpoint Magazine,* Winter 2014. http://sandpointmagazine.com/story/its-hyperbole-and-a-little-more/

Biondo, Brenda. *Once upon a Playground: A Celebration of Classic American Playgrounds, 1920–1975.* Hanover, NH: ForeEdge, 2014.

Black, M. C., K. C. Basile, M. J. Breiding, S. G. Smith, M. L. Walters, M. T. Merrick, J. Chen, and M. R. Stevens. *The National Intimate Partner and Sexual Violence Survey: 2010 Summary Report.* Atlanta, GA: National Center for Injury Prevention and Control, Centers for Disease Control and Prevention, 2011. https://www.cdc.gov/violenceprevention/pdf/nisvs_report2010-a.pdf

Blackford, Holly. "*Raw Shok* and Modern Method: Child Consciousness in *Flowers for Algernon* and *The Curious Incident of the Dog in the Night-Time.*" *Children's Literature Association Quarterly* 38, no. 3 (Fall 2013): 284–303.

Bogard, Billy Dean. Personal interview with the author. Transcript of audio recording for "Life Stories" theater class. April 11, 2016.

Bosman, Julie. "Flint Water Crisis Inquiry Finds State Ignored Warning Signs." *New York Times,* March 23, 2016. https://www.nytimes.com/2016/03/24/us/flint-water-crisis.html

Bowman, Isa. "The Inner Life of a Famous Man." In *Lewis Carroll: Interviews and Reflections,* edited by Morton N. Cohen, 89–102. Iowa City: Univ. of Iowa Press, 1989.

Braitman, Laurel. *Animal Madness: How Anxious Dogs, Compulsive Parrots, and Elephants in Recovery Help Us Understand Ourselves.* New York: Simon & Schuster, 2014.

British Library. *Comics Unmasked: Art and Anarchy in the UK.* Museum exhibit. May 2–August 19, 2014.

Brittain, Isabel. "An Examination into the Portrayal of Deaf Characters and Deaf Issues in Picture Books for Children." *Disability Studies Quarterly* 24, no. 1 (2004). http://doi.org/10.18061/dsq.v24i1

Brooks, Cheryl. "Race, Politics, and Denial: Why Oregon Forgot to Ratify the Fourteenth Amendment." *Oregon Law Review* 83 (2004): 731–61. https://scholarsbank.uoregon.edu/xmlui/bitstream/handle/1794/4561/83_2_731.pdf;sequence=1

Brooks, David. *Bobos in Paradise: The New Upper Class and How They Got There.* New York: Simon & Schuster, 2000.

Brosh, Allie. *Hyperbole and a Half* (blog). http://hyperboleandahalf.blogspot.com

Brosh, Allie. *Hyperbole and a Half: Unfortunate Situations, Flawed Coping Mechanisms, Mayhem, and Other Things That Happened.* New York: Touchstone / Simon & Schuster, 2013.

Brosh, Allie. "I Am Allie Brosh, the Draw-Writer of *Hyperbole and a Half.* Ask Me about Anything!" Reddit. October 22, 2013. https://www.reddit.com/r/IAmA/comments/1ozt33/i_am_allie_brosh_the_drawwriter_of_hyperbole_and/

Buck, Chris, and Jennifer Lee, directors. *Frozen.* Screenplay by Jennifer Lee. Music and lyrics by Kristen Anderson-Lopez and Robert Lopez. Disney Pixar Studios, 2013.

Carey, Allison C. *On the Margins of Citizenship: Intellectual Disability and Civil*

Rights in Twentieth-Century America. Philadelphia: Temple Univ. Press, 2009. ProQuest.

Carey, Allison C. "The Quest for Community: Intellectual Disability and the Shifting Meaning of Community in Activism." In *Research in Social Science and Disability 6: Disability and Community*, edited by Richard K. Scotch, Allison C. Carey, and Sharon N. Barnatt, 189–214. Bradford, UK: Emerald Group Publishing, 2011.

Carey, Joanna. "Michael Foreman: Life through a Line." *Guardian*, March 4, 2011. https://www.theguardian.com/books/2011/mar/07/michael-foreman-general -children-illustrator

Carroll, Lewis. *Alice's Adventures Underground*. Manuscript hand-lettered and illustrated by the author. 1862–4. British Library MS 46700. https://www.bl.uk/ collection-items/alices-adventures-under-ground-the-original-manuscript-version-of-alices-adventures-in-wonderland

Carroll, Lewis. *Alice's Adventures in Wonderland*. New York: Harper & Brothers, 1901.

Carroll, Lewis. *The Diaries of Lewis Carroll*. Ed. Roger Lancelyn Green. Vol. 1 and 2. New York: Oxford Univ. Press, 1954.

Carter-Long, Lawrence, and David M. Perry. "The Ruderman White Paper on Media Coverage of Law Enforcement Use of Force and Disability: A Media Study (2013–15) and Overview." Ruderman Family Foundation. March 2016. http://rudermanfoundation.org/wp-content/uploads/2017/08/MediaStudy-PoliceDisability_final-final.pdf

Cavanaugh, Sheila L. *Queering Bathrooms: Gender, Sexuality, and the Hygienic Imagination*. Toronto: Univ. Toronto Press, 2010.

Centers for Disease Control and Prevention. "U.S. Public Health Service Syphilis Study at Tuskegee." https://www.cdc.gov/tuskegee/timeline.htm

Chan, Melissa. "The 5 Most Important Flint Water Crisis Emails Released by Michigan's Governor." *Time Magazine*, January 20, 2016. http://time.com/4187842/ flint-water-crisis-michigan-governor-emails-rick-snyder/

Charlton, James I. *Nothing About Us Without Us: Disability Oppression and Empowerment*. Berkeley: Univ. California Press, 1998.

Chen, Mel Y. *Animacies: Biopolitics, Racial Mattering, and Queer Affect*. Durham: Duke Univ. Press, 2012.

Chess, Simone, Alison Kafer, Jessi Quizar, and Mattie Udora Richardson. "Calling All Bathroom Revolutionaries." In *That's Revolting: Queer Strategies for Resisting Assimilation*, edited by Mattilda Bernstein Sycamore, 216–37. Brooklyn: Soft Skull Press, 2004. ProQuest.

Christou, Makrina Nanette. Email interview with the author. December 11, 2015.

Chute, Hillary. *Graphic Women: Life Narrative and Contemporary Comics*. New York: Columbia Univ. Press, 2010.

Cohen, Morton N. *Lewis Carroll: A Biography*. New York: Alfred A. Knopf, 1996.

Collins, William Bootsy, George Clinton Jr., and Bernie Worrell. "Aqua Boogie (A Psychoalphadiscobetabioaquadoloop)." Sony/ATV Music Publishing, 1978.

Cooper, Carina. Personal interview with the author. November 10, 2015.

Cooper, Helen. *The English Romance in Time: Transforming Motifs from Geoffrey of Monmouth to the Death of Shakespeare.* Oxford: Oxford Univ. Press, 2004.

Cottin, Menena, and Rosana Faría. *The Black Book of Colors.* 2006. Translated by Elisa Amado. Toronto: Groundwood Books, 2008.

Crenshaw, Kimberlé. "Mapping the Margins: Intersectionality, Identity Politics, and Violence against Women of Color." *Stanford Law Review* 43, no. 6 (July 1991): 1241–99. https://doi.org/10.2307/1229039

Danforth, Scot, and Taehyung Kim. "Tracing the Metaphors of ADHD: A Preliminary Analysis with Implications for Inclusive Education." *International Journal of Inclusive Education* 12, no. 1 (2008): 49–64. https://doi.org/10.1080/13603110701683105

Daniels, Kapria. "What Teachers Never Taught and Writers Feared to Write: Disability in African American Children's Literature." *Disability Studies Quarterly* 24, no. 1 (Winter 2004). https://doi.org/10.18061/dsq.v24i1

Davis, Lennard. "Disability in the Media; or, Why Don't Disabled Actors Play Disabled Roles?" In *The End of Normal: Identity in a Biocultural Era.*, 31–42. Ann Arbor: Univ. of Michigan Press, 2013.

Davis, Lennard. *Enabling Acts: The Hidden Story of How the Americans with Disabilities Act Gave the Largest U.S. Minority Its Rights.* Boston: Beacon Press, 2015.

Davison, Al. *Spiral Cage.* London: Titan Books, 1990.

Delany, Samuel R. "Dichtung und Science Fiction." In *Starboard Wine: More Notes on the Language of Science Fiction,* edited by Samuel R. Delany and Matthew Cheney, 139–61. Middletown, CT: Wesleyan Univ. Press, 2012. ProQuest.

Department of Justice and Constitutional Development. "Biographical Notes: Minister Tshililo Michael Masutha." Republic of South Africa. http://www.justice.gov.za/contact/cv/cv_min.html

Derrida, Jacques. *The Animal That Therefore I Am.* Edited by Marie-Louise Mallet. Translated by David Wills. New York: Fordham Univ. Press, 2008.

Diller, Lawrence H. "The Run on Ritalin: Attention Deficit Disorder and Stimulant Treatment in the 1990s." *Hastings Center Report* 26, no. 2 (March–April 1996): 12–18. JSTOR.

Dodgson, F. Menella. "Do You Believe in Fairies?" In *Lewis Carroll: Interviews and Reflections,* edited by Morton N. Cohen, 14–5. Iowa City: Univ. of Iowa Press, 1989.

Draper, Sharon M. "Biography." *Sharondraper.com.* http://sharondraper.com/biography.asp

Draper, Sharon M. *Copper Sun.* New York: Atheneum Books for Young Readers, 2006.

Draper, Sharon M. *Fire from the Rock.* New York: Speak (Penguin), 2007.

Draper, Sharon M. *Out of My Mind.* New York: Atheneum Books for Young Readers, 2010.

Draper, Sharon M. *Panic.* New York: Atheneum Books for Young Readers, 2012.

Draper, Sharon M. "Sharon Draper, Out of My Mind." Television interview. *NC Bookwatch.* September 14, 2012. http://video.unctv.org/video/2278888925/

Draper, Sharon M. *Ziggy and the Black Dinosaurs #1: The Buried Bones Mystery.* New York: Aladdin Paperbacks, 1994.

Dunn, Patricia A. *Disabling Characters: Representations of Disability in Young Adult Literature.* New York: Peter Lang, 2015.

E. "Disney's *Frozen* and Autism." *The Third Glance* (blog), December 21, 2013. https://thethirdglance.wordpress.com/2013/12/21/disneys-frozen-and-autism/

Early Childhood CARES. "Circle of Friends." https://earlychildhoodcares.uoregon.edu/forparents/classrooms/circle-of-friends/

EDIN (The Eastern Disability Network) and the National Bureau for Students with Disabilities. "In Their Own Words: The Real Story of Disability in Ghana." VSO Media, September 18, 2009. Video, 5:37. https://www.youtube.com/watch?v=X9q9QwRnRUA

"Effects of the Word." *R-Word: Spread the Word to End the Word.* http://www.r-word.org/r-word-effects-of-the-word.aspx

Elliott, Lisa, Conversation with the author. July 11, 2018.

Elman, Julie Passanante. *Chronic Youth: Disability, Sexuality, and Rehabilitation.* New York: NYU Press, 2014.

Emerald, Elke, and Lorelai Carpenter. "ADHD, Mothers, and the Politics of School Recognition." In *(De)Constructing ADHD: Critical Guidance for Teachers and Teacher Educators,* edited by Linda J. Graham, 99–117. New York: Peter Lang, 2010.

Emily. "Teen Book Review: *Hyperbole and a Half.*" Cedar Mill Community Libraries website, Washington County, Oregon. October 29, 2013.

Eminem. "Cleanin' Out My Closet." *The Eminem Show.* Songwriters Marshall Mathers III and Jeffrey Bass. Eight Mile Style Music, 2002.

Eng, David L. *Racial Castration: Managing Masculinity in Asian America.* Durham: Duke Univ. Press, 2001.

Eugene Parks and Open Space. *Eugene Outdoors! Spring 2004.* Eugene, OR: Public Works Department, 2004.

Felton, Tom. "How 'Harry Potter' Helped This Fangirl's Battle with Depression." Fusion Media, October 12, 2015. https://fusion.tv/video/209972/how-harry-potter-helped-this-fangirls-battle-with-depression/

Finnerty, Cynthia Foster. Interview with the author. January 1, 2016.

Fonger, Ron. "Ex-Emergency Manager Says He's Not to Blame for Flint River Water Switch." *MLive Media Group.* October 13, 2015. http://www.mlive.com/news/flint/index.ssf/2015/10/ex_emergency_manager_earley_sa.html

Foreman, Michael. *Seal Surfer.* San Diego: Harcourt Brace, 1997.

Friedrich, Bruce. "The Cruelest of All Factory Farm Products: Eggs from Caged Hens." *HuffPost,* March 16, 2014. https://www.huffingtonpost.com/bruce-friedrich/eggs-from-caged-hens_b_2458525.html

Florez, StormMiguel. "Dear Austin Special Needs Bathroom." In *Gender Outlaws: The Next Generation,* edited by Kate Bornstein and S. Bear Bergman, 52–3. Berkeley: Seal Press, 2010.

Garland-Thomson, Rosemarie. "Misfits: A Feminist Materialist Disability Concept." *Hypatia: A Journal of Feminist Philosophy* 26, no. 3 (Summer 2011): 591–609. JSTOR.

Garland-Thomson, Rosemarie. *Staring: How We Look.* New York: Oxford Univ. Press, 2009.

Ghana Federation of Disability Organizations. "About Us." https://www.gfdgh.org/about-us/

Gibbons, Sarah. "Neurological Diversity and Environmental (In)Justice: The Ecological Other in Popular and Journalist Representations of Autism." In *Disability Studies and the Environmental Humanities: Toward an Eco-Crip Theory*, edited by Sarah Jaquette Ray and Jay Sibara, 531–51. Lincoln: Univ. of Nebraska Press, 2017.

Giles, Gail. *Girls Like Us.* Somerville, MA: Candlewick Press, 2014.

Graham, David A. "The Mysterious Death of Freddie Gray." *Atlantic*, April 22, 2015. https://www.theatlantic.com/politics/archive/2015/04/the-mysterious-death-of-freddie-gray/391119/

Graham, Linda J. "ADHD and Schooling: Looking for Better Ways Forward." *International Journal of Inclusive Education* 12, no. 1 (2008): 1–6. Taylor & Francis Online.

Graham, Linda J. "Teaching ADHD?" In *(De)Constructing ADHD: Critical Guidance for Teachers and Teacher Educators*, edited by Linda J. Graham, 1–20. New York: Peter Lang, 2010.

Gray, Eve. "An African Century." *The Bookseller*, August 23, 2002. https://www.thebookseller.com/feature/african-century

Gray, Tiffany. "Let It Go (Autism Version)." Adaptation of film lyrics by Sarah Rush (ZebraGal). February 21, 2014. https://www.youtube.com/watch?v=K2WkzP7RNYo

Green, Katie (website). https://katiegreen.co.uk/

Green, Katie. *Lighter than My Shadow.* London: Jonathan Cape, 2013.

Green, John. *The Fault in Our Stars.* New York: Dutton, 2012.

Greenblatt, Stephen. *Will in the World: How Shakespeare Became Shakespeare.* New York: W. W. Norton, 2004.

Gulick, Luther Halsey. "Play and Democracy." *Charities and the Commons* 18 (Aug. 3, 1907): 481–6.

Haddon, Mark. *The Curious Incident of the Dog in the Night-Time.* New York: Vintage, 2003.

Hadjimatheou, Chloë. "The Disabled Children Locked Up in Cages." *BBC News Magazine*, November 13, 2014. http://www.bbc.com/news/magazine-30038753

Halberstam, Judith (Jack). *The Queer Art of Failure.* Durham: Duke Univ. Press, 2011.

Hames-Garcia, Michael. *Identity Complex: Making the Case for Multiplicity.* Minneapolis: Univ. of Minnesota Press, 2011.

Hamilton, Elizabeth C. "Afrofuturism and the Technologies of Survival." *African Arts* 50, no. 4 (Winter 2017): 18–23.

Hanna-Attisha, Mona, Jenny LaChance, Richard Casey Sadler, and Allison Champney Schnepp. "Elevated Blood Lead Levels in Children Associated with the Flint Drinking Water Crisis: A Spatial Analysis of Risk and Public

Health Response." *American Journal of Public Health* 106, no. 2 (Feb. 2016): 283–90. https://doi.org/10.2105/AJPH.2015.303003

Haraway, Donna. *The Companion Species Manifesto: Dogs, People, and Significant Otherness*. Chicago: Prickly Paradigm Press, 2003.

Haze, Angel. "Cleaning Out My Closet." *Classick*. 2012. Soundcloud.

Hearne, Vicki. *Adam's Task: Calling Animals by Name*. New York: Knopf, 1986.

Hediger, Ryan. "Crossing Over: (Dis)ability, Contingent Agency, and Death in the Marginal Genre Work of Temple Grandin and Jim Harrison." In *Animals and Agency: An Interdisciplinary Exploration*, edited by Sarah E. McFarland and Ryan Hediger, 321–39. Leiden: Brill, 2009.

Higashida, Naoki. *The Reason I Jump: The Inner Voice of a Thirteen-Year-Old Boy with Autism*. Translated by K. A. Yoshida and David Mitchell. New York: Random House, 2013.

Hill, Marc Lamont. *Nobody: Casualties of America's War on the Vulnerable, from Ferguson to Flint and Beyond*. New York: Atria Books, 2016.

Hitselberger, Karin. "Harry Potter and the Inaccessible Book." *Claiming Crip* (blog). August 2, 2016. http://www.claimingcrip.com/2016/08/harry-potter-and-inaccessible-book.html?q=harry+potter

Hodson, Heather. "Interview with R. J. Palacio, author of *Wonder*." *The Telegraph*, February 21, 2012. http://www.telegraph.co.uk/culture/books/authorinter-views/9086974/Interview-with-RJ-Palacio-author-of-Wonder.html

Hollman, Mark, and Greg Kotis. "It's a Privilege to Pee." Libretto. In *Urinetown: The Musical*. Milwaukee: Hal Leonard, 2001.

Honeyman, Susan. *Child Pain, Migraine, and Invisible Disability*. New York: Routledge, 2017. Taylor & Francis Online.

hooks, bell. "Whiteness in the Black Imagination." In *Displacing Whiteness: Essays in Social and Cultural Criticism*, edited by Ruth Frankenberg, 165–79. Durham: Duke Univ. Press, 1997.

Howard, Rhoda. *Colonialism and Underdevelopment in Ghana*. New York: Africana, 1978.

Hughes, Chloë. "Seeing Blindness in Children's Picturebooks." *Journal of Literary and Cultural Disability Studies* 6, no. 1 (Jan. 2012): 35–51. http://doi.org/10.3828/jlcds.2012.3

Institute for Community Inclusion, University of Massachusetts, Boston. Think College! College Options for People with Intellectual Disabilities. https://thinkcollege.net/

International IDEA. "Constitutional History of Ghana." Constitution Net. http://www.constitutionnet.org/country/constitutional-history-ghana

"Interview with Sharon M. Draper." *Goodreads*, November 2009. https://www.goodreads.com/interviews/show/370.Sharon_M_Draper

Jacobs, A. J. "The Impacts of Variations in Development Context on Employment Growth: A Comparison of Central Cities in Michigan and Ontario, 1980–2006." *Economic Development Quarterly* 23, no. 4 (2009): 351–71.

Jaques, Irene Dodgson. "A Conversation with Dodgson's Niece." In *Lewis Carroll:*

Interviews and Reflections, edited by Morton N. Cohen, 27–8. Iowa City: Univ. of Iowa Press, 1989.

Johnson, Simon. "J. K. Rowling Contemplated Suicide." *The Telegraph*, March 23, 2008. http://www.telegraph.co.uk/news/uknews/1582552/JK-Rowling-contemplated-suicide.html

Jones, L., M. A. Bellis, S. Wood, K. Hughes, E. McCoy, L. Eckley, G. Bates, C. Mikton, T. Shakespeare, and A. Officer. "Prevalence and Risk of Violence against Children with Disabilities: A Systematic Review and Meta-analysis of Observational Studies." *The Lancet* 380, no. 9845 (2012): 899–907.

Jordan, Tim. "Troubling Companions: Companion Species and the Politics of Inter-relations." *NORA: Nordic Journal of Feminist and Gender Research* 19, no. 4 (Dec. 2011): 264–79. http://doi.org/10.1080/08038740.2011.620003

Kafer, Alison. *Feminist, Queer, Crip*. Bloomington: Indiana Univ. Press, 2013.

Kane, Emily W. "'No Way My Boys Are Going to Be Like That!': Parents' Responses to Children's Gender Nonconformity." *Gender and Society* 20, no. 2 (Apr. 2006): 149–76. http://doi.org/10.1177/0891243205284276

Keelan, Jennifer. "Climbing the Capitol Steps for ADA." YouTube. *It's Our Story Project*. July 5, 2010. Video, 4:27. http://www.youtube.com/watch?v=HesvwnM-0nE

Keller, Bill. "David Simon on Baltimore's Anguish." *Marshall Project*, April 29, 2015. https://www.themarshallproject.org/2015/04/29/david-simon-on-baltimores-anguish

Kim, Catherine Y., Daniel J. Losen, and Damon T. Hewitt. *The School to Prison Pipeline: Structuring Legal Reform*. New York: NYU Press, 2010.

Kit, Borys, and Rebecca Ford. "Julia Roberts to Play Jacob Tremblay's Mother in 'Wonder.'" *Hollywood Reporter*, May 5, 2016. http://www.hollywoodreporter.com/news/julia-roberts-play-jacob-tremblays-mother-wonder-891160

Kuusisto, Stephen. "Ann Coulter and the R Word Ride Again!" *Planet of the Blind* (blog), August 26, 2016. https://stephenkuusisto.com/2016/08/26/ann-coulter-and-the-r-word-ride-again/

Lakoff, Andrew. "Adaptive Will: The Evolution of Attention Deficit Disorder." *Journal of the History of the Behavioral Sciences* 36, no. 2 (March 2000): 149–69. http://doi.org/10.1002/(SICI)1520–6696(200021)36:2<149::AID-JHBS3>3.0.CO;2–9

Lalvani, Priya, and Chris Hale. "Squeaky Wheels, Mothers from Hell, and CEOs of the IEP: Parents, Privilege, and the 'Fight' for Inclusive Education." *Understanding and Dismantling Privilege* 5, no. 2 (2015): 28–41. http://www.wpcjournal.com/article/view/14433/Lalvani_Hale

Lamont, Bethany Rose. "What We Can Learn from *Harry Potter*'s 'Mad Women.'" *New Statesman*, June 28, 2017. https://www.newstatesman.com/culture/books/2017/06/what-we-can-learn-harry-potter-s-mad-women

Larsson, Naomi. "Out of Sight: The Orphanages Where Disabled Children Are Abandoned." *The Guardian*, September 26, 2016. https://www.theguardian.com/global-development-professionals-network/2016/sep/26/orphanage-locked-up-disabled-children-lumos-dri-human-rights

Lavender, Isiah III. "Digging Deep: Ailments of Difference in Octavia Butler's 'The Evening and the Morning and the Night.'" In *Black and Brown Planets: The Politics of Race in Science Fiction*, edited by Isiah Lavender III, 65–82. Jackson: Univ. of Mississippi Press, 2014.

Lee, Shawna J., Amy Krings, Sara Rose, Krista Dover, Jessica Ayoub, and Fatima Salman. "Racial Inequality and the Implementation of Emergency Management Laws in Economically Distressed Urban Areas." *Children and Youth Services Review* 70 (Nov. 2016): 1–7. http://doi.org/10.1016/j.childyouth.2016.08.016

Le Guin, Ursula K. "Introduction." In *The Norton Book of Science Fiction: North American Science Fiction, 1960–1990*, edited by Brian Attebery and Ursula K. Le Guin, 15–42. New York: W. W. Norton, 1993.

Leiter, Valerie. *Their Time Has Come: Youth with Disabilities on the Cusp of Adulthood*. New Brunswick: Rutgers Univ. Press, 2012. ProQuest.

Levine, Marc V. "Downtown Redevelopment as an Urban Growth Strategy: A Critical Appraisal of the Baltimore Renaissance." *Journal of Urban Affairs* 9, no. 2 (June 1987): 103–23. http://doi.org/10.1111/j.1467-9906.1987.tb00468.x

Levy, Michael, and Farah Mendlesohn. *Children's Fantasy Literature: An Introduction*. Cambridge: Cambridge Univ. Press, 2016.

Lindsey, Luna. "Reflected in Ice: An Aspergers Review of *Frozen*." *Luna Lindsey is making you think* (blog), February 24, 2014. http://www.lunalindsey.com/2014/02/reflected-in-ice-aspergers-review-of.html

Literally Media Ltd. "X All the Y." Know Your Meme. http://knowyourmeme.com/memes/all-the-things

Livengood, Chad. "Emails: Flint Water Warnings Reached Governor's Inner Circle." *Detroit News*, February 26, 2016. http://www.detroitnews.com/story/news/michigan/flint-water-crisis/2016/02/26/snyder-aides-urged-switching-flints-water-oct/80967048/

Los Angeles Times Staff. "Read the Letter From 'Little Miss Flint' That Stirred Obama to Visit Flint." May 4, 2016. http://www.latimes.com/nation/nation-now/la-na-read-little-miss-flint-letter-20160504-snap-htmlstory.html

Lowe, Nick, music and lyrics. "The Beast in Me." Recorded by Johnny Cash on *American Recordings*. Universal Music Publishing Group / American Recordings, 1994.

Lowery, Wesley. *"They Can't Kill Us All": Ferguson, Baltimore, and a New Era in America's Racial Justice Movement*. New York: Little, Brown, 2016.

Macleod, David I. *The Age of the Child: Children in America 1890–1920*. New York: Twayne Publishers, 1998.

Makarechi, Kia. "Angel Haze's 'Cleaning Out My Closet' Recounts Sexual Abuse & Eventual Triumph." *HuffPost*, October 23, 2012. https://www.huffingtonpost.com/2012/10/23/angel-haze-cleaning-out-my-closet_n_2006943.html

Maron, Mark. *WTF with Mark Maron: Allie Brosh*. Episode 550. November 13, 2014. Podcast. http://www.wtfpod.com/podcast/episodes/episode_550_-_allie_brosh

Martin, Emily. *Flexible Bodies: The Role of Immunity in American Culture from the Days of Polio to the Age of AIDS*. New York: Beacon Press, 1995.

Martin, Karin A. "Becoming a Gendered Body: Practices of Preschools." *American Sociological Review* 63, no. 4 (Aug. 1998): 494–511. ProQuest.

Maryland Department of the Environment. "480 Baltimore City Dwellings to Be Made Lead Safe." June 21, 2001. http://www.mde.state.md.us/programs/Press-Room/Pages/143.aspx

Maryland Judiciary. "Stanley Rochkind." Maryland Judiciary Case Search Results. http://casesearch.courts.state.md.us/casesearch/inquirySearch.jis

Mateik, Tara, and Dean Spade. *Toilet Training: Law and Order (in the Bathroom)*. New York: Sylvia Rivera Law Project, 2003. https://vimeo.com/85470055

Mathews, Carrie. "My Harry Potter Story." In *A Wizard of Their Age: Critical Essays from the Harry Potter Generation*, edited by Cecilia Konchar Farr, 182–4. Albany: SUNY Press, 2015.

McCloskey, Melissa. "To See Ourselves through Visuals." Unpublished essay, June 11, 2014.

McCoy, Terrence. "Freddie Gray's Life a Study on the Effects of Lead Paint on Poor Blacks." *Washington Post*, April 29, 2015. https://www.washingtonpost.com/local/freddie-grays-life-a-study-in-the-sad-effects-of-lead-paint-on-poor-blacks/2015/04/29/0be898e6-eea8-11e4-8abc-d6aa3bad79dd_story.html?utm_term=.bafafb3d3fea

McCoy, Terrence. "How Companies Make Millions off Lead-Poisoned, Poor Blacks." *Washington Post*, August 25, 2015. https://www.washingtonpost.com/local/social-issues/how-companies-make-millions-off-lead-poisoned-poor-blacks/2015/08/25/7460c1de-0d8c-11e5-9726-49d6fa26a8c6_story.html?utm_term=.a59c2fb778d9

McReynolds, Leigha. "Animal and Alien Bodies as Prostheses: Reframing Disability in *Avatar* and *How to Train Your Dragon*." In *Disability in Science Fiction: Representations of Technology as Cure*, edited by Kathryn Allan, 115–27. New York: Palgrave Macmillan, 2013.

Melson, Gail F. "Child Development and the Human-Companion Animal Bond." *American Behavioral Scientist* 47, no. 1 (2003): 31–9. http://doi.org/10.1177/0002764203255210

Meyer, Abbye E. "'But She's Not Retarded': Contemporary Adolescent Literature Humanizes Disability but Marginalizes Intellectual Disability." *Children's Literature Association Quarterly* 38, no. 3 (Fall 2013): 267–83.

Miller, Marjorie. "'Harry Potter' Casts a Spell across the Ages." *Los Angeles Times*, September 8, 1999. http://www.latimes.com/nation/la-na-potter-casts-spell-20170626-story.html

Miller, Theresa. "Rethinking Care: Disability and Care in Dinah Mulock Craik's *The Little Lame Prince and His Travelling Cloak*." *Limina: A Journal of Historical and Cultural Studies* 21, no. 1 (2015): 1–11. http://www.limina.arts.uwa.edu.au/__data/assets/pdf_file/0010/2827891/Miller-article.pdf

Mingus, Mia. "Access Intimacy: The Missing Link." *Leaving Evidence* (blog), May 5, 2011. https://leavingevidence.wordpress.com/2011/05/05/access-intimacy-the-missing-link/

Miserandino, Christine. "The Spoon Theory." ButYouDontLookSick. 2003. https://butyoudontlooksick.com/articles/written-by-christine/the-spoon-theory/

Montgomery, Cal. "Harry Potter and the Allure of Separatism." *Ragged Edge*, June 3, 2004. http://www.raggededgemagazine.com/focus/potter0604.html

Mora, Nicolás Medina. "The Short, Hard Life of Freddie Gray." *BuzzFeed News*, August 18, 2015. https://www.buzzfeed.com/nicolasmedinamora/what-freddie-grays-life-says-about-baltimores-justice-system?utm_term=.cpA18D73z#.yc-MK56V2E

Morrell, Heather. Personal interview with the author. November 22, 2013.

Morrell, Heather. Telephone interview with the author. May 15, 2015.

Mothers from Hell 2. "Home." http://www.mothersfromhell2.org

Mulock, Dinah Maria. *The Little Lame Prince and Other Stories*. Newbery Classics Series. Philadelphia: David McKay, 1927.

National Public Radio. "Hyperbole and a Half." Paperback Nonfiction Bestsellers. https://www.npr.org/books/titles/240779382/hyperbole-and-a-half-unfortunate-situations-flawed-coping-mechanisms-mayhem-and-

New York Times. "Best Sellers: Children's Middle Grade." *New York Times*, April 28, 2013. https://www.nytimes.com/books/best-sellers/2013/04/13/childrens-middle-grade/

New York Times. "Best Sellers: Children's Middle Grade Hardcover." *New York Times*, July 31, 2016. https://www.nytimes.com/books/best-sellers/2016/07/16/childrens-middle-grade-hardcover/

New York Times. "Best Sellers: Children's Middle Grade Hardcover." *New York Times*, September 17, 2017. https://www.nytimes.com/books/best-sellers/2017/09/17/childrens-middle-grade-hardcover/

Nicolajeva, Maria. "The Development of Children's Fantasy." In *The Cambridge Companion to Fantasy Literature*, edited by Farah Mendlesohn and Edward James, 50–61. Cambridge: Cambridge Univ. Press, 2012. https://doi.org/10.1017/CCOL9780521429597

Nodelman, Perry. *Words about Pictures: The Narrative Art of Children's Picture Books*. Athens: Univ. of Georgia Press, 1988.

Odom, Samuel L. "Preschool Inclusion: What We Know and Where We Go from Here." *Topics in Early Childhood Special Education* 20, no. 1 (2000): 20–7. ProQuest.

Osofsky, Audrey. *My Buddy*. Illustrated by Ted Rand. New York: Square Fish / Henry Holt, 1992.

Otto, Eric C. *Green Speculations: Science Fiction and Transformative Environmentalism*. Columbus: Ohio State Univ. Press, 2012.

Palacio, R. J. *Wonder*. New York: Knopf, 2012.

Paley, Vivian Gussin. *The Boy Who Would Be a Helicopter: The Uses of Storytelling in the Classroom*. Cambridge: Harvard Univ. Press, 1990.

Patsavas, Alyson. "Recovering a Cripistemology of Pain: Leaky Bodies, Connective Tissue, and Feeling Discourse." *Journal of Literary and Cultural Disability Studies* 8, no. 2 (2014): 203–18. ProQuest.

Pickens, Therí. "Octavia Butler and the Aesthetics of the Novel." *Hypatia: A Journal of Feminist Philosophy* 30, no.1 (Winter 2015): 167–80. JSTOR.

Plaskow, Judith. "Embodiment, Elimination, and the Role of Toilets in Struggles for Social Justice." *CrossCurrents* 58, no. 1 (Spring 2008): 58–64. https://www.jstor.org/stable/24461652

Price, Margaret. "The Bodymind Problem and the Possibilities of Pain." *Hypatia: A Journal of Feminist Philosophy* 30, no. 1 (Winter 2015): 268–84. JSTOR.

Puar, Jasbir. "Queer Times, Queer Assemblages." *Social Text* 23, nos. 3–4 [84–85] (2005): 121–39. http://doi.org/10.1215/01642472-23-3-4_84-85-121

Purdy, John. "Crossroads: A Conversation with Sherman Alexie." 1997. In *Conversations with Sherman Alexie*, edited by Nancy J. Peterson, 36–52. Jackson: Univ. of Mississippi Press, 2009.

Quayson, Ato. *Aesthetic Nervousness: Disability and the Crisis of Representation.* New York: Columbia Univ. Press, 2007.

Ravitch, Diane. *The Death and Life of the Great American School System: How Testing and Choice Are Undermining Education.* New York: Basic Books, 2010.

Ray, Sarah Jaquette. *The Ecological Other: Environmental Exclusion in American Culture.* Tucson: Univ. of Arizona Press, 2013.

Reetz, David R., Carolyn Bershad, Peter LeViness, and Monica Whitlock. "The Association for University and College Counseling Center Directors Annual Survey." Reporting period September 1, 2015–August 31, 2016. *Association for University and College Counseling Center Directors.* https://www.aucccd.org/assets/documents/aucccd%202016%20monograph%20-%20public.pdf

Rentz, Catherine. "Freddie Gray Remembered as Jokester Who Struggled to Leave Drug Trade." *Baltimore Sun*, November 22, 2015. http://www.baltimoresun.com/news/maryland/freddie-gray/bal-freddie-gray-remembered-as-jokester-who-struggled-to-leave-drug-trade-20151120-story.html

Review of *Wonder* by R. J. Palacio. *Publishers Weekly*, February 20, 2012. https://www.publishersweekly.com/978-0-375-86902-0

Reyes, Philip. "A Letter to Writers about Autism." Disability in Kidlit. April 23, 2015. http://disabilityinkidlit.com/2015/04/23/a-letter-to-writers-about-autism/

Ritchie, Andrea J. *Invisible No More: Police Violence against Black Women and Women of Color.* Boston: Beacon Press, 2017.

Rose, Damon. "When Disabled People Took to the Streets to Change the Law." *BBC News*, November 7, 2015. http://www.bbc.com/news/disability-34732084

Rose, Jacqueline. *States of Fantasy.* Clarendon Lectures in English. Oxford: Clarendon Press, 1998.

Rose, Tricia. *The Hip Hop Wars: What We Talk about When We Talk about Hip Hop—and Why It Matters.* New York: Basic Civitas, 2008.

Ross, Janell. "Why You Should Know What Happened in Freddie Gray's Life—Long before His Death." *Washington Post*, December 19, 2015. https://www.washingtonpost.com/news/the-fix/wp/2015/12/19/why-you-should-know-what-happened-in-freddie-grays-life-long-before-his-death/?utm_term=.e525db7dadfe

Roulstone, Alan, and Simon Prideaux. *Understanding Disability Policy.* Bristol, UK: Policy Press, 2012.

Rowell, E. M. "To Me He Was Mr. Dodgson." In *Lewis Carroll: Interviews and Reflections,* edited by Morton N. Cohen, 129–34. Iowa City: Univ. of Iowa Press, 1989.

Rowling, J. K. *Harry Potter and the Deathly Hallows.* New York: Scholastic, 2007.

Rowling, J. K. *Harry Potter and the Goblet of Fire.* New York: Scholastic, 2000.

Rowling, J. K. *Harry Potter and the Order of the Phoenix.* New York: Scholastic, 2003.

Rowling, J. K. *Harry Potter and the Prisoner of Azkaban.* New York: Scholastic, 1999.

Rowling, J. K. *Harry Potter and the Sorcerer's Stone.* New York: Scholastic, 1997.

Rowling, J. K. "Remus Lupin." *Pottermore.* https://www.pottermore.com/writing-by-jk-rowling/remus-lupin

Saldívar, Ramón. "Historical Fantasy, Speculative Realism, and Postrace Aesthetics in Contemporary American Fiction." *American Literary History* 23, no. 3 (Fall 2011): 574–99. http://doi.org/10.1093/alh/ajr026

Scamander, Newt (J. K. Rowling). *Fantastic Beasts and Where to Find Them.* New York: Scholastic, 2001.

Schalk, Sami. "Coming to Claim Crip: Disidentification with/in Disability Studies." *Disability Studies Quarterly* 33, no. 2 (2013). http://doi.org/10.18061/dsq.v33i2.3705

Schmitz, Mark, Prima Fillippone, and Elaine Edelman. "Social Representations of Attention Deficit / Hyperactivity Disorder, 1988–1997." *Culture & Psychology* 9, no. 4 (Dec. 2003): 383–406. http://doi.org/10.1177/1354067X0394004

Segal, Corrine. "These Young Poets Show There's More to Flint than a Water Crisis." *PBS NewsHour,* March 29, 2016. https://www.pbs.org/newshour/arts/poetry/these-young-poets-show-theres-more-to-flint-than-a-water-crisis

Serlin, David. "Pissing without Pity: Disability, Gender, and the Public Toilet." In *Toilet: Public Restrooms and the Politics of Sharing,* edited by Harvey Molotch and Laura Norén, 167–85. New York: New York Univ. Press, 2010.

Shah, Sonali, and Mark Priestley. *Disability and Social Change: Private Lives and Public Policies.* Bristol, UK: Policy Press, 2010.

Shapiro, Joseph P. *No Pity: People with Disabilities Forging a New Civil Rights Movement.* New York: Three Rivers Press, 1993.

Shin-Wheeler, Bridget. Conversation with the author. July 30, 2014.

Shute, E. L. "The Walks Were Well Worth the Cricks." In *Lewis Carroll: Interviews and Reflections,* edited by Morton N. Cohen, 55–7. Iowa City: Univ. of Iowa Press, 1989.

Shuttleworth, Russell P. "Defusing the Adverse Context of Disability and Desirability as a Practice of the Self for Men with Cerebral Palsy." In *Disability/Postmodernity: Embodying Disability Theory,* edited by Mairian Corker and Tom Shakespeare, 112–26. London: Continuum, 2002.

Siebers, Tobin. *Disability Theory.* Ann Arbor: Univ. of Michigan Press, 2008.

Simplican, Stacy Clifford. *The Capacity Contract: Intellectual Disability and the Question of Citizenship.* Minneapolis: Univ. of Minnesota Press, 2015.

Singer, Eric S. "Why Baltimore Burns." *The Nation*, May 1, 2015. https://www.the-nation.com/article/why-baltimore-burns/

Singer, Peter. *Practical Ethics*. 2nd ed. Cambridge: Cambridge Univ. Press, 1993.

Skinner, Eugene. Diary excerpt quoted on interpretive sign, Parks and Open Spaces, Eugene, OR, 2015.

Small, David. *Stitches: A Memoir*. New York: W. W. Norton, 2009.

Smith, Sherri L. *Orleans*. New York: Speak (Penguin), 2013.

Snyder, Sharon L., and David T. Mitchell. "Introduction: Ablenationalism and the Geo-politics of Disability." *Journal of Literary and Cultural Disability Studies* 4, no. 2 (2010): 113–25.

Snyder, Sharon L., and David T. Mitchell. *Narrative Prosthesis: Disability and the Dependencies of Discourse*. Ann Arbor: Univ. of Michigan Press, 2001.

Solomon, Andrew. *Far from the Tree: Parents, Children, and the Search for Identity*. New York: Scribner, 2012.

Solomon, Susan G. *American Playgrounds: Revitalizing Community Space*. Hanover, NH: Univ. Press of New England, 2005.

Spitz, Ellen Handler. *Inside Picture Books*. New Haven: Yale Univ. Press, 1999.

Staff Blogger. "Does Skool Suck?" *New Statesman*, March 6, 2006. https://www.newstatesman.com/node/163853

Stemp, Jane. "Devices and Desires: Science Fiction, Fantasy, and Disability in Literature for Young People." *Disability Studies Quarterly* 24, no. 1 (Winter 2004). http://doi.org/10.18061/dsq.v24i1.850

Sygall, Susan. "Community Conversation." University of Oregon Disability Studies Forum, October 30, 2014.

Tait, Amelia. *"Harry Potter* Didn't Cure My Depression—But for an Hour a Day, It Helped." *New Statesman*, June 26, 2017. https://www.newstatesman.com/culture/books/2017/06/harry-potter-didn-t-cure-my-depression-hour-day-it-helped

Taylor, Becky, and Dena Taylor. *Tell Me the Number before Infinity*. Capitola, CA: Many Names Press, 2016.

Taylor, Deborah. "The Voice: Sharon Draper's Storied Journey from Classroom Teacher to Acclaimed YA Icon." *School Library Journal* 61, no. 6 (June 2015). ProQuest.

Taylor, Sunaura. *Beasts of Burden: Animal and Disability Liberation*. New York: New Press, 2017.

Taylor, Sunaura. "Beasts of Burden: Disability Studies and Animal Rights." *Qui Parle: Critical Humanities and Social Sciences* 19, no. 2 (Spring–Summer 2011): 191–222.

Tettenborn, Éva. "Melancholia as Resistance in Contemporary African-American Literature." *MELUS: The Journal of the Society of the Study of the Multi-ethnic Literature of the United States* 31, no. 3 (2006): 101–21. http://doi.org/10.1093/melus/31.3.101

Thind, Rundip. "Understanding the Equality Act: Information for Disabled Students." Disability Rights UK Fact Sheet. April 24, 2017. https://www.disability-rightsuk.org/understanding-equality-act-information-disabled-students

Thorne, Jack, with J. K. Rowling and John Tiffany. *Harry Potter and the Cursed Child: Parts One and Two.* Special Rehearsal Edition Script. New York: Scholastic, 2016.

Titchkosky, Tanya. *The Question of Access: Disability, Space, Meaning.* Toronto: Univ. of Toronto Press, 2011.

Tomlinson, Sally. "Race and Special Education." *Counterpoints* 270 (2004): 76–88. JSTOR.

Trachtenberg, Jeffrey A. "Why Social Media Embraced Allie Brosh's Book 'Hyperbole and a Half.'" Speakeasy, *Wall Street Journal*, November 25, 2013. https://blogs.wsj.com/speakeasy/2013/11/25/why-social-media-embraced-allie-broshs-book-hyperbole-and-a-half/

Trapp, Brian. Conversation with the author. July 28, 2016.

Trueman, Terry. *Stuck in Neutral.* New York: HarperCollins, 2000.

Trust, Gary, and Keith Caulfield. "Eminem Marks Sales, Hot 100 Milestones." *Billboard*, March 21, 2014. http://www.billboard.com/articles/columns/the-juice/5944791/eminem-marks-sales-hot-100-milestones

Tucker, Miriam E. "Communication Lacking in Chronic Migraine Encounters." *Medscape*, July 9, 2015. https://www.medscape.com/viewarticle/847715

Unfried, Alana. Transcript of audio recording for "Life Stories" theater class. March 28, 2016.

United Nations. "U.N. Convention on the Rights of Persons with Disabilities." Division for Social Policy and Development Disability. https://www.un.org/development/desa/disabilities/convention-on-the-rights-of-persons-with-disabilities.html

US Department of Education. "Individuals with Disabilities Education Act." IDEA: Individuals with Disabilities Education Act. https://sites.ed.gov/idea/

US Government Publishing Office. "Public Law 111-256-Oct. 5, 2010: 'Rosa's Law.'" October 5, 2010. https://www.gpo.gov/fdsys/pkg/PLAW-111publ256/pdf/PLAW-111publ256.pdf

van der Kolk, Bessel A. *The Body Keeps the Score: Brain, Mind, and Body in the Healing of Trauma.* New York: Viking, 2014.

von Ravensberg, Heidi. Conversation with the author. September 16, 2014.

"Walker Contributors: Michael Foreman." Walker Books. http://www.walker.co.uk/contributors/Michael-Foreman-2741.aspx

Watkins, D. *The Beast Side: Living and Dying while Black in America.* New York: Skyhorse Publishing, 2015.

Welch, William M. "Disabled Climb Capitol Steps to Plea for Government Protection." *Associated Press*, March 12, 1990. http://www.apnewsarchive.com/1990/Disabled-Climb-Capitol-Steps-To-Plea-For-Government-Protection/id-2672c50ca9c6155ed0cc3a4e36bdc20c

Wendell, Susan. *The Rejected Body: Feminist Philosophical Reflections on Disability.* New York: Routledge, 1996.

West, Isaac. "PISSAR'S Critically Queer and Disabled Politics." In *Transforming*

Citizenships: Transgender Articulations of the Law, 61–88. New York: NYU Press, 2014.

WETA Television, Washington, DC. "Transcript from an interview with Sherri L. Smith." AdLit: All About Adolescent Literacy. http://www.adlit.org/transcript_display/33885/

WGBH Educational Foundation. "Federal Laws Pertaining to ADHD Diagnosed Children." *PBS Frontline.* http://www.pbs.org/wgbh/pages/frontline/shows/medicating/schools/feds.html

Whitt, Pamela Beth, and Scot Danforth. "Reclaiming the Power of Address: New Metaphors and Narratives for Challenging Behaviors." In *(De)Constructing ADHD: Critical Guidance for Teachers and Teacher Educators*, edited by Linda J. Graham, 143–64. New York: Peter Lang, 2010.

Wolfe, Cary. *Animal Rites: American Culture, the Discourse of Species, and Posthumanist Theory.* Chicago: Univ. of Chicago Press, 2003.

Wolitzer, Meg. *Belzhar.* New York: Dutton Books for Young Readers, 2014.

Yaghr, Christie. Email to the author. November 30, 2014.

Yaszek, Lisa. "Afrofuturism, Science Fiction, and the History of the Future." *Socialism and Democracy* 20, no. 3 (Nov. 2006): 41–60. Taylor & Francis Online.

Yaszek, Lisa. "The Bannekerade: Genius, Madness, and Magic in Black Science Fiction." In *Black and Brown Planets: The Politics of Race in Science Fiction*, edited by Isiah Lavender III, 65–82. Jackson: Univ. of Mississippi Press, 2014.

Yenika-Agbaw, Vivian. *Representing Africa in Children's Literature: Old and New Ways of Seeing.* London: Routledge, 2008.

Yoon, Nicola. *Everything, Everything.* New York: Delacorte Press, 2015.

Young, Gordon. *Teardown: A Memoir of a Vanishing City.* Univ. of California Press, 2013.

Young, Stella. "Disability—a Fate Worse than Death?" *Ramp Up: Disability. Discussion. Debate* (blog). *ABC*, October 18, 2013. http://www.abc.net.au/rampup/articles/2013/10/18/3872088.htm

Young, Stella. "I'm Not Your Inspiration, Thank You Very Much." Filmed April 2014 in Sydney, Australia. TED video, 9:16. https://www.ted.com/talks/stella_young_i_m_not_your_inspiration_thank_you_very_much

Young, Stella. "It's Not My Fault I'm Obsessed with Toilets." The Drum, *ABC*, February 5, 2014. http://www.abc.net.au/news/2014-02-06/young-accessible-toilets-offer-sweet-relief/5239932

Yozzo, Carlo, and Robin Yozzo. Personal interview with the author. January 17, 2015.

Zare, Jeffrey. "An Autistic's Reflection on Disney's *Frozen*." *Autism Support Network.* November 27, 2014. http://www.autismsupportnetwork.com/news/autistics-reflection-disney-frozen-elsa-3251111

Zephaniah, Benjamin. *Face.* New York: Bloomsbury, 1999.

Zephaniah, Benjamin. *Gangsta Rap.* New York: Bloomsbury, 2004.

Zephaniah, Benjamin. *Too Black, Too Strong.* Northumberland, UK: Bloodaxe Books, 2001.

Zimmer, Tracie Vaughn. *Reaching for Sun*. New York: Bloomsbury, 2007.
Zucchino, David, and James Queally. "'The Wire' in Real Life: The Baltimore Neighborhood Freddie Gray Called Home." *Los Angeles Times*, April 28, 2015. http://www.latimes.com/nation/la-na-west-baltimore-profile-20150428-story.html

Index

Italic page numbers refer to photographs.

249